Lasting Friendships, A Century of Friendship Sloops
Copyright © May 2014 Friendship Sloop Society

ISBN: 978-0-9904040-1-9

Illustrations by T. B. R. Walsh unless otherwise credited.

Photographs not credited were submitted by the owner, with permission, for use in this book.

Front cover: Sloops GLADIATOR and CHANCE, photo by Roger Duncan 1970.
Back Cover: Sloops OSPREY and HELEN BROOKS, photo by Judy Heininger 2013.
Frontispiece: Sloops CHRISSY and BLACK JACK, photo by Roger Duncan 1969.

The Friendship Sloop Society
Friendship, Maine 04547
www.fss.org

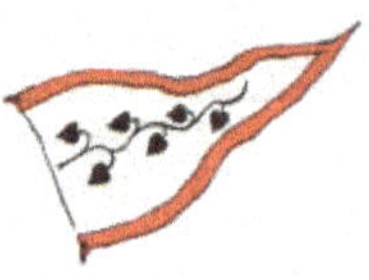

Please direct inquiries to:
The Friendship Sloop Society Book Committee
c/o 731 Tasker Hill Rd.
Conway, NH 03818

Lasting Friendships

A Century of Friendship Sloops

**T. B. R. Walsh, Ralph W. Stanley, and members of the
Friendship Sloop Society**

Foreword by Maynard Bray

Foreword:

Who could not love a Friendship sloop? Even to a layman's eye, they look just right—like they're ready for work, or play, and look as if they're up to about any weather that may come along. Above all, they're beautiful—stunningly beautiful. Most remarkable is that the builders themselves created them without benefit of a professional designer or naval architect. They're a shining example of common sense evolution as practiced by the fisherman/boatbuilders of mid-coast Maine.

It's one thing to arrive at a workboat that does its job well, but quite another to come up with one with eye-catching good looks. As with colonial housebuilders, the men who built the Friendships had an unusually refined sense of proportion and an understanding of aesthetics down to the last detail. But these boats weren't overburdened with fancy details; there were just enough of them for accent. Like the carved trailboards, for example, which serve only to enhance the curved stem and its gammon knee extension: to blend them together nicely and form a handsome and gradual transition between the boat's bow and its bowsprit. By no means did such bows originate in mid-coast Maine, but it's remarkable to me that "common" workboat builders adopted such refinements here.

From their high and handsome bow, a Friendship sloop's sheer runs aft in a curve that's low enough amidships to fish from, and then swoops up to a stern that's as graceful as the bow.

With its rake and rolled-in quarters, a Friendship sloop's stern is a good deal harder to build than a flat transom whose upper corners are sharp, but its beauty is almost indescribable with all those lovely curves coming together back at the stern. These details, too, originated "up to the west'ard" on larger craft. Elliptical sterns may have played a minor role in not snagging the main sheet as much as sharp cornered transoms, but I think beauty had way more to do with them than function.

On deck, in between the trailboard-adorned bow and the elliptical stern, there's the steam-bent oak coaming and cabin front—another spellbinding batch of curves, as that oval sweeps along the sheer and across the crowned deck. As can be seen in the early photographs of the McLain-built GENESEE, some had a half-oval cabin and a separate, full-oval coaming. How nice was that?

Speaking of the McLain family who built their boats on Bremen Long Island (and called them "Sloop Boats," certainly not Friendship sloops), I think that in hull shape and quality of construction, they're the best of the breed I've ever seen. I got to know Newell McLain pretty well while the sloop ESTELLA A., built by his father, Rob, was being restored in the early 1970s near where Newell lived in Thomaston. Because I was in charge of the work being done by Newbert & Wallace for Mystic Seaport (it was a total rebuild), I wanted to understand as much as possible how ESTELLA was built so that Rob McLain's original work could be duplicated. Although she'd been converted from workboat to yacht, and then to a museum-exhibit, most of the structure that McLain so carefully fitted together was still there for examination. And examine it I did. It had proven to be strong and the fits were near perfect even though the wood itself had rotted beyond reuse. (Leaking decks and rusted steel fastenings had just "done her in.")

I learned from Newell that, because his father had no big power saw or stationary planer—the island had no electricity, he ordered most of the live-edge oak boards finished to an inch and a half in thickness. Likewise, the backbone timbers were of uniform thickness, as was the rest of the wood, like planking, framing, and joinery. So it was a straightforward order that he placed with the sawmill, and the resulting lumber, along with galvanized nails, some lengths of "drive iron" round bar, a few threaded bolts, an anchor, a little locally-forged ironwork, rope and wire for the rig, and cotton duck for the sails that his wife would sew together, was just about it for materials. What remained was careful labor in which pride of product played a huge role. No expensive cast lead or cast iron ballast keels for these workboats; all their ballast was inside, down low and out of the way in the deep bilge. It was called "shovel ballast," and consisted of small stones that were free for the taking right off the beach.

Newell told me that Sundays was a day spent visiting each other's shops and comparing the boats they were building that winter. Friendly competition naturally took place, with each builder trying to better his neighbor—and no doubt to better mainland boatshops like Wilbur Morse's as well. Add to that the inspiration that came from all the vessels built elsewhere (think Massachusetts, especially) that fished mid-coast Maine waters and could be examined in detail, and you have the basis of some exceptionally fine sloop boats—or Friendship sloops, if you prefer.

Not much money, but skill, care, and pride, in abundance!

I always wanted to own a Friendship sloop, but never got the chance and probably never will. But I love looking at old photos of them lying cheek-to-jowl in working harbors like Matinicus or York Island and comparing rigs, hull shapes and details. You simply can't beat them for looks or for straightforward utility. Those old guys really knew how to fashion an exceptional sailboat!

The working Friendship sloop is probably gone forever, but the respect they're being given through the Friendship Sloop Society and the commitment to preserving and restoring existing sloops and building replicas in both wood and fiberglass means that, as a type, Friendship sloops are alive and well and will doubtless remain so for many years. It comes as no surprise that a Morse built two thirds of the forty or so pre-World War II surviving originals. In wooden replicas, Ralph Stanley and McKie Roth show frequently as builders, while Jarvis Newman and Bruno & Stillman take honors for turning out replicas in fiberglass. In this book you'll find nearly 300 Friendship sloops of all varieties listed, with photos of many, and stories of some.

The book is a valuable resource in and of itself and Ted Walsh, Ralph Stanley, and the book committee are to be congratulated for putting it together. It is a welcome and fitting tribute to more than the 50 years of the Friendship Sloop Society and to Friendship sloops themselves.

Maynard Bray
Brooklin, Maine
May, 2014

Contents:

Preface

On a blustery Sunday morning in September 1960 contenders gathered for the Boston Power Squadron race for auxiliary sloops. We might not know what exactly was said in conversations preceding the race, but undoubtedly sports and current events figured heavily. The imminent retirement of Ted Williams from the Boston Red Sox, or perhaps the recent Olympic gold medal wins of runner Wilma Rudolf and a pugnacious boxer named Cassius Clay may have been discussed. Perhaps the conversation was political with speculation as to who would do well in the first televised Presidential debate to be broadcast later in the month between the two candidates, Richard Nixon and John F. Kennedy. Undoubtedly there was conversation about boats. The conversation might have been centered around speculation as to which of the sleek new Marconi-rigged boats would place well, or perhaps commentary on the newer materials used in boat construction. Fiberglass was the new low-maintenance wonder-material: stable, smooth, no more leaks, no more shipworm, no more rot. There might have even been some remark passed about the one antique in today's race, clearly a sacrificial offering to days gone by, something nice for the real racers to look at as they zipped by her. Later that day, when the finish gun fired, the first boat to cross the finish line was the antique, a boat built when Teddy Roosevelt was President of the United States.

Aboard the winning boat, a Friendship sloop named VOYAGER*, owner and skipper Bernard MacKenzie, impressed by his old sloop's performance, had the first inkling of an idea. Wouldn't it be great to gather as many surviving Friendship sloops as possible for a race in Friendship, Maine. He began talking up his idea, and the result was the formation of the Friendship Sloop Society. The first race held in Friendship in 1961 drew fourteen boats and over three thousand spectators.

Half a century later the President of the United States, vacationing in Maine, was having lunch with the First Family at the Boathouse of the Claremont Hotel on Mount Desert Island. As they finished their lunch the Obamas watched twelve Friendship sloops close on the finish line of the annual Southwest Harbor Rendezvous and scratch race of the Friendship Sloop Society. We do not know what kind of impression this small fleet made on the First Family, but the event was historic. The President of the United States was in attendance, although neither he nor the First Lady might have been aware when they went out to a casual lunch, that they would be attending a Friendship sloop race. The boats that finished second, ALICE E. #23, and third, GLADIATOR #71, were both over one hundred years old—a testament to the longevity of the Friendship Sloop design and the love and care that some of these vessels engender. But perhaps most significantly, nine of the boats racing that day were built after the formation of the Friendship Sloop Society. They were built for the enjoyment of sailing on, and caring for, a type of boat that so well marries aesthetic form, practical seaworthy function, and tradition. This last fact illustrates most clearly the influence and endurance of the Friendship Sloop Society.

One week after the Southwest Harbor Rendezvous, twenty-eight Friendships converged on the docks of Rockland, Maine, for the annual Friendship sloop gathering. These sloops represented an even larger cross-section of the Friendship Sloop Society. One sloop, TECUMSEH #242, was notable both because she was an original 1902 boat and because she came all the way from Oakville, Ontario via Florida. (Her owner joked that he should have gone left instead of right at New York City). Another sloop, TAMARA #272, was notable for coming right off the building ways of Ralph W. Stanley. For three days there were races, day cruises, and lots of informal social gatherings on the dock, in boat cockpits, and under the tent at the Rockland town landing. It was an amazing collection of wonderful boats. More importantly, it was an extraordinary collection of people with diverse backgrounds and talents, united in their passion for a family of boats and the personal friendships that have inevitably developed around them.

More than one hundred years after the design was firmly established, the Friendship sloop is alive and well. Fifty years after the formation of the Friendship Sloop Society, there are many more Friendships on the water and being built or rebuilt than were in existence when the Society was founded.

While this is a book about Friendship sloops, it is also a book about people: the people who developed the original boats, those who passed them on and converted them for recreation, those who preserved the remaining original boats, and those who went on to build new Friendship sloops inspired by what had gone before. However, the best we can do is to call this a progress report. This is not a complete history, nor can it be because of the many people who are still sailing, preserving, and building these beautiful vessels. Their stories have yet to be written.

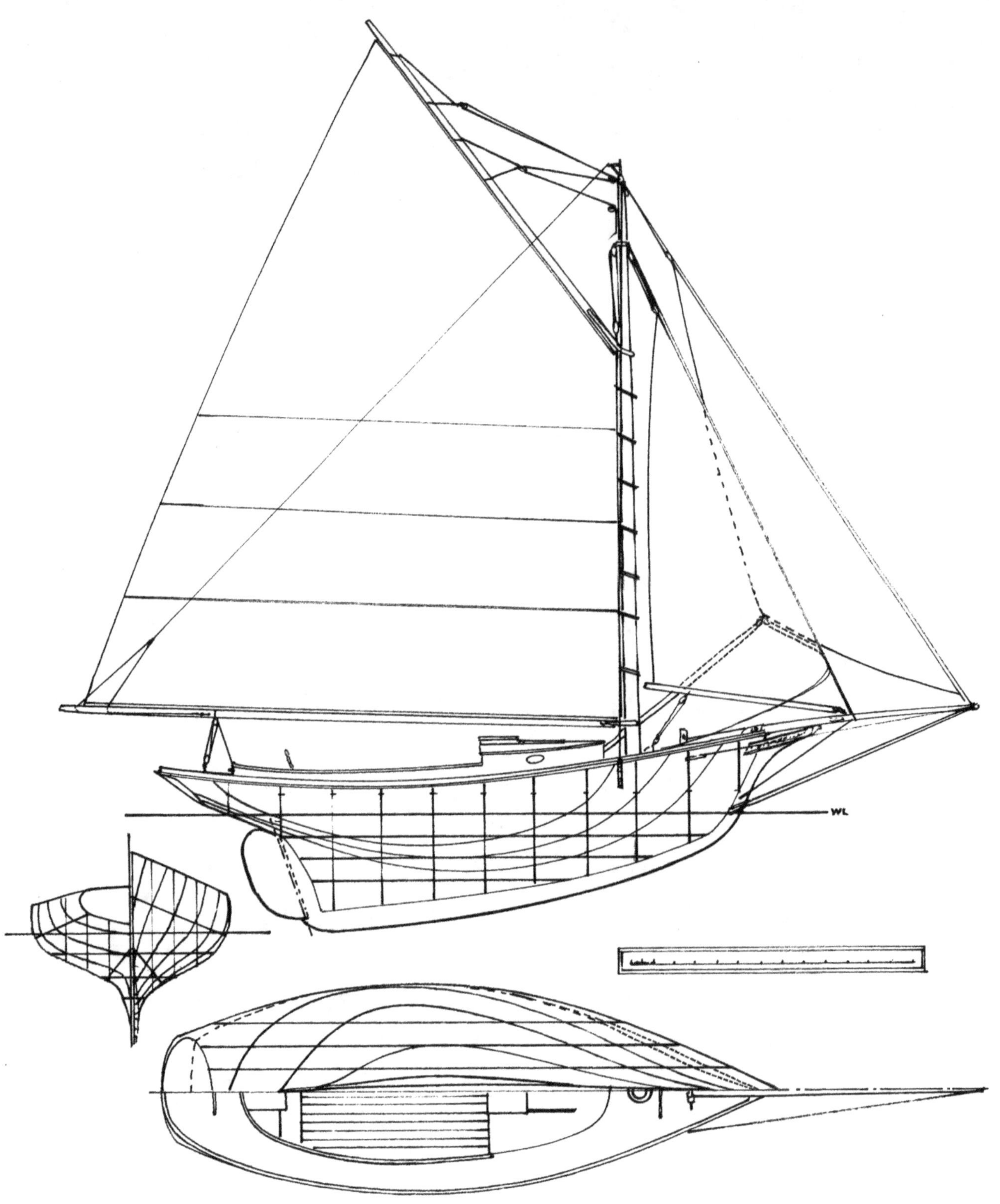

Friendship sloop built about 1900
Length on deck   28' 6"
Waterline length   23' 10"
Beam   9' 5"
Draft   5' 4"

Lines taken off by Howard I. Chapelle
Redrawn By T.B.R. Walsh 2014

Chapter One: Origins

The Friendship sloop has come to be recognized as an icon of traditional American sailing craft. Both functional and adaptable, the design evolved to meet the specific needs of a time and place in history. Why the design came about is a story of personalities, influences, and innovations. This story begins with a look at the time and place that the design evolved and the needs of the people who built these distinct and enduring boats.

The fifty years after the American Civil War was a period of transformation for much of the preserved, but fragile, Union. The State of Maine was undergoing significant change. The development of railway lines to Bangor, Augusta, Rockland, and Portland, and steamship connection to Boothbay Harbor, was turning these towns into cities. The demand for Maine lumber, granite, quicklime, and other raw materials promised growth and opportunity, at least for those Mainers who lived on the coast, near a railhead, or on one of the many rivers that led to the coast.

For those Mainers who did not live on the ocean or a major river or near a railhead, travel was slow and difficult. People commonly spoke of distance in leagues, a unit of three miles, either nautical or statute—as much a unit of time as it was a unit of distance. Three miles was the distance that an average person could walk or row in an hour under normal conditions. If someone told you that a farm was two leagues off, they were also telling you that it was two hours away. Settlements that were on the rivers or ocean were at a certain advantage because goods and materials could often be moved by boat far more easily than by cart; this was particularly true if the boat could be moved by wind rather than oar.

The settlers of the coast, while enjoying some advantages, were certainly not living in the land of milk and honey. Winters were harsh and long, the growing season was short, and the ground required backbreaking clearing of trees, removal of ubiquitous rocks, and improvement of the soil in order to provide even basic sustenance of vegetables and hay. On the other hand, unlike settlers inland, settlers on the ocean also had access to an abundance of cod, mackerel, hake, haddock, clams, lobster, and mussels all within a league of most waterfront or island homesteads. To harvest this abundance one needed skill, a willingness to work, and a boat. Most coastal homesteads were just that, the first or second, or possibly third generation attempts to wrestle a decent living by combining the harvest of the meager farmlands and the available resources of the sea. The farmer-fishermen who populated the coastal regions had to cultivate a multitude of skills in order to prosper.

In the middle of the Maine coast lies Muscongus Bay, rich in resources and with unique geographical advantages. It was a place that would be transformed as a result of its location. Fed by three rivers, the waters of the bay

Friendship sloop heading out to fish.

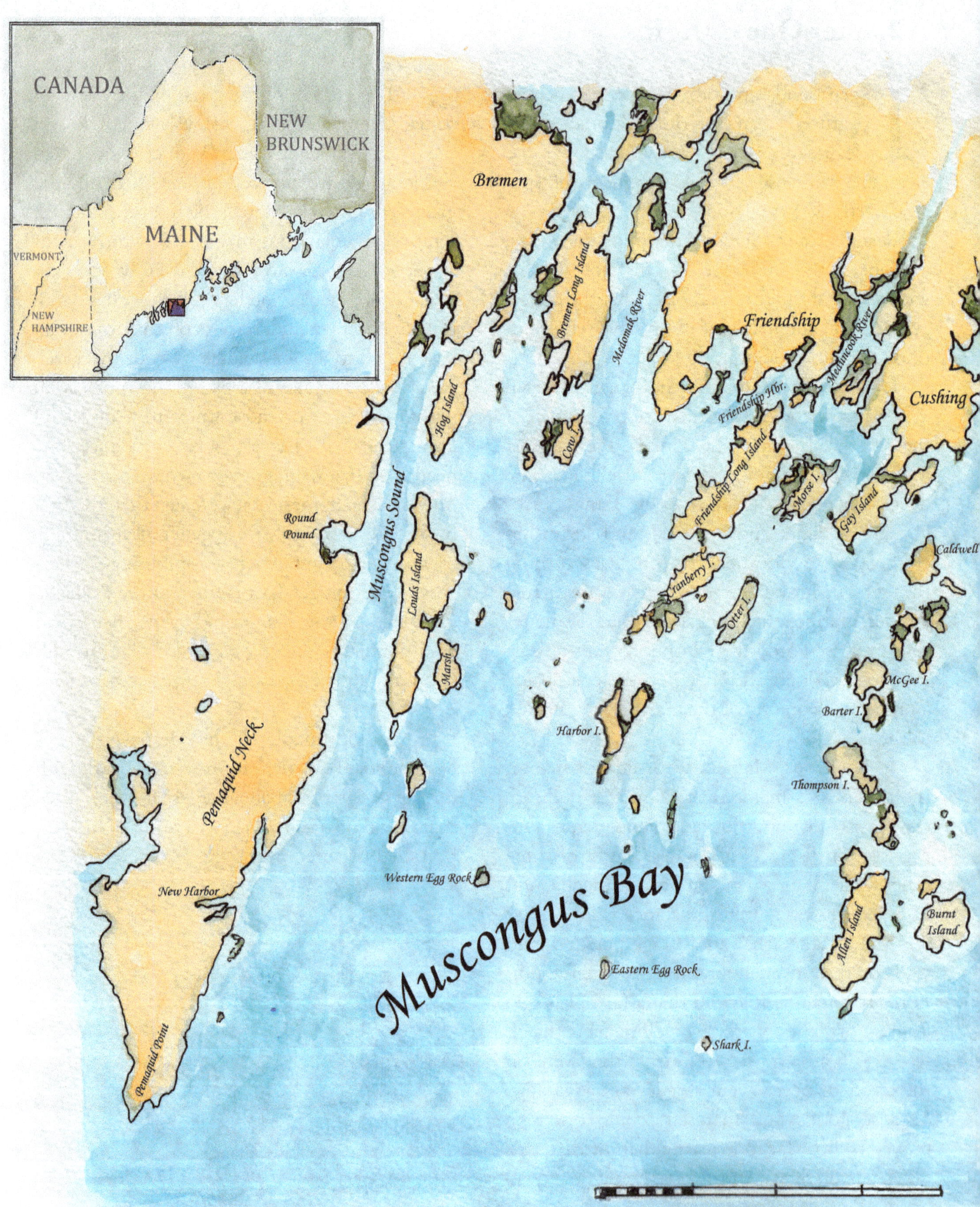

CANADA
NEW BRUNSWICK
MAINE
VERMONT
NEW HAMPSHIRE
Bremen
Friendship
Cushing
Bremen Long Island
Medomak River
Meduncook River
Friendship Hbr.
Hog Island
Cow I.
Morse I.
Gay Island
Caldwell
Muscongus Sound
Round Pound
Friendship Long Island
Cranberry I.
Otter I.
McGee I.
Louds Island
Barter I.
Marsh
Harbor I.
Thompson I.
Pemaquid Neck
New Harbor
Western Egg Rock
Muscongus Bay
Allen Island
Burnt Island
Eastern Egg Rock
Pemaquid Point
Shark I.

were rich with wildlife and sea life. The edges of the bay were crenulated with natural harbors, carved into the mainland, like New Harbor, Goose River, Cushing, and Round Pound. Others, like Bremen and Friendship, were places where the shelter of one or more islands combined with a natural harbor or cove. Islands like Louds, Marsh, Hog, Bremen Long Island, Harbor Island, Hall, Friendship Long Island, McGee, Gay, Otter, and Black seemed strategically placed to take advantage of good fishing grounds and the proximity of natural harbors. The Georges Islands chain provided a slight separation and a natural breakwater between the aforementioned harbors and islands, and Hupper Island and Port Clyde. This bay of natural opportunities had been settled since colonial times, but now, comfortably located at just about the middle of the coast of Maine, it found itself ideally located between two of Maine's growing commercial hubs, Rockland and Boothbay Harbor, each a day's sail away.

It was here in Muscongus Bay that a boat design evolved that came to represent American adaptation, ingenuity, and resourcefulness—the Friendship sloop.

Friendship Harbor 1890s

Where did the Friendship sloop come from? One would assume Friendship, Maine, but such a deceptively simple question becomes complex when one considers that the term "Friendship sloop" is not a specific design, but rather a general term for a family of craft that evolved from earlier designs to meet changing needs.

The term "Friendship sloop" is like the term "clipper ship", which came into use at just about the same period in history. Carl C. Cutler, in his excellent book *Grayhounds of the Sea*, goes to great lengths to explain why no one can definitively say what was the first clipper ship. It was a collaborative effort of designers and sailors, merchants and markets, that resulted in something uniquely American and uniquely suited to the needs of the times. The Friendship sloop followed an almost identical trajectory, and, like the clipper ships, was a product of a time, a place, and a set of needs.

In the 1970s, Bradley Beckett tried to find out who built the first Friendship sloop. This is what he wrote for the 1976 Friendship Sloop Society yearbook:

A short time ago I tried to find the original builder of the Friendship sloop. Most believe Wilbur Morse of Friendship was the mastermind. Roy Wallace, a boatbuilder and a grandnephew of Morse, said Wilbur used to lobster in a peapod on Bremen Long Island in the late 1800s. After a while, Wilbur wanted something better. What he came up with was the Friendship sloop. Then I talked with Carroll Carter, another boatbuilder. Said he, "I was told 'Waut' Prior built the first one . . . But as far as a Friendship sloop goes, there is no Friendship sloop. (That is, the first ones were built on Bremen Long Island.) Of course, a lot of builders moved to Friendship and built over there. There was Wilbur Morse and his brother Charles. Then Al Morse was down in Cushing. There were a lot of others besides."

Next I went to see Newell McLain, another grand-nephew of Wilbur Morse and boatbuilder. "The first Friendship sloop Wilbur Morse built," said Newell, "he borrowed the mold off my grandfather (Rob McLain) to build her out of. But as far as he being the first one — no. Grandfather was the first one!" How did it evolve? Newell related the tale: "Fishermen used to have little 14 or 16-foot centerboard boats. They'd sail out to the traps, take the mast out, and row around the traps.

"Well, Gramp Rob said he didn't see why he couldn't sail up to a trap, haul it, trim the jibboom, keep her off the rocks, and set the trap again. Well, 'Waut' Prior (a neighbor) said it couldn't be done. So they argued over it for years till after a while Gramp Rob said, 'Damned if I don't try it!' and he built one he couldn't take the mast out of, about 18 or 20 feet in length. So, he built the first Friendship sloop and was the first ever to haul a trap under sail in Maine waters." Shortly after, everyone was building them.

Newell told of the DICTATOR #2, a Friendship sloop that was the pride and joy of its turn-of-the-century builder, Newell's father. "Father built her out of wood, already tucked right to the tiller for $425 — sails and everything!" Jarvis Newman of Southwest Harbor in recent years bought its remains. "What he wanted was its lines. Now he's building fiberglass ones of that design and selling them." A short time after visiting Newell McLain I paid a visit to Carleton Morse on Morse's Island off Friendship. Said he, "There were a lot of people who built Friendship sloops but there was only one person who could have built the original — my father (Warren Morse)!"

Mr. Morse elaborated, "He did his own planning and designing. He had seen a good many vessels because he had been on voyages to the Mediterranean and Pacific. In addition, he had previously learned the boatbuilding trade even as a youngster in the shop with his father."

"The early boats were shallow draft. He worked on those. It wasn't much of a conversion to the deep draft." Asked when his father made the change he replied, "I would say perhaps 1872 and he continued to build them right up until 1905, the year he died."

So, who built the first Friendship sloop? Well, who really knows? What can be said is that Wilbur Morse can't be unanimously claimed the original Friendship sloop builder. There are obviously many interesting versions and a lot of family pride interwoven.

But this is what makes history interesting and keeps family traditions alive.

Design Origins

There is no question that Wilbur Morse had much to do with the branding of the Friendship sloop. He certainly claimed to be the originator of the design. In fact he went so far as to declaim that the definition of a Friendship sloop "... is a sloop built in Friendship by Wilbur Morse". However, the historical evidence not only fails to support this claim, but it points to a more collaborative effort that many people contributed to in a process of trial and error, as is evidenced by what Mr. Beckett wrote in the 1970s .

What is now termed a "Friendship" sloop was originally known by a number of names: Morse boats, Muscongus boats, yacht boats, yacht sloop boats and eventually Friendship sloops. These boats, whatever we call them, were a subset of the larger family of single masted vessels that were known from Eastport to Block island as just "sloop boats", or perhaps more colloquially, "sloop-bo'ts".

The sloop-bo't was the small truck of the late 19th century and, like the small trucks of today, they came in a variety of shapes and sizes. In Muscongus Bay the sloops that were built by the McLains, Morses, Winchenbachs, Carters, Priors and Lashes were mostly a marriage between two major influences—the earlier Muscongus Bay sloops built in the area before the war, and the design innovations that were evolving in the Massachusetts building yards of Gloucester and Essex for the Gloucester fishing fleet.

Prior to the Civil War, fishermen in Muscongus Bay used a variety of local craft ranging from simple skiffs and dories to a type of open centerboard boat that was built locally. These centerboarders were small, typically around fif-teen feet in length, clinker built, with rounded bows and frames that were either steam-bent, or bent from green wood. They were undoubtedly more maneuverable under sail than a dory or skiff, and they would have represented an improvement on the dory or skiff, but they also would have been too small to venture into deep water.

Lobstering from a dory with bow-head traps.

The needs of the local fishermen-farmers were changing. As those needs changed, boat design had to adapt to meet those needs. The demand was for a vessel that could be used to perform a greater variety of tasks, from jigging cod and fishing mackerel in a small way, to moving goods. Additionally, the lobster traps of the time were large and heavy, and as fishermen looked to place more of them in the bay, there was a need for both a larger craft and one that was a more stable work platform. The boat that evolved to meet these needs was eventually called the Muscongus Bay sloop.

Larger than the earlier open boats—anything between twenty and thirty feet in length on deck—they owed much in terms of construction to the earlier centerboarders. They were still clinker built, with bent frames that were

*Typical Muscongus Bay sloop
The design was usually clinker built and a significant step up from the early centerboard boats used in Muscongus Bay.*

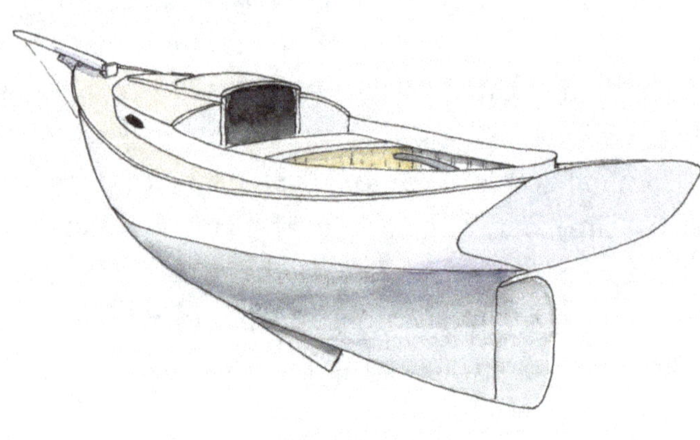

The raked transom common on Muscongus Bay sloops would evolve into an elliptical shape on Friendship sloops.

let into a heavy keel, and they had similar lines. They had the mast well forward, a bowsprit with a plumb or spoon bow, and in some cases a flat transom, though more commonly a transom set at an angle raking aft. While they retained the large centerboard and relatively shallow draft of the earlier designs, we also see new elements. These newer boats were decked over forward, and many had a small cuddy. The evolution of a more raked transom led to an inboard rudder design, and they typically had an unusual single halyard for a gaff-rigged mainsail. They carried a jib, but were often sailed with mainsail alone. Most were twenty-five to twenty-eight feet in length on deck, and could be easily handled by a man lobstering alone.

Concurrent with the development of the Muscongus Bay sloop, other influences were at work. These influences represented design changes that had their origins in the Massachusetts building yards of Boston, Gloucester, and Essex.

As in Muscongus Bay, the needs of the offshore fisheries were changing, and schooner design adapted to meet those needs. The fishing schooners in use prior to 1880 were of two slightly different designs, the sharp shooters and the clipper schooners. While the two designs were different, they shared certain characteristics. One was that they tended to be shoal draft, possibly because Gloucester Harbor is shallow. Another was that they tended to be over rigged. Although fast, these schooners needed to be sailed with great skill because despite very good initial stability, when heeled too far they could reach a point of no return, which led to sudden capsize.

As with the inshore fisheries, there was a demand for larger more stable work platforms. Multiple losses of offshore fishing boats with all hands resulted in a cry for safer schooners—

boats that were less prone to both capsizing and broaching but that were still fast so that they could get the catch to market.

According to Howard Chapelle, in his excellent book *The History of American Sailing Ships*, the first design that addressed these concerns was the ROULETTE, designed by Dennison J. Lawlor of East Boston, and launched in 1884. The new design moved to a deeper hull that drew upon his successful designs for pilot boats. ROULETTE performed well and other designers followed Lawlor's lead. Soon new schooners were being built that took advantage of and improved on Lawlor's ideas.

Two well-known examples of these new schooners were the FREDONIA, designed by Edward Burgess in 1889 and built in Essex, Massachusetts, and the SENATOR LODGE, built in Essex in 1890 and designed by George Melville McLain. These newer vessels had clipper bows—hollow entries at the waterline and topsides that flared as they rose to deck level. The result was a fast boat with a clean entry, but the flaring topsides made for a dryer ride in rough seas and a boat less likely to broach in large waves. These designs also included a raked and curved transom, and a flat run with a more pronounced "drag" to the keel, meaning that the keel was angled so that it was deeper aft and shallower forward.

What this meant in the simplest terms is that the transom design of the new Gloucestermen let a following sea lift the vessel and slide under her rather than break on her stern. The more pronounced drag to the keel meant two things, more stability and a better ability to work to windward under sail. The combination of these elements meant a faster more stable and more seaworthy offshore work platform.

The effects of these design developments were being felt in Muscongus Bay where

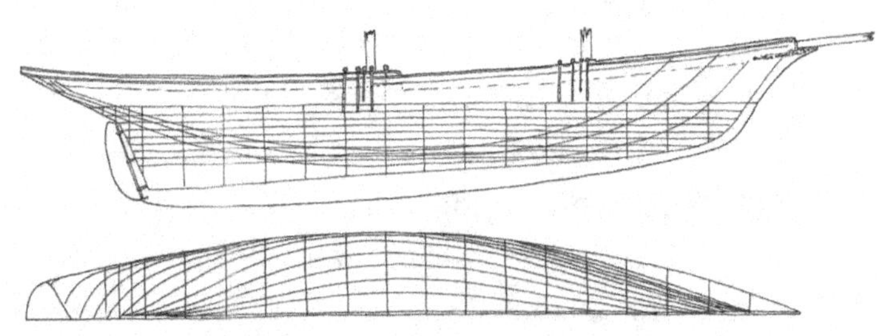

FREDONIA
*Designed by Edward Burgess 1889
and built by A.D. Storey in Essex, Massachusetts.*

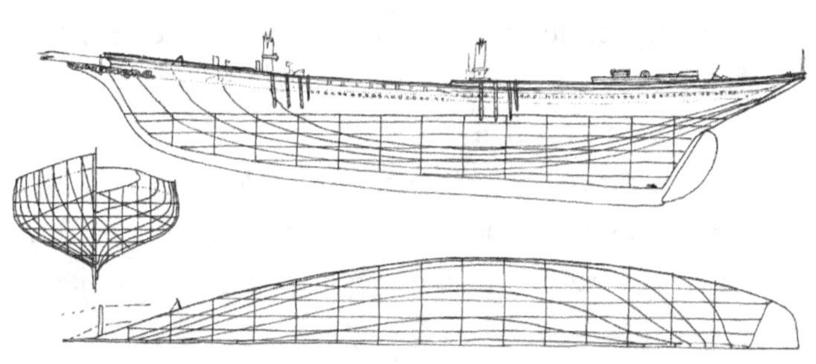

SENATOR LODGE
Designed by George Melville McLain and built in Essex in 1890.

there was growing pressure for an even larger and more seaworthy boat than the Muscongus Bay sloop.

There were clear connections between Muscongus Bay and Gloucester. The Gloucester fleet was large and always hungry for men. Men from mid-coast Maine sailed in the schooners, and the new designs. One man who shipped out on mackerel schooners was Wilbur Morse of Friendship, and another was Robert A. McLain from Bremen Long Island.

George Melville McLain originally of Breman Long Island, a well-known fishing captain and schooner designer in Gloucester, designed the SENATOR LODGE mentioned above. Some historians have attributed the awareness of the Muscongus Bay builders of the developments in the Gloucester fleet to this connection. Others feel that too much has been made of the family connection, particularly because George McLain identified himself with Gloucester and Essex and returned home very rarely. Whatever the exact nature of this connection, there is no question that the builders of Muscongus Bay were aware of the changes to the offshore fleet.

As fishermen-builders like Robert McLain and Wilbur Morse returned to their shops, the influences of the offshore fleet became apparent in a new design that was evolving to supplant the Muscongus Bay sloop.

This new design did away with the centerboard and replaced it with a deeper keel, a keel that had pronounced drag below the waterline, similar to the new schooners. These designer-builders borrowed the clipper bow and raked elliptical transom from the Gloucester fleet and adapted them to the sloops they were building. There were enough design adaptations clearly influenced by the Gloucester fleet that some have speculated that the Friendship sloop

EARLY LOBSTERING

By Ralph W. Stanley

When the coast of Maine became permanently settled after the 1760's, lobsters were plentiful, but were not regarded as a very important source of food. It is hard to believe today that during this period of early settlement lobsters were regarded as the lowest, most disgusting thing that a person could eat. It was just not the acceptable thing to do. The early settlers were very self-sufficient and proud of it, but at times when food was scarce circumstances were such that people had to eat lobsters and if people did eat lobsters they would go to great lengths to conceal the fact from their neighbors, such as burying the shells at night under cover of darkness. Lobsters could be picked up easily in the rockweed along the shore and were sometimes gathered by the people and used as fertilizer for their gardens. A steady diet of lobsters day in and day out will get pretty monotonous as they are a rich food, but not very filling. A person can eat a couple of lobsters and still feel hungry. When the summer hotels became popular in the 1870's and 80's lobsters were still plentiful and inexpensive. The summer help would insist in their contracts that they would not be fed lobster more than two or three times a week.

In the 1870's there came about a market for canned lobsters and a number of canning factories were set up on the Maine coast. Lobsters were easily caught, sometimes with a simple devise consisting of a weighted wooden or metal hoop with a net laced inside. The bait would be placed in the center of the net, and with a rope bridled from three points on the hoop, it could be lowered to the bottom in shallow water and then raised without upsetting. Lobsters would crawl on the net to get the bait. If one were careful hauling the device, the lobster would stay in place while it was being hauled to the surface. This was sufficient to catch a few lobsters in shallow water. Flounders could also be caught with this device. For deeper water, traps were built with a flat bottom and spruce bows covered with lathes spaced apart. These early bow-headed traps had a fishing head in each end. The fishing head was a net laced in the end of the trap with a hole in the center for the lobster to crawl into. In the early traps this hole had a small wooden hoop laced into it to keep it open. This was called a "funny eye". Lobsters could crawl in, but just as easily crawl out. Later traps were built more elaborately with a space called a "parlor" to hold lobsters longer. Today most traps are built with plastic-coated wire mesh.

In the early days lobsters were still plentiful and a fisherman with forty or fifty traps could, by tending the traps each day, catch sufficient lobsters to keep the factories supplied. All lobsters were keepers and were sold: big ones, small ones and those with eggs. Pictures of the factories show great piles of lobsters, ten or twelve feet high.

The factories employed many people of all ages. In 1884 Lyle Newman was 9 years old. He was sent out from the factory on the steamboat wharf at Southwest Harbor in a rowboat loaded with lobster shells to dump them in the middle of the harbor. Somehow he upset the boat, but was rescued by a couple of off-duty crew from the Little Cranberry Island Life Saving Station, who happened to be nearby. Of course, they wrote the account of the rescue in their life saving report. Any incident like this, whether they were on duty or not, would enhance the value of the Life Saving Service and prove their worth to the public and the politicians for government funding to carry out their work.

In the factories, workers cooked the lobsters and picked out the meat, which they packed in cans sealed with lead solder. People could have suffered from lead poisoning if they ate much lobster from cans.

Lobsters were getting increasingly scarce and conservation laws were instituted to protect the resource. Canning of lobsters became less feasible and factories disappeared. Demand for live lobsters in Boston and New York increased and wet well lobster smacks were built to transport live lobsters to market. The smacks were boats having a hold fitted with watertight bulkheads forward and aft. Holes would be bored through the hull planking in the way of the hold to allow seawater to circulate through the hold to keep the lobsters alive. Today lobsters are shipped in refrigerated trucks and by air, thereby increasing the range of market.

Early Hoop Trap

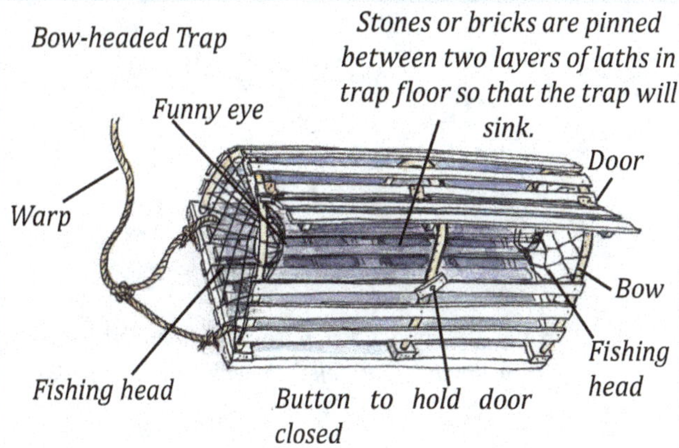

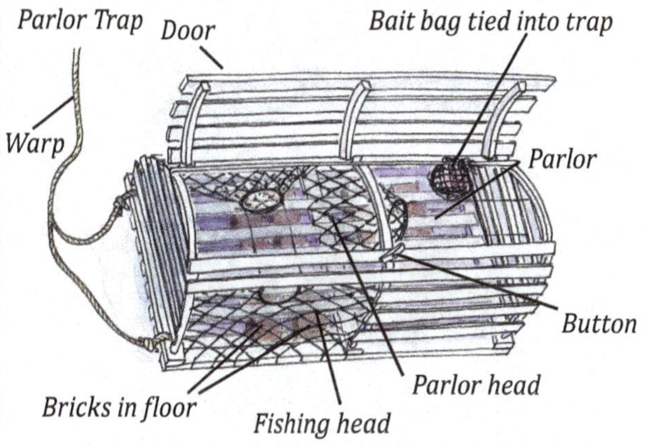

Muscongus Bay sloop owned by Melvin Simmons of Bremen Long Island.

Profile of a typical Friendship sloop based on the lines in Howard Chapelle's American Small Sailing Craft.

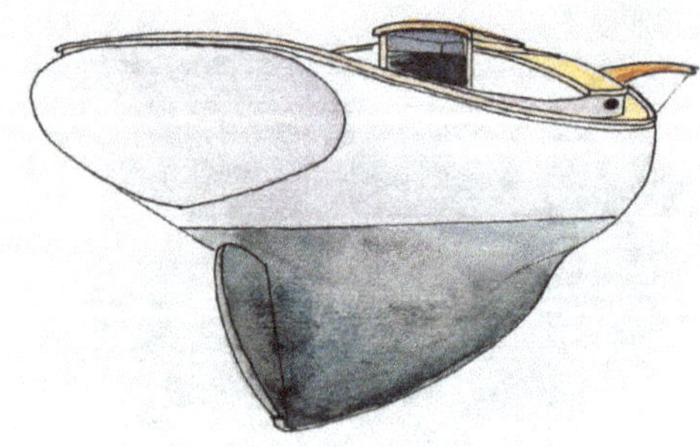

Elliptical stern.

was simply a scaled-down version of the sloop-bot's of Gloucester. But as Friendship Sloop Society Historian Ralph Stanley has pointed out, the Gloucester boats were of much heavier build with sawn frames, less sheer, and not as much homage paid to the elliptical stern as the Friendship model. It seems more likely that the builders in Muscongus were taking building methods and design characteristics that they were familiar with and that had proved successful, such as bent frames, a raked transom, and a pronounced sheer, and adapting them to newer designs. The resulting combination of old and new owed much to the Muscongus Bay sloop and to the new schooners of the offshore fleet, but was a copy of neither.

There may well have been another influence, and that is yacht design. Sailing yachts of the 1880s and 90s tended to be of deeper draft with more pronounced drag than fishing vessels. Many were weatherly sloops and it is possible that those yachts that ventured into Maine waters caught the eye of local builders who set out to emulate design elements that they had seen and liked.

Another ingredient, though difficult to quantify, was the personal experience of the builders as sailors and fishermen. Ralph Stanley speculated that one of the reasons the smooth curves of the elliptical transom became such a prominent design feature of the Friendship sloop was that the rounded edges and sleek curves made it much less likely for the long main sheet of the sloop to get caught up under, or on the edge of the transom. This is the kind of design development that results from personal experience using a boat. Fishermen, then as today, had different ways of doing things and

10

would request changes to match the way they fished, and a good idea was copied.

The Friendship sloop stands apart from other sloops in methods of construction that were not typical elsewhere, but that became fairly standard in Muscongus Bay. For example, Howard Chapelle in his seminal work *American Small Sailing Craft*, attributes the longevity of many Friendships to the unusual way deck beams were connected to the frames of the hull. There are a number of ways to make this structural connection. Most often it is a combination of a shelf running under the deck beams and a clamp, or plank, that follows the curve of the inside of the frames at the sheer. The two are fastened together in a sort of "L" shaped configuration. In Friendships, however, a type of sheer timber was developed that was not a single plank, nor a combination of shelf and plank, but rather a series of heavy timbers, usually made of oak, scarfed and through-bolted together to follow the curve of the sheer, resulting in a heavier, stronger, and more rigid shelf than was typical of other sloops of the time. The heavy keel combined with these heavy sheer timbers resulted in a stiff boat, one that has been described as "three keels with a boat between them".

Despite these heavy timbers the construction, on the whole, was considered light, perhaps a holdover from the clinker built Muscongus Bay sloops. Bent frames, for example, are very strong and can withstand a lot of stress and flex, while being much smaller in cross section and weight than sawn frames. Another unusual construction detail that Chapelle comments on, is the inclusion of a ceiling inside the frames that went almost the whole length of the hull. While usually of light planks bent to follow the

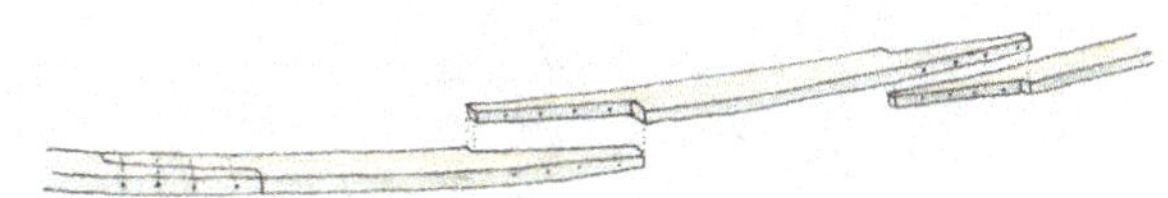

The sheer timbers are constructed of heavy pieces scarfed and bolted together.

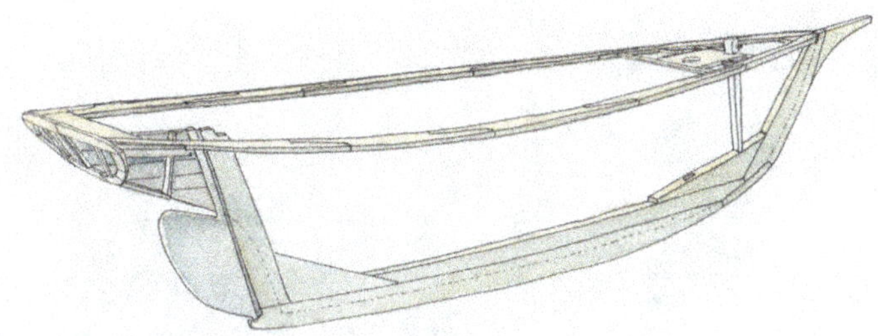

The heavy sheer timbers, sometimes called a lock strake, and the heavy keel of a Friendship sloop have been referred to as "three keels with a boat between them".

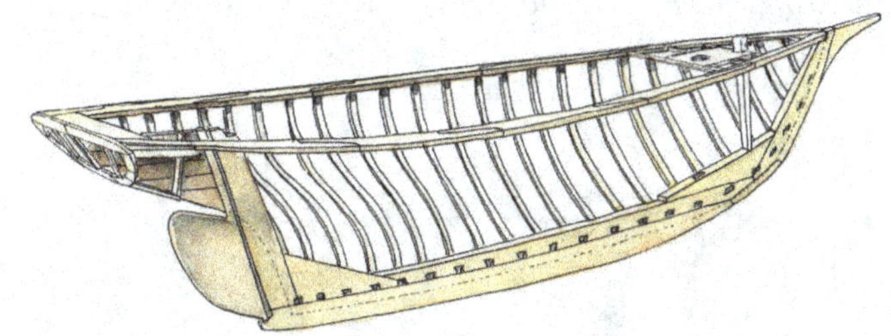

Framing on a Friendship sloop was typically bent, either green wood or steam bent.

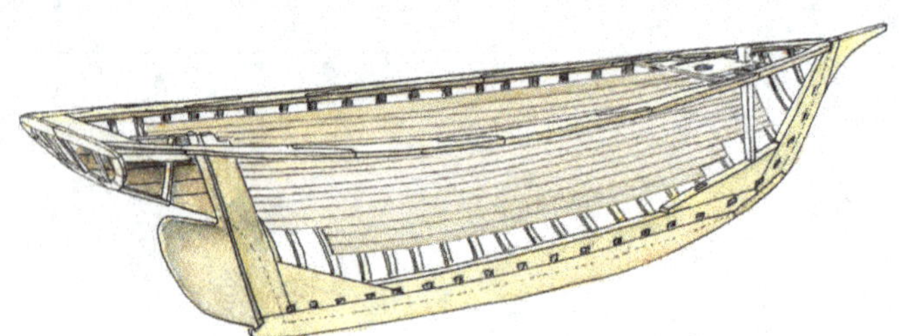

The interior ceiling of a Friendship sloop acted like an interior second skin.

The LOLA MARION in South Brooksville, Maine, 1908.

Carvers Harbor frozen over 1918.

shape of the frames, the result, as he points out, means that these boats had essentially a double skin, another element making them strong and stiff while reasonably light.

These innovations that helped to add strength to the hull seem strangely at odds with other building conventions, however. One convention being that there were very few floor timbers in Friendship sloops. Chapelle maintains that there were never more than five timbers, and that some Friendship sloops were built without any floor timbers at all. Another standard construction method was to set the heel of the mast directly into a socket in the keel instead of some form of mast-step. This practice often put great stress on the keel and garboards at the foot of the mast and caused many boats to "work" and leak badly at this part of the hull.

Returning to the question of who built the first Friendship sloop, it should be apparent that there was not a first, but rather many firsts. Trial and error led to an amalgamation of design elements and construction techniques that became standard ingredients of the Friendship sloop.

The development of the Friendship sloop should be seen in a different light than the development of the offshore fleet. Schooners that came from the yards in Gloucester and Essex were large in scale and represented a significant investment in both time and money, and perhaps predictably, the influence of individual vessels is both more obvious and more likely to be recorded. Unlike their big sisters, Friendship sloops were built by the hundreds, and mostly by individuals. The individual investment was less, and since many people built them, it is much more difficult to trace which builder came up with which specific innovation. As Ralph Stanley has pointed out, there

First hand account of fishing from a Friendship

Friendship Sloop at Work

Interview with Albert D. Cushman

Adapted from the 1964 FSS yearbook

No one will deny that lobstering is a difficult job. For most anyone merely trying to maintain his balance and stay on his feet while the boat pitches and rolls would be a day's work, or finding and keeping his bearings in a thick fog or blinding snowstorm might discourage the wary. Add to this the finding, hauling, baiting, and resetting of a couple hundred traps a day and you have a rough idea of a lobsterman's lot. Admittedly the winch for hauling traps, the depth finder, and the radio telephone, not to mention the standing tops and gasoline engines have eased things up considerably.

For a comparison between today's fishing and that 50 years or more ago we talked to Allie Cushman, a veteran lobster fisherman who has fished for lobsters for more than seventy years. Allie has fished from a Wilbur Morse sloop. She was the thirty-four foot WAWENOCK. We asked Allie how it was possible for one man to manage the sails, warp, traps, lobsters, and bait and still manage to keep clear of the ledges and rocks, and he said the secret was to "lead out the sheet of the mains'l quite a way, and trim the jib tight while you're hauling. The boat would lay good then." He added, "When you hauled, the trap would come to the top of the water quite a way off, and you would have to pull it over to you, of course."

Usually two men would team up for winter fishing, and they would always take a dory along. If the weather was moderate and calm, one man would haul traps from it, while the other stayed with the sloop. During a good breeze, it took all the skills of both men to sail the boat and haul the traps, with wind, waves and spray keeping them pretty well wet down most of the time. When asked if it wasn't bitter cold with no spray hoods or standing tops, Allie explained that one man would stand down in the "cuddy" and watch his partner's face. "When his nose started to turn white, it was time to change places."

"Lobstering was altogether different 50 years ago," said Allie. "In those days a man had one gang of traps. About 60 was all he could haul in one day, and we couldn't put them in close to the rocks the way we do now."

Out of curiosity, we asked Allie how old he was when he first went lobstering. His answer was something like this — "Well I couldn't say exactly, but my folks thought I was too young to be out in a boat, so I lugged a trap down on the point and set it out at low water as far as I could. The next day I'd go haul it in to see what I'd caught."

And Allie's been at it ever since except for a time when he went seining with his father in a 48-foot Friendship they named NORTH STAR.

But seining's another story.

Vinalhaven waterfront 1911.

were some fishermen-builders who built a sloop over the winter, fished that boat for a season, sold the boat, and started a new boat the following winter. This cycle of building followed by experimentation followed by more building, contributed to the overall development of the Friendship sloop, but it makes it even more difficult to attribute a specific innovation to a particular boat or builder. Further complicating the issue is the fact that many of the builders were related to one another either by blood or through marriage, and trying to figure out who got which idea from whom becomes something of a quagmire.

Having said that, different builders did indeed have different reputations, and were known for design features of the boats that they built. Boats built by Robert McLain were reputed to be of the very best construction. Wilbur Morse, the most prolific of builders, built many well-constructed sloops, but he also produced some that were much less well built. Again to quote Ralph Stanley, "It looks like he may have built some sloops to fit the wallet of the owner". Even within families there were noticeable differences. The sloops built by Wilbur Morse differ slightly from those built by his brother Charles. To the uninitiated the differences might seem miniscule, but ask a current owner of either a Charlie Morse or Wilbur Morse boat what those differences are and you are likely to get an earful.

The result of these influences and collaborations is not so much a type of boat as it is a family of boats. As is sometimes the case with families of people, a strong family resemblance can be apparent, while each person is also recognizable as a unique individual.

For the Friendship sloop, the family resemblance consists of a boat whose beam is equal to roughly one-third the length on deck. The mast is set about a fifth of the way aft of the bow. The boom is roughly the length of the boat on the waterline, and the gaff is long enough to reach the rudderpost from the mast. Other features include an inboard rudder, with either a tiller or wheel, and a bowsprit that is one-third the length of the boat on deck, and a heavy keel originally with a ballast of beach stone inside. How the boats were ballasted changed over time to some boats having iron ballast inside, and eventually ballast, either iron or lead, was used both inside and outside the keel. We would be remiss not to include the elliptical transom mentioned earlier, and the clipper bow, which is almost always adorned with a pair of trailboards carved with a curving vine or similar design, and in some cases the name of the builder.

These variables can differ from boat to boat, but as is the case with family resemblance, each boat is immediately recognizable as a Friendship sloop.

The Early Builders

It is not within the scope of this book to list the individual histories of all the early boat builders that worked in Muscongus Bay. Unfortunately, a fire in Friendship destroyed a lot of original records, which would make such a task even more difficult if that were the objective. However, we can give a pretty good run down of the most influential builders who worked, either together or independently, in the early development of this family of vessels.

Wilbur Morse is the name that many people think of when they think of Friendship sloops, and that is not unreasonable when you consider how many he built. Roger Duncan, in his excellent book *Friendship Sloops*, attributed between 400-500 sloops to Wilbur Morse. It is also understandable when you consider that, like many other early builders, Wilbur Morse was gifted at self-promotion. There is another difference between Wilbur Morse and most, if not all of the other builders in Muscongus Bay, and that is that while most builders worked alone or with a helper, Wilbur had a relatively large crew of men, and they often were working on more than one boat at a time. While it would be unfair to say that Wilbur had a production line going in Friendship, a photograph taken of one of his last shop crews shows ten men, and even if the ten-man crew is representative of a short period in the career of Wilbur Morse, it does represent a different scale of production than other builders in the area.

There are a good number of Wilbur Morse sloops still alive and kicking. AMITY #9, BLACK JACK #19, TERN #24, WHITE EAGLE #31, NOMAD #32, CHANCE #37, SAZERAC #44., and VENTURE #66 have all survived.

Wilbur was not the only member of the Morse family building sloops though. His older brothers Albion and Charles built many fine sloops. MORNING STAR #82 and MUSCONGUS #154 are two built by Albion that have survived, and CHRISSY #18, RUTH L. #13, VERA JEAN #164, TECUMSEH #242 and WESTWIND #95, which were built by Charles, are still with us today. The youngest Morse brother, Jonah, was foreman at the Wilbur Morse yard, so he should be included in the list as well.

Not everyone in Friendship was a Morse. James Winchenbach, Leroy Wallace, Archie Thomson, and Irwin and Stacy

The early Goose River shop of Wilbur Morse.

The Wilbur Morse shop in Friendship.

CHRISSY #18 built by Charles Morse.

Maine Sloop Boats
A Story of Two Scallop Fishermen

By Ralph W. Stanley

The scallop fishery of Penobscot Bay developed on a limited basis about the year 1900 or before. Scallops were caught by means of dragging a dredge on the bottom at first by boats under sail. The Maine Sloop Boat, known today as the Friendship sloop, was the boat of choice for towing a dredge under sail. However, dredging for scallops under sail without power involved a lot of hard work and really was not practicable. Hauling up a dredge full of scallops, rocks and other bottom debris could be back breaking work. Dredges were necessarily small and consequently the catch would be small. With the advent of the gasoline engine, fishing for scallops became a more viable fishery. Many Friendship sloops were fitted with two-cycle engines—the Knox engine, produced locally, was a popular engine. Some sloops were fitted with a stationary engine for hoisting the dredge.

The Maine Sea and Shore Fisheries Report for 1909-10 states that the scallop fishery was comparatively new being largely developed since the advent of the motor boat, although scallops had been caught for a number of years before. It was not unusual on a good day in winter, to see from sixty to one hundred boats dragging in Penobscot Bay. Many of these boats were undoubtedly Friendship sloops. These boats were usually crewed by two or three men and the catch varied from thirty to one hundred gallons a day according to the supply, demand and conditions of the weather. Penobscot Bay was closed to scallop fishing during the summer months.

The following narrative by Tinker Crouch of Oceanville, Deer Isle relates the experiences of her grandfather and his brother, yacht captains who sailed on yachts in the summer season and fished from their sloop in the winter. She writes about her grandfather, Francis Claude Gross, of Oceanville,

He got his start one day when he was under twenty years (Probably about the year 1893) out fishing with his father, Capt. Thad, (Thaddeus Gross m. Eunice Margaret Greenlaw). A yacht (the schooner yacht FROLIC, 26 tons and 58-feet length overall built in 1879 at Islip, New York) belonging to Herbert H. White of Marblehead, for many years treasurer of the Cambridge University Press, came along side to ask if they knew anyone who would go cook for him since they had had to put their cook ashore in Rockland because of illness. Grampa decided he'd like to go and so began a yachting career lasting many years, thirty of them with Mr. White. He often went to school to upgrade his license ending up with an unlimited captain's certification for the Atlantic coast and a limited certification for the world (because he did not have the tonnage) He would go yachting in the summer and scalloping in the winter in their Friendship sloop with his brother, Ray (Raymond Clayton Gross, who also was a yacht captain during the yachting season.)

Grammie Gross (Lucy Ellen Lane) lost her father (Joseph Lane) at sea when she was thirteen years old. He left four daughters, Ada Trundy Dow (adopted), Alice, Lucy and Nina. She only finished eighth grade as was the custom unless one planned to teach school. She was working as house help in the Gross house when she and Grampa decided to get married. They quietly went to Stonington and were married by the minister and then came home to his house. When her sister, Nina and his brother Ray found out, they were outraged because they also planned to marry and she (Nina) had wanted a double church wedding, something Grampa would never have gone along with. Sometime later they moved to a wing of Aunt Cad and Uncle John Gross' house in Oceanville. When they had five hundred dollars saved they built their own house in Oceanville.

One winter Ray and Grampa fished over near Rockland all winter, so the next winter the two families moved there and rented a house (about 1915-16). (In 1899 Benjamin Thaddeus Gross of Deer Isle, Maine, father of Francis and Raymond, had a sloop of nine tons named VIXEN built at Friendship, Maine, probably by Wilbur Morse. Francis and Ray also owned a sloop but unfortunately the name of their sloop is not known. In 1914, according to Deer Isle tax records, Capt Thad's sloop is valued for taxation at $150 while the sloop belonging to his two sons is valued at $224.)

That winter their boat was run down and sunk by a Boston fishing smack, the fishing schooner EDITH B. THOMPSON, Ray was below and got out through a port. Grampa was thrown overboard. Neither could swim but both were picked up by the fishing smack.

The Deer Isle Messenger of November 12, l915 re-

Sloop owned by Frank Raymond Gross that was run down in 1915, (we believe her name was the AGNES) note the club-footed staysail.

ports the incident, "The scallop sloop owned by Frank and Raymond Gross, of Oceanville, was sunk near the United States trial course, in west Penobscot bay, on Wednesday of last week, by the Boston fishing schooner EDITH B. THOMPSON. The Stonington craft was returning from the day's fishing on the Monroe Island beds, when the clutch broke and it became stalled near the trial course. The Boston smack came along at this time and so absorbed was the helmsman in watching the superdreadnought NEVADA's trial run that he failed to notice the helpless scallop boat directly in his path. The latter was struck directly amidships, and sank immediately. Frank Gross, who was in the cockpit, jumped overboard, and the mainsheet was thrown to him by one of the THOMPSON's crew, and he was drawn safely to the fisherman's deck. Raymond Gross made his way over the shattered side and jumped aboard the schooner. With its equipment the scallop sloop represents a loss to her owners of about $1200."

They commenced to have a new motor boat built in Thomaston named DORIS. (The DORIS was thirty-two feet in length with a beam of nine feet. It seems that Frank and Ray very quickly received a settlement from the owners of the THOMPSON for enough money enabling them to buy the new boat. Perhaps Mr. White, being from Boston, put some pressure on the owners of the THOMPSON. Usually it takes some time to settle a situation such as this.) They went back to Rockland the next year and all the good fishing was in the Eastern Bay so they were seldom home. In such cases the wives would do a lot of cooking when the men were home for the weekend and send them off well-provisioned for the week, which they would spend on the boat if they were too far away to get home every day. The next year they bought the house in Stonington making that headquarters. Three children were born (to Francis and Lucy) Margaret Ellen in 1902, Doris Lane in 1910 and Francis Lane in 1913. Doris started school in Rockland at age six in the third grade.

With Mr. White, Grampa often raced. The winnings, which they took, often were paid in gold pieces, which Mr. White always gave to Grampa and he gave to Grammie. The oak sideboard always in her dining room she bought with the first twenty-five dollar gold piece he won.

Their wedding present from Mr. White was a tea set from New York City, gold and white china. (Tanya Gross Riva granddaughter now has this.) Grampa was invited to go to England one year as Mr. White's companion to play golf (he went) and he once asked Grampa what kind of a vacation trip he would take if he had three weeks all expenses paid. His Answer was, "Sail down the coast, through the Panama Canal to California and back across by train". Grammie wouldn't go on a ship so they went to the Grand Canyon round trip all expenses paid.

Following are the vessels in which Francis Gross served as Captain:

FROLIC, a 26-ton schooner yacht owned by Herbert H. White built at Islip, New York in 1879.

WILD GOOSE

CACHALOT I, a 41-ton schooner yacht owned by Herbert H. White built at Tottenville, New York in 1899.

CACHALOT II, a 77-ton auxiliary ketch owned by Herbert H. White built at Damariscotta, Maine in 1928.

CACHALOT III, auxiliary schooner built at Shelburne, Nova Scotia.

AJAX

ROBIN, 49-ton auxiliary schooner owned by Norman H. White (Herbert's brother) built at City Island, New York in 1902.

MARIE, a 38-foot overall sloop owned by Herbert H. White built at South Boston in 1902. This must have been the boat that they raced to win the gold pieces .

BEATRICE B., auxiliary schooner owned by Fritz B. Talbot built at Boothbay Harbor, Maine in 1930.

The crew at the Wilbur Morse Yard. Left to right: James Franklin Winchenbach, Leroy Wallace, Archie Thompson, Wilbur A. Morse, Ray Simmons, Irvin Simmons Sr., George Carter, Harold Benner, Stacy Simmons, and the last man is unidentified .

Eugene McLain on the far left, Steven Prior and Ed Merry seated in the front row. Standing left to right are Leslie Collamore, Crosby Prior, Norman Carter, Orrin McLain, Chester Carter, and Elmer Willey. All but Merry are believed to have been involved in building sloops. The picture is dated August 1906.

ESTELLA A. #200

Simmons all worked for Wilbur Morse at some point, along with two of the Carter family. Some of these men built boats on their own as well, and should be considered builders in their own right.

The McLain family dominated Bremen and Bremen Long Island boatbuilding. Robert A. McLain Sr., who was married to Wilbur Morse's oldest sister Mary, was perhaps the best-known member of the family, but his four sons, Robert E., Alexander, Eugene and Almond, were also building boats.

Robert E. McLain built the lovely ESTELLA A. #200 in 1904 for Jack Ames of Matinicus Island for a contract price of $425.00. ESTELLA A. now resides at Mystic Seaport as part of their permanent collection. Of the boys, Alexander may be the best known. GLADIATOR #71, built in 1902 is still going strong and is a nice example of Alexander McLain's work.

In addition to the McLains, George Washington (Wash) Carter and his two sons, (Abdon and George), Vincent Collamore, William Prior, and George Prior were all building sloops.

This list of builders is by no means complete, but it does give a pretty good idea of how many builders were cheek-by-jowl building Friendships in the two generations that preceded World War I. This incredibly prolific period of boatbuilding, design and development was to have a far-reaching influence, as we shall see.

On Sailing Characteristics of Individual Sloops

By Ralph W. Stanley

Friendship sloops were not at all perfect boats, and builders were constantly seeking ways to improve their model. I have talked with men who fished from sloops, and one thing that I learned was that some sloops would drag their sterns under when sailed hard. Apparently, when heeled over, the boat did not have buoyancy enough in the underbody aft, and that, together with the forward motion of the boat, would tend to drag the stern under water. Once this happened, it would be hard to get the boat up into the wind.

If the stern is too buoyant when heeled, the bow tends to go down and creates a weather helm. Cliff Robbins of Southwest Harbor had a sloop named the ALICE G, and she had such a weather helm that he had to rig a tackle on the tiller to steer her. A lot of sloops had faults, but many balanced very well. Richie Stanley of Cranberry Isle had a sloop named the ALICE MARION, built at Hatchet Cove, Friendship, by Charles Morse in 1908, with a round bow. Fishing with a crew of three, they would be off shore for several days. When they got ready to sail home, they would trim the sails, drop the tiller in the comb, and let her sail herself while they went below to play cards, looking out now and then to check their course.

York Island, Maine, circa 1900.

Paul Stubing photo courtesy of the Penobscot Marine Museum

Sloop GENESEE

by Ralph W. Stanley

Adapted from the 1991 FSS yearbook.

The sloop GENESEE, built in 1900 by Robert E. McLain, was for many years owned by Oscar W. Sellers at Stonington, Maine. Typical of many Friendship sloops of her day, she started out as a sailing vessel, eventually having an engine installed. She was engaged in the fishing business for at least 25 years. Her long life no doubt reflects the care she was given over the years.

One photo right shows GENESSE with a fishing party. The photo above shows her at the Johnson and Young lobster dock at Stonington. The building at the right of the lobster dock is the steamboat wharf. Note the fine peapods in the picture. One is well-equipped with sail, oars and other gear, and perhaps had just got in from hauling traps. Also note the rub strips on the afterquarters of the sloop. Sometimes when hauling traps, the sloop would range ahead and the trap would trail astern. These strips protected the planking from wear and

chafing of the rope hauled over the side. Traps were hauled by hand in those days.

GENESSEE is very similar to the DICTATOR #2, built by the same builder in 1904. She has the same deck layout that DICTATOR originally had with the oval cockpit. GENESSEE was slightly smaller than DICTATOR, GENESSEE being 30'0" on deck, 10'0" beam and 5'3"draft at 7 gross tons, and DICTATOR being 31'4" long 10'6" beam 5'4" draft at 8 gross tons. These sloops were close enough in size to have been built from the same model.

In 1925, GENESSEE was listed in *Merchant Vessels* as a motor vessel with a crew of two with an 8 h.p. engine being used for fishing. At this time, she was owned by Henry Roberts of South Portland, Maine, who was her owner for the next ten years. In 1936, she was owned by Morgan Upton of Cambridge, MA. and home ported in Portland. In 1937, ownership changed to A. Morris Hughes and her home port was still Portland. This is the last year she appears in the *list of Merchant Vessels*.

Courtesy of the Deer Island Historical Society

Friendships Still Work

By Bill Thon

Adapted from the 1974 FSS yearbook

It does not seem likely that many of that hardy breed who started hauling lobster traps with a sloop would still be active.

Ernest Maloney of Port Clyde, now in his eighties, not only is a working lobsterman, but can still roundly cuss the price and quality of trap stock. His daughter, who is our postmaster, once told me that the first time she was on a sloop was when she was carried aboard in a basket.

I may as well admit to an inordinate interest in anything about boats in general, and working craft in particular. So it was not long after putting ECHO #54 in commission that I began pestering Ernest with questions about how fishing was managed, and how a sloop behaved while hauling traps. It seemed best talking about it on winter afternoons in the little fish house on the wharf with the odor of oak, cedar, rope, paint, and burning wood from the stove, with now and then a whiff of bait when you got too loo'rd of it. Ernest would sit in a beat-up old Morris chair, one arm missing and the stuffing half out of the rest, I would find a stool or capsize a bucket and fire away. Ernest would recall how often the sloops had to be rowed out of the harbor in the flat calm of early dawn. Perhaps about sun-up there would be a bit of wind so the big sweep could be lain aside. "Well Sir, you come up on your buoy and cast off the stays'l sheet and give the mains'l about half of the sheet," etc., etc.

The following summer one fine day Ernest and I were headed out of the harbor for an afternoon sail. We had rounded the Brothers and were standing toward Burnt Island, all the while passing many pot buoys, and it occurred to me to say to Ernest, "If one of these was yours how would you handle the boat?"

He looked at me with a kind of twinkle in his eye and said, "You want to haul a lobster trap?" I guess I didn't waste any time in saying "Yes." Here it was — not talk or reading about it in books. This was a real live lobsterman going to haul traps in a Friendship sloop.

"First," he said, "take in that jib." This left us with the stays'l and the main and we were in business.

We were about a mile off the southeast side of Magee Island where he had some traps. Fortunately I had a camera on board and went forward and stood by the mast while I watched the clock turn back more than a half century. Ernest, with a gaff in one hand and the tiller in the other rounding up to snag the buoys, handling sheets, knee against the tiller to keep her up in the wind, bringing the trap in, hand over hand, (ECHO is not equipped with any hauling gear).

He was able to bring in the heavy trap without scratching my paintwork.

ECHO has always been nimble: she will come about nearly in her own length. Old timers would say she is handy, and it was a joy to watch Ernest work with her and see how well she performed her intended purpose.

After we had a good lobster I was satisfied but Ernest insisted on getting a "few more for Mrs. Thon."

Later when we picked up our mooring there were a half dozen prime, unplugged counters crawling about under the seats in the cockpit.

Rowing back to the wharf in the dinghy I was, as usual, admiring the tumble home around ECHO'S stern when Ernest looked at her and smiled and said, "You know I haven't done that for more than fifty years."

There is something heroic about these men and when they are gone, something will be missing from this area, for their like is not soon to be found.

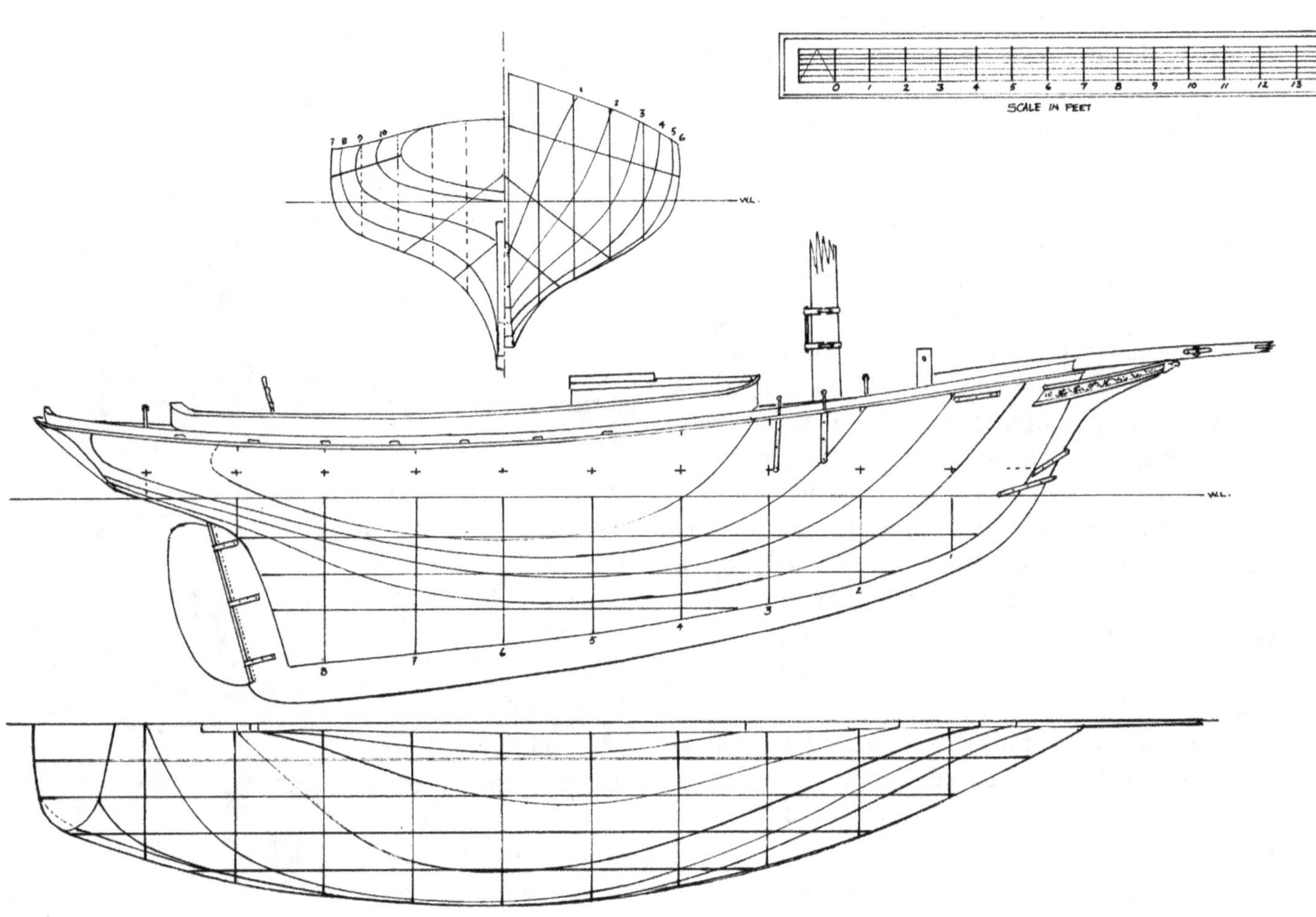

Lines of a typical Friendship sloop
Length on deck   29' 5"
Waterline length 25' 0"
Beam   10' 0"
Draft   5' 7"

Lines taken off by Howard I. Chapelle
Redrawn By T.B.R. Walsh 2014

Chapter Two: The Conversion to Recreational Sail

As early as the first decade of the twentieth century, Friendship sloops were starting to make the transition from prosaic tools used to fish and move basic goods to pleasure craft.

The first phase came from the fishermen themselves. Since the end of the Civil War, rusticators had been coming to Maine to escape the heat of the city in the summer. Many farmers realized that catering to the needs of summer visitors presented an easier way to make a living than farming. Some farms became boarding houses for summer visitors, and some of those boarding houses developed into hotels. By the beginning of the twentieth century there were well-established summer colonies along the coast, from the southern Maine beaches to Mount Desert Island. Just as many farmers saw this invasion of the summer visitors as an opportunity, so did many fishermen. A small investment in cleaning and repainting their sloops at the beginning of the summer, perhaps even the addition of a few cushions, and fishermen could take out summer people and sail them around, often for better money than could be earned fishing. The term used for this new form of alternative income was "sailing parties," with emphasis on the second word. Sailing parties were not limited to sloops, nor was this actually a new idea. A small pinky schooner built in Essex, Massachusetts in 1827 was taking sailing parties out of Christmas Cove as early as 1899. However, the sheer number of sloops available meant that there were more opportunities for sloops than other types of craft.

Most of the boats engaged in sailing parties did not give up fishing altogether. Taking out rusticators for a day sail on nice afternoons was an experiment, one which some fishermen embraced and others found more challenging than winter fishing. For those who took to it, the relationship that developed between the early charter captains and the parties they took out often had a different flavor than the usual servant-master relationship. The fishermen, turned charter captains, were typically fiercely independent individuals, who were taking out parties as much to be obliging as for any financial incentive. Other than cleaning up their sloops a bit, these captains saw no need to change the way they spoke, or how they behaved. Most treated their new cargos with the same respectful diffidence with which they treated all strangers. The rusticators in their turn recognized the sailing ability, local knowledge, and weather wisdom of these mariners and, by and large, accepted any eccentricities as part of the package. In fact, sailing together and facing a sudden fog or summer squall often forged a closer relationship between captains and summer people. In many cases those bonds, unusual in people of such different backgrounds and social standing, became very strong and important to both parties. Three examples of sloops that sailed parties: SIREN II, owned by Ed Leeman of Round Pond, used to sail parties out of Damariscotta. Archie Spurling had a sloop called the DOLPHIN out of Cranberry Island, and sailed parties out of Southwest Harbor. SWEET PEA, owned by Charles E. "Peter" Richardson also sailed out of Cranberry Island (see sidebar pg. 24-25). According to Ralph Stanley, "SWEET PEA was originally to be called ALERT, but someone else launched a boat at about the same time with that name, so Richardson was going to call her LITTLE FLIRT, but then some wag painted SWEET PEA on her, and the name stuck".

SIREN II sailed parties out of Damariscotta.

Sailing parties was not a full time occupation, and most sloop skippers continued to fish, haul traps, and use their boats as they had when there was no one to take out, although some of them became a little more mindful of the paint.

The true transformation to recreation craft came for the Friendship sloop as a byproduct of another transformation, and that was the evolution of many summer boarders into cottagers.

As more and more people from away discovered the glories of Maine, many, particularly the well-to-do, did not cherish sharing their vacation time rubbing shoulders with other people from away. Some began buying land and building cottages for themselves so that they could have their own little private slice of Maine. Some of those slices were not so little.

While the Maine summer cottage could be a small camp on a secluded point, it was just as likely to be a grand shingle-style mansion on the same scale as a hotel, but intended for the use of one family, and in some cases, one person. Sometimes it was the true intention of the owner to escape the social commitments and pressures that were a part of everyday life for

24

'Peter' Richardson and SWEET PEA

Adapted from the 1987 FSS yearbook

In November 1986, Ralph Stanley and his wife Marion agreed to an oral history interview by Bob Brooks and his wife Judy O'Neal. The following conversation concerning Peter Richardson was extracted from those recordings.

The conversation starts with the identification of the photograph on page 25.

Ralph: That was the SWEET PEA. She was a 25 footer which belonged to Charles E. Richardson. Everybody called him "Peter Richardson". Peter was a smooth, crackerjack sailor and could do anything with that sloop.

Bob: You recognize him from the photo then?

Ralph: He wasn't sailing her that day. My great-uncle Lewis Stanley was sailing the boat that day. Sometimes Peter might be indisposed and Uncle Lew would take the boat for him.

Marion: A nice way of saying he was drunk!

Bob: Is Peter the gent whom you wrote something about a couple of years ago? The same gent who used to backwind her upside the dock with a bottle of rum in one hand?

Ralph: Yep! [chuckle] Yep, that's him! He was a character, but he could really handle that sloop— he could put her anywhere. He used to sail the Appalachian Club and had a standing order to sail them whenever they wanted to go out. He was out to Baker's Island with a party of people one time and they decided they wanted to stay later.

"Alright," he said, "but it'll turn thick o'fog."

"Oh, no!" They didn't think so. "It doesn't look bad."

"Alright," he said, "I'll stay. If it doesn't bother you, it doesn't bother me."

The longer they stayed, the drunker he got as he was sipping rum all the afternoon and all the evening. Well, finally they came down about ten o'clock to take her back to Northeast. It was dungeon-black thick o'fog. He had an old make'n'break Knox in that sloop. He started her up and headed for Northeast and they didn't see a thing. They

SWEET PEA with Lew Stanley at the helm. Peter Richardson was "sick" the day the photo was taken.

Ralph wrote the following about Peter Richardson for the 1985 Yearbook:

Most every harbor on the coast had one or two men who became legends through their ability to sail and handle Friendship sloops. Peter Richardson of Cranberry Isles was one such person. I can remember him in a fresh afternoon breeze sailing by Beal's dock in Southwest Harbor to pick up a party at the public dock. He would be leaning against the tiller waving his hat with one hand and a bottle of rum with the other, shouting some remark to those watching on Beal's dock, punctuating it with a good swig of rum. With the wind blowing directly on the public float, he would luff into the wind, drop his tiller straight in its comb, leave the main sheet, go up on the bow and by backing the jib first one way and then the other, he would back his sloop in beside the float. Someone would hold the shroud and the party would pile aboard. He would take the tiller, trim the main, fill away and be off for an afternoon sail.

Peter Richardson in legend may exceed the reality of his life, but tales abound about his feats of seamanship, his quirks of character, his stentorian voice, and his use and abuse of spirits. Peter, noted for his fetish for keeping his sloop clean and for his crankiness when hung over, had a charter of lubbers on board and convinced them to fish without removing the shells from the clams used for bait. Peter kept SWEET PEA spotless that day, but the fishing wasn't too great!

knew he was drunk and they were worried to death about whether they would make it or not. Finally, they heard the bell on the Bear Island lighthouse, so they wanted to turn right there.

"Oh, there's the lighthouse. Let's turn right now!" All Peter would do was sing, "Give Me Five Minutes More!" And he sung them that song and went five minutes more, then hauled her up 'round north and went straight into Northeast Harbor. He could hardly stand up.

Judy: Now, is that where he sailed out of?

Ralph: No! He'd sail out of Southwest, Northeast, anywheres. He was at Cranberry Island.

Bob: Do you know what happened to her?

Ralph: She was down at Uncle Lew's boatyard and she just fell apart. Jarvis [Newman] has got the eagle from her. Somebody else took the trailboards, I think. There are still pieces of her kicking around.

Bob: Now, who did her?

Ralph: Wilbur Morse. Peter had her rebuilt in 1931 by Chester Clements at Southwest Boat.

Sailing Parties and a 1907 Race
By Ralph W. Stanley

Adapted from the 1994 FSS yearbook.

Rock End Hotel dock, Gilpatrick Cove. Great Cranberry Island in background.

Many fishermen in the 1890s and early 1900s fixed their sloops up with new paint and varnish and sailed rusticators in the summer before the lobstering and fishing season in the fall. Wherever there was a summer colony, sailing in sloops was popular. Many families would engage a fisherman with his sloop for the whole summer, and many did this year after year.

Fishermen were pretty skillful sailors, and the summer people were quite impressed by the way they could sail their sloops to a dead stop at the dock or the mooring and the way they handled their sloops in difficult situations. It was considered great sport to sponsor races among the sloops. The following account from *The Bar Harbor Record* of August 28, 1907 is of a sloop race off Northeast Harbor.

"The annual race for sloops owned in and around Northeast Harbor by year-round residents was sailed last Saturday in wind enough to make it interesting, though they had to beat it out on the first leg of the course, which was from Northeast Harbor to the whistling buoy off Baker's Island, then to the red spar buoy in Western Way and back to Northeast Harbor, a distance of 8 ½ miles.

"There were two classes, large and small sloops, over 30 feet and under 30 feet, cash prizes and pennants offered by the summer colony. Eight large and four small sloops entered. In the large class the ALERT, Capt. W.D. Stanley of Cranberry, won the $10 first prize and pennant, with Capt. Freeman Gott second ($5 and pennant). The LOUISE A, Capt. Ernest Spurling, was third ($3). In the small class the COLUMBIA, Capt. Henry Spurling of Southwest Harbor, took first prize, $10 and pennant. The next two were L' SPERENCE, owned by Lewis Stanley, Cranberry, and sailed by Capt. Will Black; and the NELLIE FRANCIS, Capt. Fred Spurling, Islesford. There were two other Islesford entries, the MARY ALICE (under 30 feet), Capt. George Henry Spurling, the HELEN, Capt. Arthur Joy, the ROVERS BRIDE, Capt. Harvey Bulger, the DEFENDER, Capt. Freeman Stanley, and the SEA GULL, Capt. Fred A. Birlem. It was a top race, and if the wind was fluky at the start, the boats finished in a whole sail breeze."

Captain Freeman Gott's sloop was named the MERRY WINGS.

them, and sometimes it was just an extension of that same life. Whether the intention was to get away or to impress the same neighbors one saw in Boston, Philadelphia, or New York, the effect was the same, cottagers became a set unto themselves—or almost.

One area where many cottagers still preserved their connections to the community was in boating. Just as these summer visitors did not favor sharing space in a hotel lobby or dining room, many were unenthusiastic about sharing a particular sloop or captain. Cottagers began the practice of contracting with a captain and his sloop for the season. This might go on for a season or two, but as has already been described, fishermen rarely kept a sloop for very long, but went about building a new sloop, or having one built every few years. By the end of World War I it was common for a fisherman, particularly one who sailed parties, to sell the old sloop to summer people. Sometimes the new owner would pay the former captain a small retainer to act as the agent for the boat to oversee maintenance and to be available to sail the boat for the family, or simply to give advice.

Buying older sloops for use as pleasure boats made sense for everyone involved. The fisherman usually got far more money than he reckoned the boat was worth, and the summer person was buying a boat with which he was often already familiar, and at much less cost than having a yacht built. After the Great War, the number of people coming to Maine for summers grew, and sloops that would have previously been considered worn out were bought and fixed up enough to use as pleasure craft. These boats were almost always leaky, and to use the expression of the time, some had been "bobbed". The enormous rig—long bowsprits and booms that fishermen needed to get home, or out to haul when there was little wind, put too much strain on a worn-out hull, and it was

RUTH LOGAN
Adapted from the 1992 FSS yearbook.

RUTH LOGAN comfortably double-reefed.

My grandfather, James Logan, first came to Friendship at the behest of his good friend Robert Armstrong to inspect the Y.M.C.A. camp on Crotch Island. The Logan family liked Friendship so much that, in 1907, he had a summer cottage built on Davis Point overlooking the harbor. Grandpa considered oil lamps and candles to be too dangerous so he had a gasoline engine installed in the garage to charge the array of wet cell batteries which supplied electricity to the house. There was no public electricity on the Point at that time.

Since the family would be in residence all summer, while Grandpa would be away most of the time, he hoped to find someone who could maintain the generator, take care of the property, and also take him and the family on picnics and trips around the bay. Thus, one day, he went down to the wharf and asked if anyone had time to take him on a little trip around the harbor. Elbridge Albion Winchenpaw volunteered to take him in his Friendship sloop. While sailing, Grandpa told Mr. Winchenpaw that he needed someone to take the family and friends around Muscongus Bay and on picnics. He also hoped that that person would have time to do chores around the cottage. Thus, Ellie, as everyone soon came to call him, took on the Logan family and the care of the Logan property. To complete this story, Ellie renamed his Friendship sloop RUTH LOGAN for Grandpa's youngest daughter and moored it in front of the house.

MYRTLE E.

MYRTLE E. later in her career as JOLLY BUCCANEER #17.

common to cut down the sails and shorten both boom and bowsprit to make the sloop stiffer and safer, and to alleviate some of the strain on the hull. Some of these boats were treated by their new owners as fairly disposable, while others became cherished objects linked with memories of summer vacation, childhood, and family fun, and were lovingly cared for, outliving their intended life spans by decades.

MYRTLE E. was built by Eugene McLain in 1909 and was fished for a year before being sold to the Boynton family where she was renamed SKY PILOT. For the next 39 years the Boyntons sailed SKY PILOT, cruising her extensively before selling her. (See sidebar p. 29). She went on to another life under the name JOLLY BUCCANEER #17, and was a crowd favorite at the Friendship races for many years. She fell apart after a sinking in 1973 while being lifted from the water. Her end, while sad, came after 62 years of use, mostly as a much loved family boat. When you consider that she was built for a short life of hard work in an unforgiving environment, six decades is a remarkable lifespan.

We have already mentioned ESTELLA A. #200, built on Bremen Long Island in 1904 by Rob McLain, and now in the collection of Mystic Seaport Musuem. According to Newell McLain she was the first sloop built on Bremen Long Island to be launched with an auxiliary engine—a two cylinder, nine horsepower Knox. She was fished and ran cargo, and then between 1930 and 1935 was in the coasting trade before being sold as a yacht. At one point she even had a Marconi rig. Even for a museum ship, 110 is a ripe old age for a wooden boat.

Another original mentioned in Chapter One is GLADIATOR #71, built in 1902 by Alexander McLain for Dan Simmons. She worked in her early life and then there is a period of

A Family Love Affair With a Boat and Its Hand

by Reverend Edward C. Boynton

Adapted from the 1994 FSS yearbook.

As a family, the Boyntons for three generations have made their summer home on Maiden Island, one of the Five Islands on the eastern shore of Georgetown Island. My father, Reverend Nehemiah Boynton, loved the island and loved the sea. At long last he had his chance to acquire a boat when he inherited a modest amount of money. It was arranged for Henry Kingsbury to come over to the cottage to talk over the proposition. The "dickering" went something as follows:

SKY PILOT

"I don't want a yacht, Henry; I want a boat." Would Henry know where he could get such a boat as father wanted? He knew "just the boat." Would he go with father in the summer and use the boat for his own purposes the rest of the year? He would.

"Go and get it, Henry." No fussy business to foul the thing up. Just a simple act. "Go and get it, Henry."

Soon after, we saw Henry row past the cottage and down the bay to the open ocean. In three days he was back, at the helm of a large Friendship sloop, towing his dory behind. It was "just the right boat" of which he had spoken. She was built in 1909 by Gene McLain on Bremen Long Island and had been used that winter for fishing. She came to us the following summer, Father immediately re-named her SKY PILOT, the name she bore for the following 39 years.

SKY PILOT was 43 feet and some inches on the waterline, 15-some feet in beam, and drew 8 ½ feet. As they expressed it down there, "she had a holt on the water." She cost father $1200, all found, a typical bald-headed gaff-rigged Friendship sloop with flush deck carrying a jib, jumbo and mainsail. Father later had a topmast put on her with a topsail and flying jib. The mast was stepped fairly well aft, her boom extending well beyond the taffrail, giving her a large mainsail. When she came to us, she carried a tiller. She was not only a handy boat, but a smart boat as well, and a comfortable, not a wet, boat. And she was tight.

She had a flush deck, a chain locker in the fore-peak and a Shipmate stove in the forecastle, together with two—in a pinch three—bunks, two lockers and a dish cupboard. Aft of the forecastle bulkhead was the fish hold, aft of that the tiller cockpit, and finally the lazarette.

As we no longer needed the fish hold but could turn that space into a main cabin, father had this and other jobs done: lowering the floor of the fish hold, substituting scrap iron for the rock ballast under it, and installing a cabin roof with skylight and companionway running up the cockpit. This gave her a forecastle with two bunks and lockers up forward, a main cabin with three bunks and two lockers, excellent accommodations for comfort on a cruise. She also had a Gloucester fisherman wheel substituted for the tiller and a wooden backrest behind the wheel box, making a comfortable seat for the helmsman.

SKY PILOT was a family boat enjoyed by young and old. Her ample deck space made her ideal for large parties to have a day's sail. I have known 15 or more aboard at times, from the old folk in steamer chairs to the toddlers, whose safety was assured by being attached to a line the other end of which was made fast to a cleat or bitt, already at their tender age getting their sea legs and coming to know the feel of a deck under their feet. The children were required to wear life jackets until they were 12 and to crawl along the deck on their hands and knees.

When Henry Kingsbury left us, what seemed a major blow turned out to be a blessing, for it brought us Captain George Hanna, who took care of the boat and went with us in the summers until his death 30 years later. What distinguished Captain George was not his nautical expertise alone. It was his spirit. His instincts were fine instincts. He had a sense of the fitness of things. And he had a delightful sense of humor. Which reminds me –

We were all down in the cabin playing whist when we heard the rhythmic chug of a powerful motor alongside. Looking out the companionway, we saw a large chrome-and-mahogany job out of Providence, whose owner was a friend of my father's. They came aboard, and when our

Continued on next page

visit was over, we came on deck to see them off. As they were disappearing out of the harbor, I said to George,

"She's a pretty boat, George."

"Yes," replied George, "she's a pretty boat."

"But," I added, "I suppose, George, that in a hard chance you would just as soon be aboard SKY PILOT."

"Lor bless you, yes. Why, we'd be just comfortable and she'd be all unsoldered."

Another time, when we were crossing Frenchman's Bay, a thick Fundy fog descended on us. When we reached the whistler off Schoodic, we decided to run in for Prospect Harbor. As we poked along, one of the lookouts called out, "Breakers off the starboard bow." And soon the other man on watch called out, "Breakers to leeward." Those of us who were aft could just see the foam of the crested breaking rollers, but we could distinctly hear the roar of their breaking long before we could see them. We were running a true course and we were where we ought to be, but enveloped in that all-but-opaque gray blanket with visibility almost zero, and to hear the booming of the breaking waves on either hand and more from the general direction in which we were headed was not too comfortable a situation.

Seeing my brother and me at the wheel, and quite likely with anxious looks, George came quietly aft and reassuringly said, "Keep her headed into the silence and you will be all right." We did and we were.

With passing of the years, changes came. My father and Captain George had died. Three of us bought the boat from the family. One evening in December of '49 I received a phone call to tell me that a few days before, SKY PILOT was discovered sunk up to her trussle-trees at her winter mooring near the steamboat dock at MacMahans Island. Mr. Sample over in Boothbay heard of the happening and offered to buy the boat "as is." It seemed the sensible thing to us to sell, which we did, and so ended the family ownership of 39 years — years of happy and indelible memories.

Editors Note: SKY PILOT was raised, ballasted with 9,000 two-pound axe heads, and sold to Richard Swanson. Under her new name of JOLLY BUCCANEER #17 she joined the Friendship Sloop Society, serving as flagship for two years, and in 1967 was sold to Bill Johnson and taken to Florida. In 1973 she sank in the Dania Waterway and fell apart when lifted by a crane. As Reverend Boynton wrote, she was built by Eugene McClain, but first named MYRTLE E.

Reverend Boynton's article was written in 1973.

ANVINITA
by Dr. Peter Latella

Adapted from the 1989 FSS yearbook.

Friendship Sloop Society Archive

ANVINITA

In 1937 I was looking for a boat that was broad of beam, tough of timber, and could handle rough weather. I had two small daughters, and we were sailing a small 16-foot sloop. I found "the boat" in a Cos Cob, Connecticut shipyard. The boat—it had no name—had been in dry dock for three years and had weathered rather badly. She looked neglected and forlorn and seemed to beg and plead to be refurbished. I bought her for $400 in 1938.

The sails, fortunately, were in excellent shape and had been kept in good condition. The motor, a one-lunger Palmer, was easily gotten into condition by a mechanic. The boat was another story. With the help of my brother and friends, we scraped, burned, sanded, primed, caulked, replaced rotten timber, scrubbed and cleaned and painted and rigged the ship, named her ANVINITA, and launched her in September 1938. We sailed her down to Hudson Park, New Rochelle, and anchored in the harbor which would be her new home.

She slept two forward, one on each side of the mast. The head was on the port side; on the opposite side was a locker. The cabin slept two, and the galley was against the cockpit. Headroom was about 5 feet 6 inches, and we kept bumping our heads and this was annoying. With winter setting in, we decided to re-model again. Fortunately, the hatchway to the cabin (my little girl referred to it as the cellar) was on the starboard side of the cabin, leaving the center clear to establish headroom. I fashioned a "box" of 2 inch by 8 inch lumber, 10 feet long and 4 feet wide, and placed it on top of the cabin unattached. Then either my brother or I stood on the pier, and the other motored about the harbor, so we obtained a good eye-picture of the addition. I lowered the forward end by 3 inches and finished the top by adding a skylight and added port holes to the sides and bolted it to the cabin top after removing the portion of the cabin covered by the addition. Over all, the addition was very pleasing to the eye, comfortable in the cabin, and we received many compliments on the finished product.

Due to my limited time available, we did little cruising but spent many days swimming, sunning, picnicking, and sailing locally around Long Island Sound. We kept the boat in the water all year round. There were many excellent sailing days in November, December and January. Twice a year we would beach the boat and scrape and paint the bottom. The name. ANVINITA was coined from the three matriarchs of our family: Angela, my mother; Virginia, my wife, and Anita, our niece.

In 1939 or 1940 we ventured to the World's Fair in Flushing Meadows. We had a lovely sail to the "meadows" but were receiving radio reports that the weather was changing, so we lifted anchor and headed back home. We were caught in the storm and an adverse tide. We reefed sail, started our engine, and fought tide and wind and rain all the way home. We suffered a dislodged bowsprit, a smashed skylight, and a loose stay. From that day on, my wife refused to leave the harbor.

War was declared. I went away, and the boat went on dry dock in 1941. I returned early in 1946. I was quite busy putting my practice together and found little time for sailing. We made an honest attempt to refurbish ANVINITA but gave up in 1948. We sold her to two young veterans. In 1949 they ran up on the rocks between Mamaroneck and Rye. The boat sank, and she was beyond salvage. Hearsay said alcohol got tangled in her rigging.

When I purchased the boat, Mr. Scott gave me her papers. I did not realize then that I was purchasing a National Treasure, so paid little attention to them. I do recall the boat was built by W. Morse in 1910. Her mast and spars were spruce and the timbers oak. Overall length was listed as 39 feet 9 inches. The papers, charts and maps were all given to the purchaser when I sold the boat. She carried ballast of cast iron sash weights in the bilge.

her history that we know little about, but somehow she ended up in a boatyard in New Jersey where, in 1966 the Zuber family found her with the name "DOWNEASTER". She has been a part of the Zuber family ever since. (See sidebar p.35). Bill and Caroline Zuber have done extensive work to her over the years, even building a beautiful boat shed for GLADIATOR, which she graciously allows them to live in too. The three Zuber boys refer to GLADIATOR as their older sister.

VERA JEAN #164 was built in 1906, supposedly by Charles Morse. She started her life fishing in Muscongus Bay without an engine. Somehow in the 1920s she made her way to the Great Lakes Chicago area. She appeared in a story in the *Lake Michigan Yachting News* in 1929, which describes a cruise aboard her the previous year. A U.S. Coast Guard Certification form dating from 1955 states that she was built in 1906 and rebuilt in 1936. During the 1930s and 40s she passed through the hands of several members of the Columbia Yacht Club in Chicago. Not much is known about her history over the next decade until Stan Gratt bought her in 1960. Mr. Gratt kept her in the Chicago area until he sold her in 1978 to Dennis Mayhew, who has owned her ever since. Dennis rebuilt her in 1978 and was almost finished with a second rebuild at the time of this writing. Between the two rebuilds Dennis estimates that he has sailed her some 20,000 miles in 35 years, first in the Great Lakes, then the U.S. east coast, the Caribbean, and Gulf of Mexico. Her home now is in Florida.

Then there is ALICE E. #23, launched in 1899. She may be the oldest surviving Friendship. Although her builder is unknown, she was cared for well enough to have survived. She is owned by Karl Brunner and is still sailing parties out of Southwest Harbor, Mount Desert Island. Members of the Friendship Sloop Society are looking for any early records that relate to her. She is an original that is sailing into her second century, but given that she is still working, wouldn't it be interesting if it turned out that she was one of those early fishing sloops that turned to sailing parties?

While the boats listed here demonstrate a pattern of ownership and use that led to their survival, they also demonstrate the hold that they took of their owners and the important role they played in the lives of those people. The five sloops listed here are just a sampling of the early fishermen to have managed the transition to recreational boats. Twenty-six sloops built before 1920 are registered with the Friendship Sloop Society, a remarkable number of wooden workboats that have passed, or are fast approaching the century mark.

But even summer people get tired of bailing, and during the two decades between the wars there were people who wanted a new Friendship sloop built specifically as a yacht. Many of these new boats lacked a yacht-like finish, but were built with some small concessions made to comfort, the most common of which was a more comfortable space below decks. Many were also constructed with the recognition that they would likely last longer than fishing sloops, and most were launched with the reduced rig that recreational owners had become accustomed to. Not only were the shorter rigs easier to handle, but also recreational sailors did not need to venture offshore the way fishermen did, and by the 1930s, auxiliary engines were becoming part of the package for these boats.

Winfield Scott Carter of Friendship built three Friendships as pleasure craft in the 1930's. In 1936 he built the 30-foot sloop FLYING JIB #45. In 1937 he built the 38-foot TANNIS #7, and in 1938 he built another 38-foot sloop, ELEAZAR #38.

FLYING JIB #45 was built for Dr. A.J. "Bill" Derbyshire, of Port Clyde, Maine. Interestingly, when Dr. Derbyshire approached Scott Carter, he was accompanied by his neighbor Rodney Davis, a local fisherman who had fished in Friendships before engines were common. Bill Derbyshire owned FLYING JIB until 1964. Her next five owners either took good care of her or found her a new owner who could take on the work she needed. For example, Sara Beck bought her in 1997, cruised her extensively and made significant repairs to her hull during her ownership. She was in the process of further restoration work, helped by Harold Burnham, in 2011, when she had the opportunity to move to Ireland. She found FLYING JIB a new owner, Ryan Graham, who was willing to continue the restoration work that was needed.

In 1937 Carter built TANNIS #7, a 38-foot sloop. As was the case with FLYING JIB, TANNIS has had something of a charmed existence. She had had a number of owners before John "Jack" Cronin bought her in 1968 and she became the weekend destination for the Cronin family. The Cronins have owned and cared for her ever since. Today TANNIS carries a full rig more typical of the early Friendships, but if you look at the picture taken in 1961 (P. 34), when Douglas Randal owned her, you can see a pretty good example of the smaller rig that was typical of the recreational sloops of the 1930s and 40s.

In 1938 Carter built ELEAZAR #38 and like TANNIS she is also a 38-foot boat. She was built for three Dartmouth men and named for Eleazar Wheelock, founder of the school which became Dartmouth College. She has spent time in Maine, Delaware, and New York waters. Today her home port is Rochester, New York; so all three of Scott Carter's sloops from the 1930s are still around a decade into the twenty-first century.

FLYING JIB #45 in W. Scott Carter's shop 1936.

Bow view of FLYING JIB 1936.

FLYING JIB with Bill Derbyshire at the helm.

TANNIS #7, 1961 races. Compare the rig here with the photo on page 104.

RETRIEVER #16

RETRIEVER #16

W. Prescott "Scotty" Gannett

The desirability of a Friendship as a pleasure boat reached beyond Maine as well. Builder Warren Prescott Gannett of Scituate, Massachusetts, was approached to build several sloops in the 1930's and 40's. The boats that "Scotty" Gannett built tended to be slightly smaller boats, and we know about five of them: DEPARTURE #151, a 15-foot sloop built in 1936, 24-foot OLD FRIENDLY #11, built in 1938, 22-foot RETRIEVER #16, built in 1942, 27-foot PAL-O-MINE #34, built in 1947, and SURPRISE (not to be confused with the later SURPRISE #49 built by Phil Nichols.) Gannet was building from lines of earlier sloops in a scale fitting for day-sailers. Of these sloops DEPARTURE and PAL-O-MINE are still afloat, OLD FRIENDLY and SURPRISE are lost, and RETRIEVER's fate is in the balance.

While Maine in the 1920s saw an increase in summer visitors and cottagers that helped bring about the transition of the Friendship sloop from work platform to yacht, the continued interest in sloops and the building of new sloops during the Depression years of the 1930s is perhaps even more significant. Given the sheer number of sloops built at the turn of the century and just before, there were still plenty left three decades later, and it is only logical that a number of them would be recycled into pleasure boats. But the building of new sloops as yachts by Scott Carter and Scotty Gannet speaks of something more, it speaks of a design that is both evocative of time gone by, and at the same time, still practical. The very simplicity of the design and the challenge to the sailor to make the most of that simplicity, has an almost addictive quality for some people. Add to that the beauty of the form that goes with the function, and the end result can have an almost hypnotic attraction.

THE DEVIOUS SOJOURN OF THE "GLADIATOR"

By Bill Zuber

Adapted from the 1969 FSS yearbook.

From the time I was 5 months old I began being infected by the common salt water malady "Boatius Nuttius." The patriarch of the family succeeded in firmly implanting it in my bloodstream, after suffering himself with it through the course of some 30-odd vessels, crab cars, lobster floats, oyster wagons and other floating debris. So it was a natural thing for me, thus weakened by exposure to the disease, to graduate from college and come home to run father's boatyard for him. Thus he was freed to romp the warm waters of the Caribbean in yet another manifestation of the prevailing infection.

My wife and I decided that no known cure existed, so to make the treatment as pleasant as possible we began to build a Friendship sloop. The gestation period for boats must be fantastic because after three years of hard, sporadic labor, the hull is finished. After two years of turning a deaf ear to repeated remarks such as "When are the animals coming, Noah?" we were understandably anxious to escape the boatyard as often as possible, especially on rainy spring Sundays when you live on the premises and your door is constantly rapped upon by do-it-yourselfers wanting to know if you think it is dry enough to paint in the cabin while dripping water all over the living-room rug. We mopped up and left precipitately for Stu and Dot Hancock's peaceful abode away from the boatyard. While sitting in Dot's kitchen by the perpetually lit-off coffeepot, it wasn't long before the germs began floating around and the conversation turned to boats.

"A fella was telling me that there's a mast just about right for the Friendship over at Carver's Boat Works," I said. "What are we sitting here for?" says Dot. We piled into Stu's wagon and shortly arrived at Carver's. The mast was exactly the right dimensions and thoroughly rotted. "I think I saw two Friendships around the corner at Johnson Brothers the other day," said I, "Let's have a look. Maybe we can get some ideas." We pulled up to the end of the dock and sure enough, there were two Friendships laying side by side, which is a rather unusual sight in Central Jersey. Stu and I walked down the dock in the rain. "Look at that! Both are named 'DOWNEASTER!' Sort of appropriate," said Stu. I whistled to the girls to come have a look at the extraordinary find. One of the

two vessels was obviously older than the other and we noticed on the trailboards of the younger, "Lash Bros. 1963." Whoever had owned her had neglected her rather badly. As we turned our attention to the other older boat we noticed the companionway was not locked. I remarked that her construction showed some similarity to that of an icebreaker, and that it appeared she might be an original. Not being able to restrain ourselves we all went aboard to have a closer look. We went below and noted ample accommodations for four, full standing headroom, large galley, exceptional storage, a little rot here and there, and more rain dripping below than topside. The ladies soon became disenchanted with the waterfall effect on their hairdos, and disembarked. As I poked around for further clues to the boat's possible origin I noticed some digits crudely carved into a deck beam in the after partition in the head. "Look here!" I said to Stu. "There are some numbers carved in here that are probably from some previous documentation. I'm sure she must be an original!" We prowled around some more below and then went topside to inspect her rig like antique collectors in the Smithsonian. I looked down over the bow and saw a "For Sale" sign and a telephone number. Well, the old delirium was really beginning to work on me, and Stu's eyes looked a little glazed. Completely forgotten were the half-finished Friendship hull, finances, the 30-ft. Tancook Schooner the bank and I owned,—"What do you say we go in together and buy her?" I blurted. "Write down the phone number," said Stu, "just for the hell of it."

We returned to the Hancock residence. Conversation consisted of scattered phrases; "She really has character." "Y'think she really could be an original?" "What about all that iron in the bilge?" "Iron! What about the concrete?" "Think the engine runs?" "You guys aren't thinking something stupid!" "He'd better not be! We already own one boat and are building another!" "Think you could sail that one, Daddy?"

The "Boatius Nuttius" virus being what it is, and helped along by a few whiskey sours, I became the owner of one-half of an original(?) Friendship sloop named "DOWNEASTER." Which half is mine varies, depending on which half is in the most danger or in the worst shape so my boatyard can fix it. And fix it we did, because we had also decided to sail her back to Friendship for Homecoming in July. This was the year (1967)

Continued on page 36

Continued from page 35

of the rain and fog, even in New Jersey, and trying to repair the leaks topside took many sun dances, for as soon as we thought it was fixed so it wouldn't leak, it rained again, and it leaked again—always in a new and more inaccessible spot. Finally time ran out, and ready or not, supplies were stowed aboard with numerous back-up systems in case of disaster. The crew—Stu, Stu, Jr., a power-boat owner friend and myself—gathered on the dock in the early summer morning mist. The newly-painted waterline loomed murkily under three inches of water, as the supplies weighed more than anticipated. Three five-gallon jugs of emergency rations for the gasoline engine were lashed securely in the wooden sailing dinghy, which floated merrily behind on a long painter.

With fond farewells ringing in our ears we motored down to the sea, set all sails in a brisk south-easterly non-wind of about 2 knots, and drifted out Manasquan Inlet with the tide. The first entry in the log reads: "All hands on deck! Dinghy sinking! Rescued dinghy and gasoline and stowed dinghy aft against gallows." From that point on we never looked back—mainly because we couldn't see aft past the dinghy. Four days later, on a beautiful clear morning (the second day that month with no fog), we sailed into Friendship harbor, returning "DOWNEASTER" to her presumed birthplace. Assorted wives and children met us at the wharf and great plans were formulated for the first race the next day. Thursday morning, the handicap list was posted and "DOWNEASTER" drew handicap No. 26 out of 29. Having sailed the boat only five times prior to sailing her to Friendship, and having no racing experience whatsoever, we finally decided that we weren't in too good a position. Being placed in the replica category because we had no proof that she was an original contributed to our handicap. But we gave our first race the old college try, and managed to beat the Coast Guard back into the harbor.

The next day the fog closed in and the race scheduled for that day was canceled. We decided to try to track down the origins of "DOWNEASTER" and prove our suspicions that she might be an original. We drove to the nearest customs house, which was in Rockland, armed with the number we had found carved in the beam in the head. The customs agent, Mr. G. A. Boulier, was most helpful, but not too encouraging. He explained that unless "DOWNEASTER" was the original

Roger Duncan

GLADIATOR #71

name it would be almost impossible to trace her by numbers. The numbers in the documented vessel listing are not in numerical order, but in alphabetical order according to the original name. He offered us the use of the attic at the customs house, where all the old books by year were stored on rather dusty shelves. We each took a volume and soon determined that "DOWNEASTER" was not the original name, if she were indeed an original. But we also discovered that by some coincidence that many numbers very similar to ours were located in the "G" section of various volumes. Time was fast running out as Mr. Boulier had to go down to the harbor and check in a cargo. As a last effort I grabbed the book for the year 1902 and turned to the "Gs." I could scarcely believe my eyes when I found the number we had all been searching for, but there was the entry:

Official No. 86611 — Rig Sip. — Name of Vessel, "GLADIATOR" Gross Tonnage, 7 — Net Tonnage, 7 — Length 28.5 — Breadth, 5.3 — When built, 1902 — Where built, Bremen, Maine — Home port, Waldoboro, Maine.

We all were so excited that even Mr. Boulier seemed to catch our enthusiasm. He took the time to copy the entry on official stationery and certify that such an entry existed in the "List of Merchant Vessels of the United States, 1902 Edition." He signed the letter with a flourish, and we dustily bade him good-by. We drove madly back to Friendship, down to Betty and Al Roberts' wharf, and ran noisily up her stairs. We waved the paper at her and finally made enough sense to let her realize that we had indeed brought another original back home to Friendship and the Friendship Sloop Society. The committee came out to inspect the now-famous numbers 86611 carved indelibly in our lowly head. The head on the "GLADIATOR" (ex. "DOWNEASTER") was the most popular spot in the harbor for the next few hours.

The next day dawned bright and foggy, and we managed to find our way in the parade of sloops past the crowded wharves of Friendship out to the starting line. After two postponements, the race finally began but it soon became apparent to us that one island looks pretty much like another in the fog, when all that's visible of it are lobster buoys, a few rocks, and trees looming through the mist. Not being natives of the area we declined to risk our now-venerable original and returned to the relatively clear weather of the harbor. Dot had wisely declined to join us on this adventure, and had been busy trying to find a native of Friendship old enough to possibly remember "GLADIATOR" in her youth. When we rowed ashore we found that Dot had located a Mrs. Dwight Stanley who thought that her father, Mr. Charlie Murphy, might possibly remember back to 1902. We had to wait patiently two wharves down for Mr. Murphy to come in from lobstering—he still kept busy although well past his 90th birthday. The news had traveled through mysterious channels that we were looking for him, for when he stepped ashore he said, "I hear you're looking for me. What can I do for you?" Dot asked him, "Do you remember a boat named 'GLADIATOR'?" He recollected that she was about 34 ft., built for Dan Simmons about 60 years ago by "Bugs" McLain over Waldoboro way. These facts later proved accurate when we located the original fisheries license issued in 1902 to Daniel Simmons of Waldoboro. "Bugs" McLain was Alexander McLain, one of the family of father and brothers who built Friendship sloops on Bremen Long Island, and "GLADIATOR's" bill of sale showed her cost to be $450.00. Thus with a great deal of luck, the remarkable memory of a Maine native, and much help from many of those notoriously cantankerous "Mainiacs," we had a wealth of information about a wandering daughter of Friendship who had come home.

From 1941 to 1945 the world was at war. With a few exceptions, like RETRIEVER #16 that had been started before the war, the building of pleasure boats came to a stop. Recreational boats were laid-up for the duration, many ashore, and many were simply beached. The upheaval after the war was also a significant factor. Some boat owners went off to war and did not return, leaving sloops beached without a future. Other owners came home from the war and, like Dr. Peter Latella who owned ANVINITA (see sidebar p.30-31), found that with starting families and adjusting to a new civilian life, there simply was not time for an old Friendship sloop. The neglect of five years took its toll as well. When the war was over a good many of those boats had gone beyond the point of no return. But some sloops, although basically worn out, still had a little more life in them, just enough to infect some poor unsuspecting fellow with the Friendship sloop bug. One of those post-war individuals infected with the bug was Bernie MacKenzie. Writing about finding his own sloop VOYAGER #1, he described the tremendous affection that Friendships engender:

> Perhaps if some knowledgeable friend had come along and tried to make us listen to reason, emphasizing that we were buying a boat that was built in Teddie Roosevelt's era, we might have listened, but I doubt it. Once we climbed that ladder to her deck, we were hopelessly lost. It didn't make any difference to us that the cockpit was a jumble of loose boards and the accommodations were little better than when the fish shared the hold, or that the gaff mainsail was in patches and the jibs black with mildew. To two bachelors in their twenties, Voyager was just what we had been looking for as we crawled over every aging Friendship from Marblehead to Cape Cod. An hour later we were at the owner's home to sign the bill-of-sale.
>
> Through the happiness of the occasion, I noticed the man's wife and children were in tears. This was my first insight into the feelings these sloops engen-

Courtesy of the Gannett Family Archive

ORIGINAL WILBUR MORSE FRIENDSHIP SLOOP IN BRIGHAM'S S/Y
GREENPORT NY
1950

Snyder collection courtesy of T.B.R. Walsh

der. I thought about this later, wishing that I knew the full history of all the generations that had owned this boat. How many had reacted in like manner when she was sold? Who were the fishermen that owned her before the curse of gasoline engines, and where were the children that grew up on this boat and learned to sail and care for her?

Another fellow infected with the Friendship sloop bug was Frank Snyder. In 1946 Snyder was discharged from the U.S. Navy. He had served in the Pacific submarine fleet and had not expected to survive the war. His brother, who had also served in the Pacific, was equally surprised to be alive. The two decided that before they went off to start their professional civilian lives, they should take a summer to celebrate being alive. They headed to Maine looking for adventure. While in Eastport, they spotted an old Friendship sloop sitting in the mudflats, looking abandoned. They did some investigation and bought her for the princely sum of $400. She had been built by Wilbur Morse in 1903 and was named RITA. The two men floated her out of the mud. They did some basic repairs and spent the summer on her, according to Frank, mostly bailing. In an interview just before his death in 2006, he said, "You know I have owned a lot of boats since then, from small racing sloops to transoceanic yachts, but I don't think I ever had as much fun as I did on the old RITA." Frank sold RITA in 1951 so that he could get back into small boat racing, but he did not lose track of her and had her lines taken off by a marine architect. In 1955 RITA collapsed on her cradle under a heavy load of snow. Frank Snyder bought some of her hardware from the yard that had the job of breaking her up. He did not know it at the time, but he was not done with RITA. He also did not know that Friendship sloops were about to make a comeback.

Remembering DIXIE

Adapted from the 1988 FSS yearbook.

Friendship Sloop Society Archive

My father had a summer home at Haven (Brooklin, Maine) in Center Harbor on Eggemoggin Reach. In 1920, when I was 15 and my brother 13, my father bought a Friendship sloop from a man in Castine whose name I either never knew or have forgotten. I remember that she had no name on her stern as she was brought over and anchored just off the beach in front of our house amidst great excitement on my brother's and my part. At the dinner table that night, by family vote, she was named DIXIE. She was about 28' on deck, rigged with a jib-boom on a single jib with no topmast. She had a tiller, not a wheel. We learned that she had been built by Wilbur Morse in either 1898 or 1899. She was in tolerable condition and we kept her up well through the years as my father first taught us to sail and eventually turned us loose, at first with the Reach as a limit, and later any and everywhere on the Maine coast. We loved that little vessel.

In 1933 DIXIE was sold to a man from New York (cannot recall his name) who came up to Brooklin with his teenage son to take delivery and sail her back to Long Island Sound. My brother and I hated to part with her but the urgency of earning our livings prohibited the long summer vacations of years gone by. The New York people spent the night with us, had breakfast, and sailed off in clear weather. We heard,

a few days later by word of mouth from a lobsterman from Stonington, that DIXIE had "come up on a ledge, hard" in the Fox Island Thorofare, knocked some of her bottom out, and had sunk. The people got ashore safely. That's all we ever heard! A sad and stupid end to a splendid little vessel.

We bought her 68 years ago, lost her 55 years ago. My memory of any further details has faded, but I'd love to have old Dixie in the record book one way or another. I enclose a few faded old snap shots of her and would very much appreciate their return in the self-addressed envelope.

By the way, my model is in the Friendship Museum at Friendship, not in the museum at Bath which you mentioned. I fashioned her showing the fish well which we had removed in 1920 so as to make a larger cockpit, and named the model after my wife, Barbara. My own model here at home is of course named DIXIE, along with many other models which I've built in past years.

Sincerely yours,

Winston T. Kellogg

Friendship Sloop Society Archive

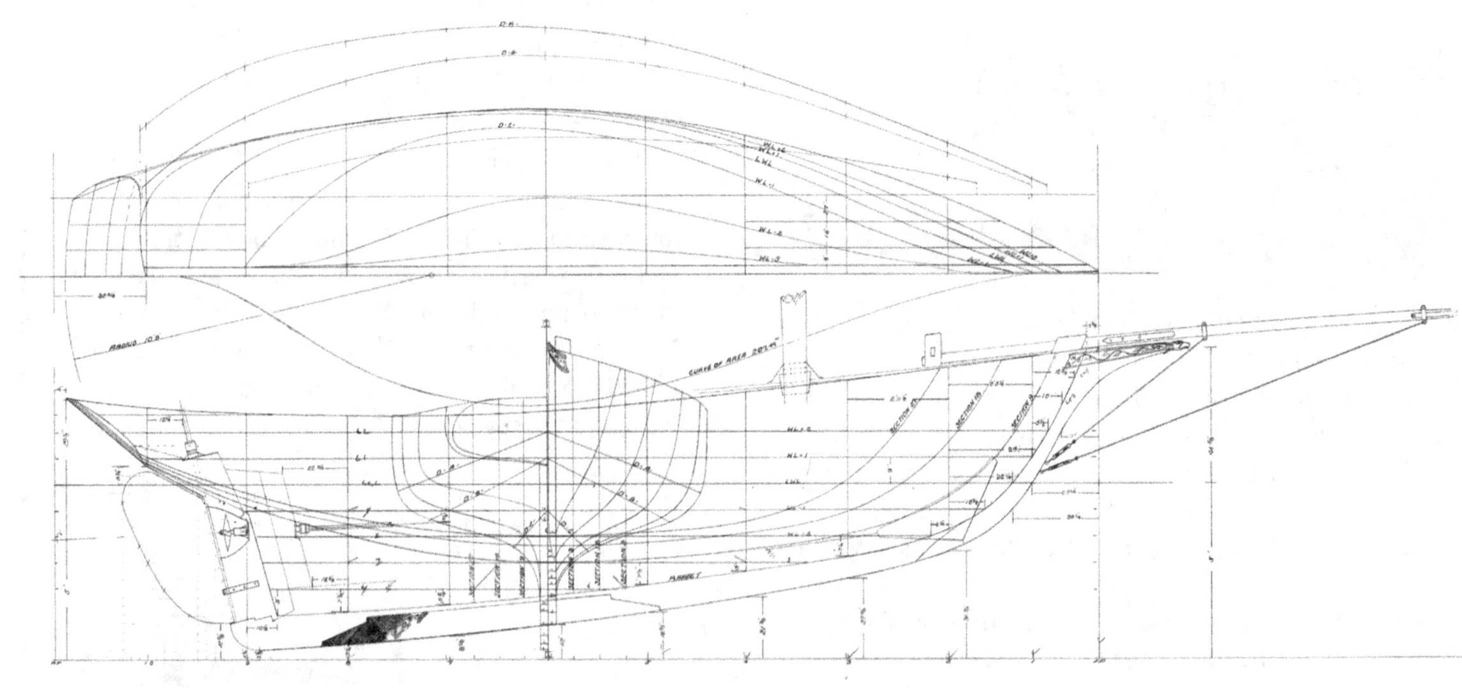

Friendship sloop
Wilbur A. Morse model
Length on deck   30' 5"
Beam   9' 5"
Draft   4' 9"
Drawn by W. C. Lash
Friendship, Maine 1971
Drawings courtesy of Nancy and Peter Toppan

Chapter Three: An Organization of Friendships

"The purpose of this Society shall be to encourage the building and sailing of Friendship sloops. To provide a medium for owners and friends to meet and enjoy each other around a common interest, and to promote the history and traditions of the Friendship sloop."

Constitution of the Friendship Sloop Society
Article II Section A

The story of the formation of the Friendship Sloop Society has been told in many places, most notably in the 1965 publication, *It's a Friendship.*

Bernie MacKenzie certainly was one of the driving forces behind the foundation of the FSS, but in reality an unusual number of extraordinarily talented individuals came together at just the right place and time to form the Friendship Sloop Society. A most delightful description of this coming together is reprinted here, also taken from *It's a Friendship.* It was written by Herald Jones, who was a key figure in founding the Society.

A SMALL VILLAGE TACKLES A LARGE JOB

One mid-winter afternoon I answered the jingle of my phone and found myself talking to Carlton Simmons, our local Postmaster. "I'm sending two men down to see you. I hope you have time to talk to them."

If I had said "No," it all might not have happened, but a retired professor is not very busy in mid-winter, so I said "yes," and went up to stand by my garage so they could find the right place.

They soon were introducing themselves as Bernard MacKenzie and John Gould.

"Not the John Gould who writes those delightful essays we've been enjoying in *The Christian Science Monitor!*" This was a delightful surprise, and I hustled them down to the house where my wife met us at the door.

Bernie MacKenzie

VOYAGER #1

Friendship in the early 1960s.

Herald Jones and Bernie MacKenzie

John Gould

Once seated, I was in for another surprise; for they had Friendship sloops on their minds. Bernard MacKenzie had entered his sloop VOYAGER in the Boston Yacht Club's race for Auxiliary Sloops at Marblehead. The appointed day had brought a smoky breeze that stood the tall-masted racing sloops on their beam ends, while the weather-wise Friendship had breezed along in merry fashion to cross the finish line first.

With the exhilaration of victory came an idea: why not promote a homecoming race for Friendship sloops in the town where they were made! He took his idea to his good friend Earl Banner of the *Boston Globe*, "It's a natural" was his reaction, and he sent Bernard to John Gould. "He knows all the important people in Maine, and has promoted most of the worthwhile ventures of recent years."

So here were Bernard MacKenzie and John Gould outlining their ideas. It didn't take much imagination on my part to see the possibilities of such a "Homecoming Race" for Friendship: unfortunately, I could also see the difficulties involved. Friendship has only 800 inhabitants; no motels or hotels; no restaurants or lunch counters; no public toilets. Such a race coming at the height of the lobstermen's harvest season might meet a good deal of resistance. But on the other hand, boat building here needed a shot in the arm, and the publicity attendant upon such a sporting event might be just what it needed.

Before the men went their separate ways, I had agreed to stir up as much interest as I could among the townspeople. In further discussion with Carlton Simmons, we decided we would need some well-organized group to get behind such a big operation, and lay it before a meeting of the Village Improvement Society. They turned it down flat—too big to tackle—too costly a venture. In view of this setback, we dropped the whole thing, for we certainly couldn't handle it alone.

About two months later, we were amazed to see Bernard MacKenzie's sloop VOYAGER sailing across the front page of the *National/Maine Coast Fisherman*, under the caption, "Friendship Sloop Race being considered for Friendship." Similar clippings came in from the *Boston Globe* and from Fred Hunt's *Quincy Patriot.*

Now this was different! With national publicity of this sort to reach the sloop owners and the yachting people, we surely could find enough help in Friendship to handle the local arrangements, so we called a group together in April and incorporated the Friendship Sloop Society. John Gould didn't get there in time for the picture-taking, but his suggestions and leadership were invaluable. Saturday, July 22nd was selected for the Homecoming Race out of Friendship in Muscongus Bay.

Bernard MacKenzie became the first President of the Society; Ralph Winchenpaw was made Vice President; Herald Jones, Secretary; and Carlton Simmons, Treasurer.

Publicity was never a problem. As Earl Banner of the *Boston Globe* and Nate Fuller of *Down East* had said, "This is a natural!" Bob Elliot contacted Don Guy of Associated Press, and sent news releases to a wide mailing list, and soon Friendship sloops winged their way across the pages of most of the important papers of the country.

All the yacht clubs from Connecticut to Canada received application blanks and before long 30 sloop owners had been heard from and over 80 persons from near and far had joined the society.

A group of Friendship people were called together to consider the local arrangements. After one meeting, half of them dropped out: it was too big a job; it couldn't be done. But a handful were left, and they went to work.

Bob and Sarah Wallace said we could use their wharf for Headquarters, and could put up loud speakers on the roof of one of their buildings: we could establish an information center, and could make three toilets available to the public. Sumner Whitney and John Armstrong gave permission to use adjacent lots for parking cars, and Al Roberts said we could hold a lobster feed and a chicken barbecue on his property. We found the Davis property could be used for additional parking of cars.

Friendship in the 1960s.

Nona Culver March was a summer resident of Friendship. She became a self-taught expert in identifying all the sloops of the fleet to become the first "Official Spotter" of the Friendship Sloop Society races held in Friendship Harbor in the 1970s. She could be found assisting Betty Roberts and Everett Walker in announcing the Finish Line results to the anxious crowds gathered at Robert's Wharf.

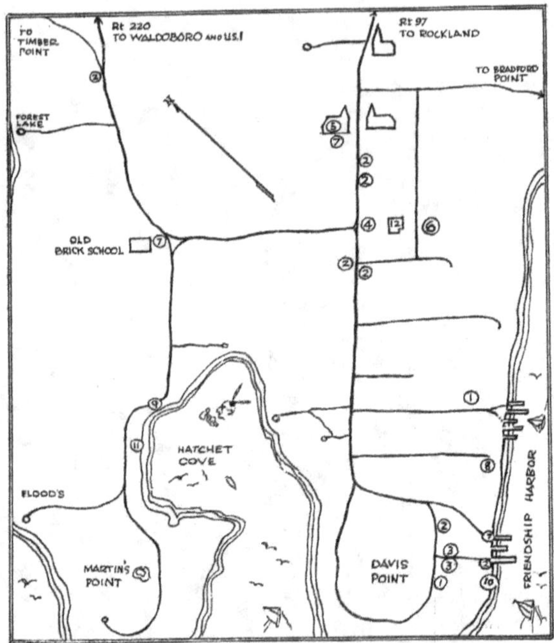

1. Parking Lots
2. Snacks
   Bob Wallace's Lobster Stand
   Al Roberts' Wharf
   VFW — Wallace's Lawn
   Pythian Sisters — Masonic Lodge
   Friendship Market
   Archie Wallace's Store
   Faulkingham's
3. Location of 5 o'clock Lobster-Clam-Bake
4. Town Hall
5. Churches (For Rest)
6. Ball Game
7. Information Points
8. Original Tool House of Wilbur Morse Boat Shop
9. Lash Brothers Boat Yard
10. Frank Winchenpaw's Boat Shop
11. Jim Murphy's Boat Shop
12. Village School

Hand-drawn map from the first Friendship Sloop Year-book 1961.

Cy Hamlin

Carlton Simmons

A college professor and his brother who taught Manual Training built and erected a "seven-holer" public toilet on a corner of this lot where the Davises said we might dig a hole.

Jim Napier agreed to place needed signs to direct the crowds, and the *Courier-Gazette* of Rockland printed them free of charge. Al Roberts arranged with camp Oceanward, Harold C. Ralph and Waldoboro Garage Co., to furnish cars to use as a free shuttle service between the harbor and the village.

Dr. Harold Frost made himself available in case of accident, and set up a first aid station in the local schoolhouse. Lerm Rowe found townspeople to man the three information centers and the first aid stations so that they were attended all day. The Women's Auxiliary of the Fire Department had their ambulance on call.

One of our biggest problems was food, but the Pythian Sisters, the Veterans of Foreign Wars and their Auxiliary, the School Community Club, the Women of the Methodist Church, a girls' class from the Advent Church, the two stores in the village, and Bob Wallace's Snack Bar, plus a paid caterer for the Skippers' Banquet combined forces to keep everyone well fed.

For the race committee, we drew heavily on our friends with experience. John Gould was able to interest his friend George Morrill to the extent that he sailed his DOWN WIND into the harbor to act as committee boat. Bill Danforth of Boothbay Harbor brought his WHITE FALCON and took Albert H. Chatfield, commodore of the Camden Yacht Club to help police the stake boats and judge the finish. Leon E. Nickerson, former commodore of the Edgewood Yacht Club of Rhode Island served as chairman.

Through his friendship with Carlton Simmons, we were most fortunate to secure the services of Cyrus Hamlin, naval architect of no mean ability from Southwest Harbor, for our handicapper.

Through the good offices of Bill Danforth, the Wawenock Power Squadron patrolled the race course.

Ronald Greene of the Sea and Shore Fisheries sent Captain Farmer and the GUARDIAN to set the handicap buoys and patrol the race in addition to carrying the host of photographers and reporters that came to record this unusual event.

To help handle the traffic ashore, and to handle the crowd, we secured the services of two Knox County Sheriff's patrol officers, and Lieutenant McKinney of the Thomaston State Police Barracks had seven men on the job.

Trophies had to be provided. Bob Elliot of the Department of Economic Development agreed to donate a trophy for the first of the original sloops across the finish line: Lash Brothers Boat Yard donated a trophy, and Eda Lawry, granddaughter of Wilbur Morse donated a trophy. Governor Reed himself came to present these to the winning skippers.

Clinton Lawry, a retired advertising executive planned and executed our souvenir program and secured enough advertising to more than cover the costs.

Our vice president, Ralph Winchenpaw planned and built the handicap buoys with the assistance of Fred McGlaughlin, retired Sea and Shore Fisheries warden.

On the appointed day, fourteen sloops answered the starting gun, and the first Friendship Sloop Regatta became a part of the Maine summer scene.

Two important after-results: the secretary spent the rest of the year writing thank-you notes; the treasurer was able to pay all bills and still have $21.00 left to start the second year!

The most extraordinary thing about this first Friendship Homecoming was its very improbability. A gathering of this type for a race was completely beyond the resources of the town. Who knew how many Friendships were left? How could one find them if they did exist? Even if the sloops could be found, what if no one came? And even if several sloops did show up, who would want to come and see them? No ordinary person in their right mind would take on such an impossible task, just to see a bunch of old sloops get together and race.

What the town had not reckoned with was that someone devoted to a boat design that was considered outdated before World War I, was not necessarily in their right mind.

Furthermore, the individuals in question were not ordinary. In fact the talents and skills that they brought to this endeavor were striking. Bernie MacKenzie was a naval draftsman for the United States Coast Guard. This put him in an excellent position to facilitate a legitimate race that would meet with the approval of the Coast Guard, and it allowed him to woo significant personalities from the world of marine architecture to take part as officials or as members of the race committee. Earl Banner of the *Boston Globe* proved invaluable for the publicity he brought through his paper, and for introducing John Gould into the mix. Gould, at the time a resident of Friendship, enjoyed a national following as an essayist and humorist. As Herald Jones demonstrates in the piece above, Gould's name and reputation were instantly recognized. Gould had written for well-known newspapers and periodicals and could drum up free publicity from his connections. Herald Jones himself was a talented writer and a gifted organizer. He pursued leads that otherwise might have fallen by the wayside. Carlton Simmons was roped into the original group. As postmaster and descendant of Wilbur Morse, he was a Friendship local who was influential in the community.

The idea that a Friendship homecoming race could gain notice in the national press speaks volumes to the extraordinary nature of the founders of the Friendship Sloop Society.

As Bernie MacKenzie would later write:

I remember writing a lot of letters during the winter of 1960-61, trying to track down other sloop owners from nebulous sources, and traveling up to Friendship to meet with Carlton Simmons, (grand-nephew of Wilbur Morse), Herald Jones and John Gould. My plans for a homecoming regatta to be held that coming summer were put before the Village Improvement Committee and promptly turned down as being too big and too costly a venture.

This surprised me, because I thought it was a pretty good idea. I kept on with my correspondence- this time to the news media: *Maine Coast Fisherman, Quincy Patriot Ledger, Lisbon Falls Enterprise, Down East Magazine, Boston Globe* and *Associated Press*. There must be a few more Friendships up there in Maine that would rendezvous with me in Friendship Harbor. Earl Banner of the Globe told me I would never find anyone, as I was the only one that had a Friendship sloop still able to float. At times I thought Earl might be correct and it seemed we were searching for survivors of an endangered species. But every bit of publicity helped the cause and soon the Friendship sloop *Associated Press* wire story appeared in newspapers nationwide.

Finally the first reply appeared in my mailbox, and then another, and we were in business. Lots of people from far away places phoned and requested more information and others wrote and sent contributions to start up the proposed association of Friendship sloop owners.

The Maine Department of Economic Development met with John Gould and me, and subsequently we got the ear of Maine's governor, John Reed. The governor thought it was a natural, and with the support of his office, the town was urged to climb on the bandwagon.

The new Friendship Sloop Society became a legal body through election of officers and signing of incorporation papers in February of 1961. Ralph Winchenpaw was my first vice-president; Herald Jones, secretary; and Carlton Simmons,

treasurer. The purpose of this non-profit group was to incorporate all past and present owners of Friendship sloops, along with other interested persons, and promote an annual race and regatta out of Muscongus Bay. We were filled with enthusiasm for perpetuating the world-famous design of this sloop and for furthering its existence by promoting an interest in building new sloops in local boatyards and beyond.

1990 FSS yearbook

The next big finds were Al and Betty Roberts. Al was a local lobster buyer, and both Al and Betty were part of the original town committee for the Friendship races. Betty became secretary for the Society in November of 1961 and later historian. Al made sure things on the waterfront went according to plan, and acted as an intermediary to the lobstering community. Al worked closely with the Friendship Museum, and Betty became a major force in the Society.

Her contributions were described in the 1976 Friendship Sloop Society yearbook in the following way:

She is Friendship's sweetheart, and although honored only by the term "secretary," she is everything to the Friendship Sloop Society from custodian of cannon ammunition to garde-malade in sickness and cheer-leader in health. The Society will never have, and neither will Fort Knox, enough money to recompense her for her unstinting faithfulness to Friendship sloopers. Smiling, she answers the good letters, and smiling she does the drudgery of replying to odd correspondence that she should (probably) file in the cuddy. As secretary, only she can do a good part of this booklet. She arranges, manages, and supervises all meetings, and her notes at the speakers' table are explicit, competent, adequate, ample, and correct. ("What's next?" . . . "Ask Betty.")

She buys the trophies, calls the newspapers with race results and other stories, tells inquiring tourists about motels, arranges accommodations for reporters and photographers, finds waitresses for the skippers' banquet, takes orders for the beer run, finds berths for would-be crew members, feeds transient sloopers, remembers everybody, loves everybody, and finds time to do many other things.

Locally, she fritters her idle time in good deeds—visiting shut-ins and elderly on schedule, bringing goodies and brightening each corner. She is a registered ambulance attendant and drops all else if the 'phone rings and a run to the hospital comes up.' She paints better than most, does needlework, and she could teach Oscar how to cook. Each morning she telephones about half the homes in Friendship to be sure all is well, and if all is not well—"What can I do?"

Unfortunately, Betty is "from away." Born in Lexington, Massachusetts, her training in Phys Ed brought her to Friendship (with Al) as an attendant at Oceanward Camp. They bought a home here, and bought the Wallace lobster wharf. Thank God, they'll never leave.

For so many things, and for being you, we thank you, Betty Roberts, we love you—and with no strings attached we dedicate this Sloop Days booklet and the Bicentennial Regatta to you. To the Friendship Sloop Society, Queen Elizabeth is here.

The following is her remembrance of that first Friendship Sloop Day:

Picture the smile of pride and satisfaction on the face of Bernard MacKenzie that summer day in July when he sailed into Friendship Harbor for the first homecoming race of Friendship sloops. Bernard's successful winning of a Boston Power Squadron Race in Voyager had germinated the idea of this homecoming event; and after six months of intensive planning between Bernard and the Friendship Town Committee, the race was finally to become a reality. This was a dream come true. Now, twenty-five years later, this dream like the measles, has turned into an infectious one. Year after year more proud owners of Friendship sloops appear for the annual regatta and many more land lubbers dream of the happy day

Al Roberts and Herald Jones.

Betty Roberts

Sketch by Bill Thon of handicap buoy reproduced from Enduring Friendships *published by the Friendship Sloop Society in 1970.*

Photo of the leaders in the first race 1961.

when they can leave the shore and join the fleet in their own sloops. This being our Silver Anniversary allows us the privilege of looking back at the past regattas with their good times and hard sailing.

That first year had three outstanding features. First and foremost, it was a huge success, secondly it was a one-race event, and lastly it set up a unique handicapping system. The regatta is still a great annual event; the one-race event soon turned to three races; the distance handicap stayed in existence many years. In this special handicapping, every sloop sailed a prescribed distance in "handicap alley," rounded a buoy set the exact distance for his handicap and snagged a lobster buoy tied to an anchor buoy to take back to the Race Committee as proof of completing his course. This was to simulate the Friendship sloop as a working lobster boat. Now one would suppose this task of grasping a small buoy would be fairly easy with an alert crew and a boat hook. It is said that Roger Duncan aboard EASTWARD #6 retrieved his buoy but in the excitement of getting it aboard jammed the gaff handle through his mains'l. Fortunately Clarence Hale, sailmaker to EASTWARD and to many others, was aboard to repair the damage at once. SARAH MEAD's crew lost the buoy overboard and someone had to jump in to get it. Easy? By 1973 the fleet had grown so large it was deemed unsafe to have so many sloops jamming handicap alley. Thus, retrieving the small buoy was stopped in favor of group roundings of similar handicapped sloops. There are those skippers who still to this day regret dropping the fun of snagging the buoy.

1985 FSS yearbook

In the paragraphs below, quoted from Roger Duncan's excellent 1985 book *Friendship Sloops*, we have another concise summary of that first race, as well as an overview of the following banquet and the first annual meeting of the Society.

The day of the race was clear and warm with a pleasant southerly breeze. On the beat down to Block Island, the fleet sorted itself out. As they passed Hall's Island on a reach across toward Thompson Island, three replicas, EASTWARD #6 [Roger's own sloop], John Dallett's MARY ANNE #10, and John Thorpe's ELLIE T. #22, were ahead and within a biscuit-toss of each other. The two reaches and the ensuing run up the west side of Friendship Long Island separated them, and they finished in that order, EASTWARD #6 the winner by 20 minutes. As she crossed the line, the 1812 cannon fired a magnificent charge of black powder, emitting not only a loud report and a cloud of smoke, but also a flaming wad of oakum that landed in EASTWARDS' cockpit. EASTWARD was awarded the Lash Brothers trophy; and MacKenzie's VOYAGER #1, the fourth boat and the first sloop built before 1920 to finish, won the Governor's Cup.

At the banquet that evening, Wilbert Snow of Spruce Head, a 77-year-old poet, read by the light of a shaky candle a long and colorful poem that he had written about a fourth of July fisherman's race. John Gould served as master of ceremonies. Governor Reed presented the awards, and the first annual regatta was over—a great success.

MacKenzie continued writing letters indefatigably, gaining coverage for the regatta in Rockland, Portland, and Boston papers as well as *Down East* and various yachting publications. He then planned a meeting of the Society at the Boston Yacht Club in Marblehead for November 25. Bill Haskell of GOLDEN EAGLE #4 made the arrangements.

No one took attendance, but the minutes state that the dining room was "filled to capacity." After a brief movie and Carlton Simmons financial report, it was resolved to hold a three-day regatta in 1962. It was proposed that a course be laid out to bring the contestants through Morse Bay and Garrison Island passage to finish in the harbor. It was also proposed that the start be made with all boats anchored on the line, sails furled and crew below. These schemes were tried and found too complicated.

Poet Wilbert Snow reads his epic poem at the first Friendship sloop banquet while Bernie MacKenzie (right) looks on .

Sloops in Morse Bay.

Sloops racing.

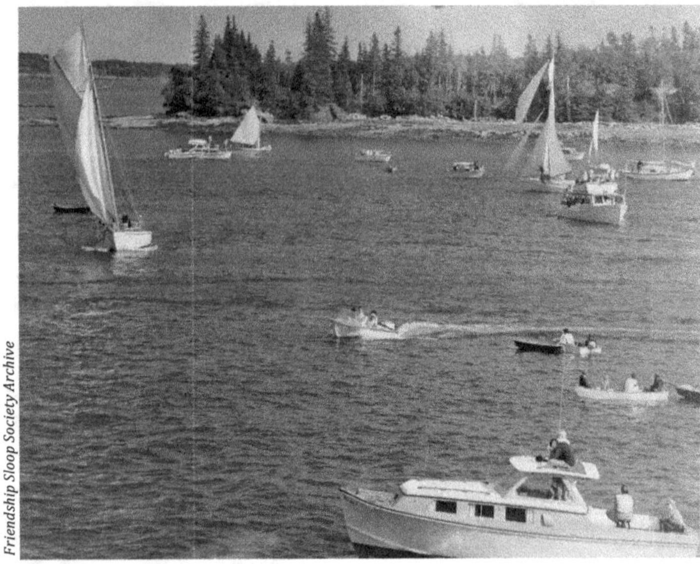

Early race in Friendship.

The only other matter of lasting interest was the election of Betty Roberts as secretary. She had served on the town committee and assumed much of the committee's responsibility. As secretary, she became a force that held the Society together for many years. She has been quick to make friends, thoughtful, sympathetic, and very accommodating. She has also been efficient and energetic, quick to answer letters, respond to requests, and take care of the innumerable details that arise day after day, year after year.

Bernie MacKenzie continues the story of those first few years in Friendship:

That first race, when fourteen sloops sailed into the harbor for their first "Homecoming" ever, was filled with excitement! It was a one-day affair on Saturday, July 22, 1961, that attracted 3,000 spectators. There were more boats in Friendship Harbor that day than residents could remember since the town was incorporated 154 years before. Perfect July weather blessed the fleet and the hundreds of people that crowded onto spectator boats to view the race. Governor Reed flew into Thomaston and traveled by car to the Friendship Town Hall that evening to present the trophies. A capacity crowd jammed the hall to hear the governor proclaim the fourth Saturday in July as "Friendship Sloop Day." It was cited as a significant milestone in the history of the little town and its people. I thought it was proper appreciation for the world-class little fishing smack that was built there in such numbers so long ago. Many of the town's residents, however, could not understand what all the fuss was about. Those old sloops built more than fifty years ago by the Morses had been forgotten and none built locally in thirty years. There was only one old sloop left in Friendship harbor—the DEPRESSION #23. Since the younger residents had not been told about the town's glory days, it was necessary for the elementary school art teacher to show the kids what these boats looked like and gaff-rigged sloops began to

50

appear on blackboards in the art class. A couple of these school girls came out to VOYAGER #1 before the race and presented me with their crayon sloop sketches. Somehow this meant more to me than the trophy from Governor Reed.

The first event was so encouraging that I took a chance and proposed three days of racing for 1962. I took another chance and sent an invitation to President Kennedy at the White House. Pierre Salinger wrote back and said the President would try to make it. I had learned that he was to be Gene Tunney's guest on John's Island that weekend and thought he might find a sloop race hard to pass up. After all, he sailed a 19' gaff-rigged sloop every summer at Hyannisport. During the race, a black Naval Academy yawl sailed into Friendship with Jack Kennedy at the helm, accompanied by Senator Muskie and others. We noticed an unusual number of Coast Guard utility boats following us at a distance, but it was not announced till afterwards that the President had actually been there watching the 1962 race.

1990 FSS yearbook

It would be hard to surpass Betty Roberts' own writing on the next few years of the Society. She was there taking notes and fills in some of what Roger left out. She wrote:

After the second year's regatta of three races, the race committee decided to vary the start for 1963. Why not try something new? The plan was to have all participating sloops at anchor with crew below and only the skipper on deck. At a cannon shot all were to up-anchor, up-sails and set off to the westward on a race course which took them around islands and back into Friendship Harbor from the eastward. The leading sloops were becalmed in Morse's Bay just before entering the harbor. The slow boats caught up with the leaders and a great drifting match of the entire fleet ensued. Suddenly a swing of the wind brought a good strong breeze and the entire fleet charged through the narrow channel into the harbor. What chaos! Everyone ashore held his breath as near misses, shouting, fast tacking, and a flood of sloops tried

Pictures of skippers from one of the first homecomings.

Skippers meeting in Friendship.

1962 Winners. Left to right: Ted Brown, James Wiggins, Roger Duncan, Bill Pendleton, Gerald Kinney, Ernest Wiegleb.

Friendships in the fog.

to maneuver for the finish line. This could have ended the regattas right there. When all the sloops were safely at anchor, the only casualty had been CHRISSY'S #18 dinghy which was "diminished" acting as a buffer when two sloops almost collided. To show the fine caliber of these skippers, there was not one protest. Needless to say, that race course has never been used again.

A cruise-race of sloops to the 1964 World's Fair in New York added a great deal of interest. Also, DIRIGO was launched and named on Maine Day of that Fair. 1964 also saw the start of an annual regatta in Marblehead sponsored by the Corinthian Yacht Club. The sloops' popularity has also been proven by invitations to participate in OP-Sail, a reenactment of Arnold's trek to Canada, and the last Tall Ships celebration in Boston.

"Homecoming Day" has always been the oustanding race of each regatta. Saturday, the last day of the races, the sloops hoist up their sails and glide by the wharves. The name of the sloop, the name of the skipper and crew are broadcast for all to hear. People from all parts of the country arrive to see this spectacular sight as the boats sail down to the starting line.

The fog has presented many interesting facets to running the regattas, mainly cancelling them. Contrary to public opinion we have held more races than we have called off. However, remember 1967? On Thursday we had a full race, Friday we cancelled on account of fog, but Saturday dawned bright and clear. So off they went. No sooner had the race started than the fog came in to join the fun. You guessed it—race cancelled. The next problem was to let the sloops "out there" know there was no more race, and this was more difficult as the fog became thicker. As we recall, EASTWARD #6 and SURPRISE #49 were the only sloops that navigated and finished the entire course. WHITE FALCON with Bill Danforth and his race committee became a search/escort service.

With the aid of radar they never gave up until all but one sloop was safely back on its mooring. The lost sloop turned up safe in the next town. The whole thing was finally accomplished about 9:30 p.m., but in the meantime the Awards Banquet back ashore looked like a deserted dinner party. Presenting trophies that year was a difficult job.

Fog again attended the regatta full force in 1971, making this the only year all three races were called off. Remark heard around the wharf, "In spite of fog, we had a good time, made new friends, and used more ice."

Remember the joking between sloops, singing, and water balloon fights that marked the wait for the start of the race, only to fall dead quiet and serious once the first gun was fired?

We could provide a list of sloops that have had rocks move right in their way. There was the Coast Guard handy to tow JOLLY BUCCANEER #17 back to port when she sprang a leak during a strong wind, and TANNIS #7 lost her topmast and mast head, dropping sails and wood on the deck without hurting anyone. Eight smiling faces of Cronin children clawed their way out from under the sails to the relief and joy of everyone.

Dr. Hahn on DEPRESSION #23 was more concerned in catching mackerel during the race. He bragged at catching 51 during one race. As a matter of fact, he came in last every year. Thus he bought a trophy for the "Last one in" so he could win a prize, and that year someone was slower than he was.

There was the "Honeymoon Sloop," WINDWARD #61. The Bracys gave the sloop to each other as a wedding present and the families deviated from the normal wedding gifts by presenting them with an anchor, sails, rope, you name it.

Jim Rockefeller on Howe Hill in Camden rebuilt OLD BALDY #57 and to launch her took her down the mountain with a pair of oxen in the old traditional way, only to put her in the water with a modern travel lift.

"Spooky," a very pregnant black cat, jumped ship from the JOLLY BUCCANEER #17 to EASTWARD #6 one calm night when everyone was off to the awards banquet. EASTWARD thought someone was playing a trick on them—JOLLY BUCCANEER mourned the loss of their cat. It all ended happily, however, with the cat restored to her proper owner.

Bill Danforth on WHITE FALCON.

WHITE FALCON.

Jim Rockefeller moving OLD BALDY #57 by oxen.

Crew of JOLLY BUCCANEER #17.

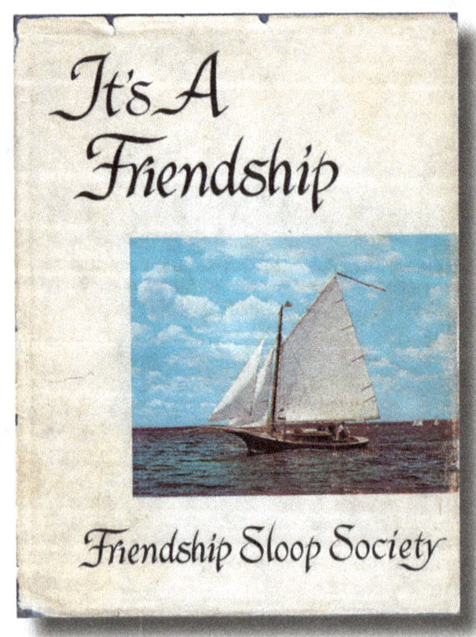

One could keep on going with all the fun and good times, but through these past years there has been a great dedication to Friendship (the town), Friendship sloops, and to friendships. Strong ties, good times, camaraderie, good hard sailing, and lack of serious protests have created lasting bonds and a great Society. This account would not be complete without mentioning a scholarship fund which the skippers have set up for Friendship students to obtain further education after high school. The Pendleton Memorial Scholarship has been in existence seventeen years and has helped many Friendship students with educational expenses. This was the skippers' way of saying "thank you" to the town for letting them monopolize the harbor for three days each year and of having a part in continuing the Friendship tradition.

1985 FSS yearbook

What these wonderful first-hand accounts fail to mention is that at the same time, Herald Jones put together the first publication of the Friendship Sloop Society, *Ships That Came Home.* Published late in 1962 and only 44 pages long, it was nonetheless a further accomplishment of the Society and a way to both record the history of the sloops in existence and to draw further attention to the goings on in Friendship during the last weekend in July. By 1965 Herald produced a more ambitious book, *It's a Friendship.* This hardcover book of 95 pages again listed existing sloops with short biographies of each boat, and it featured essays and historical pieces by John Gould, Bernie MacKenzie, Cy Hamlin, and, of course, Herald Jones. One notable contribution to this book was the preface written by the icon of American marine history, Howard I. Chapelle.

Meanwhile Al Roberts took advantage of all of the publicity and the large crowds of spectators that descended each July on Friendship, to push for a museum in Friendship. He had been collecting articles for such a museum for years. In February 1964 the Friendship Museum opened its doors in the old brick one-room schoolhouse. It had been abandoned in 1923 and then bought by the Condon family and renovated in 1927, and was used by the town as a community meeting place until Al had the idea of turning the building into a museum. Since the Museum represents the town of Friendship, it is neither a museum dedicated to Friendship sloops, nor is it the museum of the Friendship Sloop Society. However, much of the original material donated to the Museum came from members of the Society, and since so much of the town's history was dedicated to boatbuilding, there have been strong ties between the Friendship Museum and the Society ever since.

A boon to the Society in the 1970s were the continued publicity connections provided by some of its members, especially Malcolm Barter and James "Russ" Wiggins. Barter had been involved with the Society since the early days, and when he advanced to the editorial seat at *Down East* magazine, he was able to continue the work started by John Gould and Earl Banner of spreading the word about the Society.

Russ Wiggins owned AMITY #9. He was also senior editor at the *Washington Post* throughout the 1960s. Intending to retire in 1968, he instead accepted the post of U.S. Ambassador to the U.N., finally retiring in 1970. Retirement for Russ meant moving to Maine and buying a newspaper, *The Ellsworth American*, which he continued to run for years. Russ had a gift for making friends, and to quote one newspaper, "mixed with fishermen and farmers with the same ease that he mixed with senators and ex-presidents." He lived near the irascible and talented writer E.B. White, and the two were close friends. One of his long time cruising companions was well known broad-

The Friendship Museum

Russ Wiggins (in the white hat) aboard his sloop AMITY #9.

Robert's Wharf about 1970.

Friendship Homecoming about 1970.

cast journalist Walter Cronkite. Cronkite loved Maine, gracious when recognized, and appreciative when he was not, he crewed for Russ many times on AMITY #9, and even came to one of the Friendship homecomings.

Throughout the 1970s the gathering in Friendship became an annual pilgrimage. There are many members of the Society today who look back on those times with great fondness. Throughout the 60s and 70s the race committee—a long suffering bunch if ever there was one—experimented with different starts, finishes, and courses, to challenge the skippers while keeping the course safe. The handicapping system known as "handicap alley" was, as Betty Roberts mentioned above, an attempt to have faster boats sail a longer course so that the fleet could finish together, allowing spectators to see who was winning. One of the great advantages to racing in Muscongus Bay was that there was a lot of latitude for the race committee to lay out different kinds of courses and see what worked best.

In 1976 a Memorial Flagpole was donated to the town and dedicated at the annual races (See sidebar p.58). As with previous accomplishments, this tribute to memorialize those "Friendship Sloopers" who had passed over-the-bar was only achieved because members and officers of the Society stepped up and volunteered to make things happen. The memorial was not only a tribute to deceased members, but to the way things have always gotten done in the Friendship Sloop Society—by a combination of enthusiasm, volunteerism, and passion.

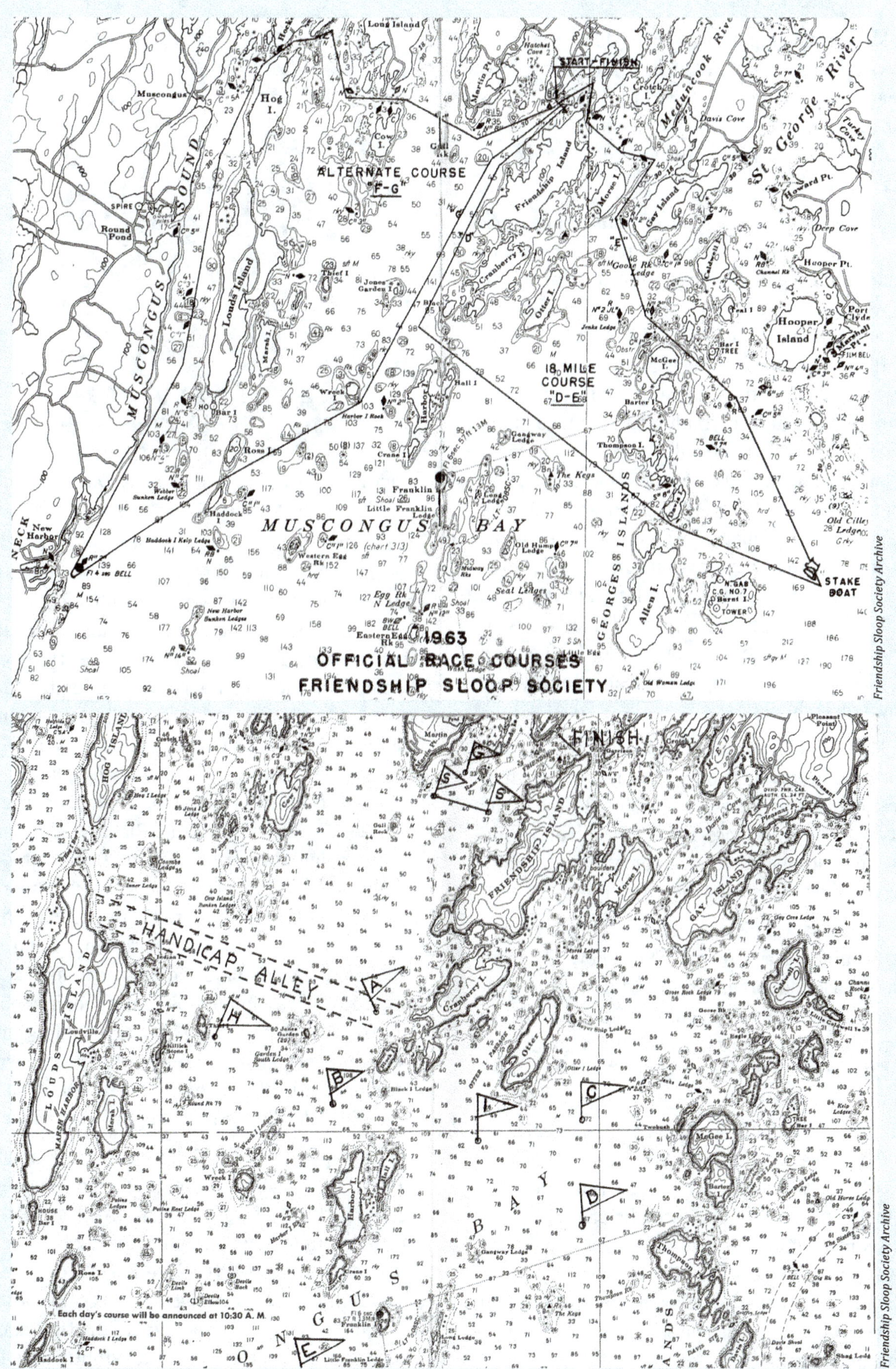

Friendship Sloop Society Archive

Friendship Sloop Society Archive

Race course for 1971 showing "Handicap Alley".

The Memorial Flagpole

Adapted from the 1977 FSS yearbook.

The Memorial Flagpole of the Friendship Sloop Society was dedicated last July 29th as the kick-off for the American Bicentennial Regatta in 1976—bringing to fruition a project that had taken much time and effort. As to the physical nature of the flagpole, Al Roberts recalls the details:

"For two years a committee of Hank White, Jack Cronin, and John Gould worked on plans for obtaining and erecting a suitable flagpole. After many false starts which included ideas for steel, aluminum, spruce, and fiberglass, Jack offered a mast he had removed from Tannis a few years ago when he decided he wanted one a little less hefty. That settled the question of material; everybody agreed a true Sloop mast was ideal. The only trouble was that the mast was at Jack's home in Sturbridge, Massachusetts, and the flagpole was to be erected in Friendship. The usual Friendship badinage ensued. John offered his pickup truck if the Society would install over-load springs. Hank said he'd tow the thing around with SARA MEAD #59 if the Society would fix him a two-year leave of absence from his practice. Sumner and Harold offered to carry it up if Virgil and Doug would lift it onto their shoulders.

The Maine Truck Owners Association would have brought the mast to Friendship, but ran into technical questions that frustrated this. Mostly, it was the inability of a trucking concern to do the job under ICC and PUC regulations—there was something about delivering off route, Friendship being off route.

Unless you saw the solution, you'd hardly believe it. Jack Cronin had a van truck. Somehow he rolled the heavy mast and topmast to the top, lashed it with many fathoms of line, and successfully moved the top-heavy load to Friendship. The only anxious moment of the trip came at the Bath bridge, which was then under repair. All who used that bridge during the summer of 1976 will shudder at the thought. The highway engineers had devised a series of arches, so the passage of the bridge was like a roller coaster, and somehow they resurfaced the bridge while motorists humped up and down and across. Jack was still sweating after he made the passage and got to Friendship. Once there, he unlashed his timbers and they were rolled onto carpenter's horses for fitting, painting, and rigging.

July 29, 1976, Jack Cronin owner of TANNIS #7 gets ready to raise the flag on the new Memorial Flagpole.

Ben Kaler dug the hole six feet due east and west, the same deep, and filled it with rocks. Two 10-inch channel irons ten feet long were imbedded in cement and a two-foot cement slab was poured over all. The mast required a substantial base. After two weeks of preparation, the volunteers were assembled for the raising. Doug Lash and Ernie Wiegleb engineered bolt holes in the mast to coincide with the pre-drilled holes in the channel irons. Hank and Marion White had come over from Camden, Alan Bellhouse (who did the rigging) was on hand. Richard Simmons was up on a neighboring roof shingling, and came down to help. Sidewalk superintendents were numerous. A derrick would have been fine, but none was on hand, so the crowd went to work with blocks and tackle, come-alongs, crow bars, poles, and muscles. While some said it was impossible, and people would get hurt, the pole went into position and nobody got hurt. It was all over in a few minutes, thanks in particular to the precision of the holes made by Doug Lash and Ernie Wiegleb. She stands straight for all to see."

The esoteric values of the Memorial Flagpole began with the deaths of two good Sloop members — Sandra Belknap of the crew of MARY ANN #10 and Jim Hall, builder, owner, and skipper of LUCY ANNE #68 and builder of RENASCENCE #141. But Sandra in particular. The lovely young lady was called aft all too soon, and her closer friends made the first contributions to the project. From this beginning, the idea of memorializing deceased members of the Friendship Sloop family resulted in the effort recounted above.

The ceremony of dedication derived some extra sentiment from the occasion of the American Bicentennial. Dr. Henry O. White, then the Society's president, commenced the program with the National Anthem, and incidental music during the exercises came from the Society's official piper, Donald Duncan, in kilt and plaid. It was one of the finest mornings the Sloop Society has ever had, and the waterfront was calm and attentive.

Those who had planned the occasion were agreeably surprised at the considerable crowd. Various members of the Society offered short remarks, and the roll of deceased Sloopers, now being memorialized, was read. Besides Sandra and Jim, the list included Arthur K. Watson, our first honorary member; Robert Gardiner, builder, owner, and skipper of RED JACKET #138; Dr. Myron Hahn, owner of DEPRESSION #23 and a past vice president; Philip Lauriat, SALATIA #90; Howard I. Chapelle, honorary member; Winnie Doane, charter member; Stuart Ford, builder and owner of CONTENT #5; Reggie Wilcox, builder and owner of EMMIE B. #78; Robert Montana, WHITE EAGLE #31; and Dr. A. Marshall Smith, APOGEE #88. All had participated in previous regattas. Other Sloop owners who because of time and distance had not been able to participate in regattas were also entered on the roll of those remembered.

The flagpole is on a square of land donated for the purpose by Al and Betty Roberts, just uphill from Al's wharf—the wharf the Society designates as official. Capt. Bellhouse rigged it with yardarm halyards, so various colors and ensigns may be flown together. Special flags were used at the dedication, including an oversized sloop burgee provided by the secretary, an original sloop streamer, and the streamer of our sister Society, that of the round-and-flat-bottom craft of Holland. And, of course, Old Glory. A plaque on the base, which will be the permanent designation of the memorial, was provided by owner Ernst Wiegleb and race skipper Bruce Morang of CHRISSY #18.

Non omnis moriar.

Jack Cronin's van with the flagpole unloaded in front of the van.

The crowds at the commemoration of the Memorial Flagpole.

The Memorial Flagpole eventually rotted away and has been replaced by a stone marker.

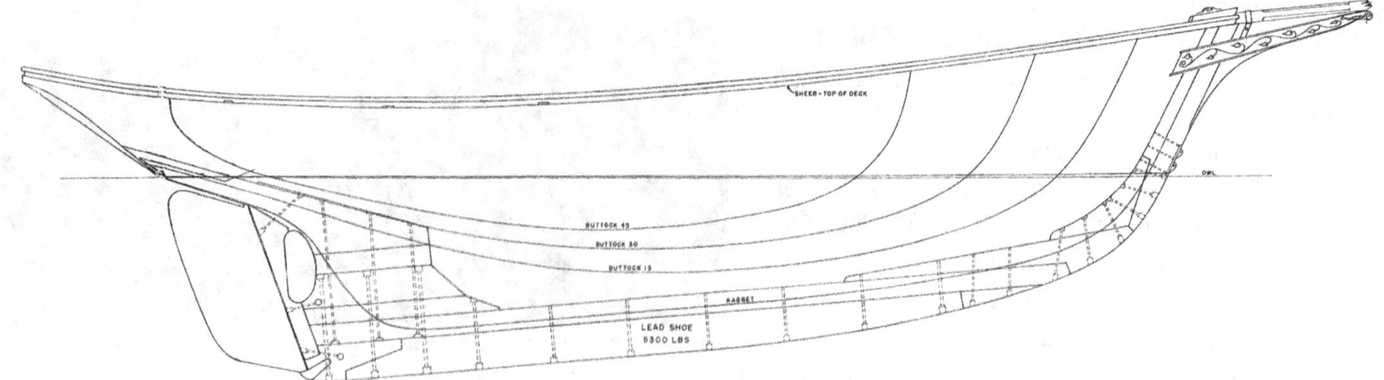

Backbone construction of 31' Friendship sloop
DICTATOR, as designed and rebuilt by Ralph W. Stanley
in 1972.
Originally built in 1904 by Robert McLain
Lines taken off by Ralph W. Stanley in 1972
for Jarvis Newman

Chapter Four:
The Revival of a Type

Part One: an Expanding Organization

By 1983 the annual gathering of sloops in Friendship had become too much for the little town and working waterfront. The decision was made to move the venue. Throughout the winter, an in-depth investigation was underway to find a different site for the annual gathering. Bruce Morang worked tirelessly as chairman of the race committee. Bruce and his wife Marcia investigated possible locations that might better serve the growing fleet. Finally a deal was struck with the Boothbay Harbor Yacht Club. According to Dick Salter, who was vice commodore at the time, the move was not really thought of in terms of a permanent shift. To quote Dick, "Bruce was telling everyone, this is a movable feast."

To see the shift to Boothbay Harbor as a purely logistical change is to ignore other influences. One of those influences was the realization that many of the older fishermen who had lived in Friendship and who had observed the activities of the Friendship Sloop Society with a tolerant eye, had passed over the bar, not to sail these waters again. Some of them were the last to have actually fished for a living from Friendship sloops. The Society had been around long enough by this point that several prominent members had passed away. This last fact was underscored in 1984 by the death of Bill Pendleton, former commodore of the Society, founder of the Pendleton Scholarship fund, and former owner of BLACK JACK #19. These losses caused many in the Society to push for a greater effort to preserve the history of the Friendship sloop and of the Society. While the annual gathering had moved to another location, the Society continued to support both the

Sloops racing 1974

Bill Pendleton

BLACK JACK #19

MAINE MARITIME MUSEUM

Adapted from the 1984 FSS yearbook

Everyone knows that Friendship sloops (and their owners) will live forever pretty much on their own power, but there are less hearty vessels which need the assistance of outsiders for assuring their preservation. That is where the Maine Maritime Museum in Bath comes in.

The museum, which has been keeping track of Maine-made ships for 20 years, will host the crews and craft of the Friendship Sloop Society July 21-23 at its Percy and Small Shipyard on the Kennebec River, and intends to make quite a fuss over them, with a lobster feed, tours, and concerts.

Sloops will sail up the Kennebec River to the restored and working shipyard that, for 24 years around the turn of the century, turned out some 40 of Maine's finest wooden ships. The Wyoming, the largest wooden sailing vessel ever put to work, was built at Percy and Small in 1909, her proud bowsprit overhanging Washington Street and her transom, some 329 feet away, shadowing the shoreline of the Kennebec.

Also mooring at Percy and Small that same weekend will be two tall ships, the WESTWARD, an educational training vessel from Woods Hole, Mass., and the PRIDE OF BALTIMORE, a replica of a Baltimore clipper, from Maryland. The SHERMAN ZWICKER, a Grand Banks fishing schooner, has hoisted anchor from Boothbay Harbor and will be alongside the shipyard's pier. She will be open as a floating exhibit on the traditional fishing fleet for Friendship sloop crews and other visitors.

After their passage up the Kennebec, Friendship crews can get their land legs back by touring the yard's original mill and joiner shop, oakum shed, and mold loft, as well as the small craft collection and exhibits on traditional ship building. They may see work in progress on several vessels, including reconstruction of the steam tug SEGUIN, the oldest registered wooden steam tug in the United States; construction of a new 40-foot pinky schooner; and restoration of one of the oldest Muscongus Bay sloops in existence.

CHANCE #37 seen at the 1983 races.

Friendship Museum and the Pendleton Scholarship Fund.

Every year since the 1961 race, the Society has published a yearbook. Originally just a program for the races that included some advertizing. The yearbook had evolved into a mini-magazine, with articles and tall tales mixed in with information on the races and on the Society. Started by Al Roberts and John Gould, it had been taken on by Roger Duncan who helped develop it into something of historical importance. There was concern about storing back issues and the original materials that went into them.

Concern for conservation of the Society's history and of the sloops themselves, led to other developments. Largely through the efforts of Bill Rand (of the WILLIAM M. RAND #218 who would later be commodore in 1991 and 1992) a dialog opened with the Maine Maritime Museum in Bath. A similar dialog had developed with the Penobscot Marine Museum, but there were several reasons to pursue a liaison with the Maine Maritime Museum. One reason was that the Museum had taken into it's fold the Apprenticeshop, a boatbuilding school founded by Lance Lee, next door to the Museum grounds, and now part of the conservation department of the Museum. Another was the Friendship sloop CHANCE #37 in the M.M.M. collection, which had been successfully campaigned in the 1983 races in Friendship, winning the class "A" trophy. In addition, the Apprenticshop had recently built a Muscongus Bay sloop. Many saw these two sloops and the maintenance shop that tended them, as physical evidence of the common purpose shared by the M.M.M. and the Friendship Sloop Society.

The combination of a teaching center for traditional boatbuilding and a museum with proper archival storage looked attractive to a number of members who felt the move from

Friendship had left them without a physical home. Another seductive element to the relationship with the Maine Maritime Museum was that they had a function-friendly waterfront. There was some thought that if the relationship between the Friendship Sloop Society and the Maine Maritime Museum were to develop, the Society might have a physical home as well as a place to store increasingly valuable historical information.

Whether holding races in the Kennebec River fronting the Museum was ever discussed is difficult to determine given the remaining letters that survive between the Society officers and the Museum staff, but there were certainly discussions of shared mailing lists, and even the possibility of handing over the secretarial aspect of running the Society to the Museum staff.

In any event, in 1984, the Museum hosted a gathering of Friendships at their waterfront facility the weekend before the races in Boothbay Harbor. They made a big effort to lay out the welcome mat, providing moorings, launch service, and tours of the Museum. The sloops that were in attendance were joined by the replica Baltimore clipper PRIDE OF BALTIMORE, the school-ship WESTWARD, and the Grand Banks fishing schooner SHERMAN ZWICKER. Despite the hazards associated with the significant tidal currents of the Kennebec River, there was good attendance, and the "Bath Rendezvous", as it came to be called, became a regular event over the next decade. In 1989 the Society even held their annual meeting and banquet at the newly completed and renovated facility. Some members recall what a grand venue it was. But, the location was not convenient for the majority of members, and the location was not used after 1989.

The Bath Rendezvous was not the only development of the early eighties. On the North Shore of Masachusetts something was brewing that

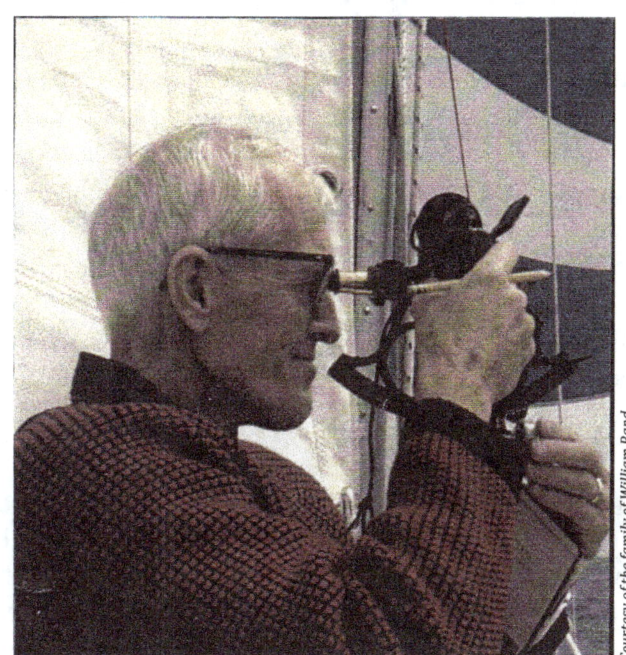

Bill Rand, commodore of the Society 1991-1992

Annual Meeting held at the Maine Maritime Museum.

Mass Bay Friends of Friendships

Adapted from the Summer 1993 newsletter

Another season of pot belly stove meetings started on November 4th when the Mass Bay group met aboard the Gloucester schooner ADVENTURE. The meeting notice read: "Our first meeting of the season starts off aboard a large Friendship sloop. She's bigger than TANNIS #7 or WESTWIND #95. In fact she's a peculiar type of vessel - has two masts and no bowsprit! The locals refer to her as the fishing schooner ADVENTURE. We'll need a good turnout to get her properly re-rigged in true Friendship sloop tradition. ...the ship's stove in the galley will be working and I've heard that the 'Joe' pot may be on..."

We've lost track of the number of years that we've been meeting at various locations in Massachusetts and New Hampshire, but we can't forget the friendships that we've made over those years. We have no president or commodore, but we do have Dick Salter, who serves as scribe, organizer, sends out the notices and passes the hat to keep the postage and "slush" fund in the black.

Last year's meetings were tours of "boatyards" to see, review, comment on, and criticize the progress, or lack of progress as the case could be, of various re-building and building of sloops. This year, the annual Christmas dinner at Manchester had its usual good turnout of 40+ members and wives.

January's meeting was held on a cold January night at the Gloucester Coast Guard station where members were provided with a guided tour of the station including their patrol craft, communications center, and maintenance building.

The New England boat show in February has become a tradition of sorts where our members look to see what's new in those modern rigs and equipment.

April's meeting was hosted by Ralph Anderson, owner of Lowell's Boat Shop on the shore of the Parker River in Newbury. The shop known for its building of the Town Class sloop, is also one of the few shops in the world that makes mast hoops. Ralph, assisted by member Larry Plumer, made a number of hoops that night to demonstrate the process.

May's meeting was a very special celebration for it was held in honor of Ted Brown's 80th birthday. Members met at Teddy's favorite place, Rosa's in Portsmouth, where we were entertained by Ted's favorite band, the Memorial Bridge Jazz Band. We also enjoyed watching Ted open "presents".

This year's series of meetings will end on a grand note: the launching of the Plumer Family sloop DESIREÉ #226 which Larry has been working to complete for a number of years. The launching is scheduled for noon on June 19th in Newburyport.

If you're interested in attending the meetings, give Dick Salter a call. More importantly, if you have an idea for a future meeting, or wish to have the group critique your building/rebuilding project contact Dick. We're always looking for a new meeting site.

Op sail '80

Courtesy of John and Carole Wojcik

One of the events that helped bring about the formation of "Mass Bay Friendships" was Operation Sail 1980 in Boston. Seventeen Friendship sloops participated in the event following the replica of the racing schooner AMERICA in the parade of sail. In many ways it was the perfect place to be, after all from our perspective AMERICA is nothing more than a really big Friendship sloop with an extra mast.

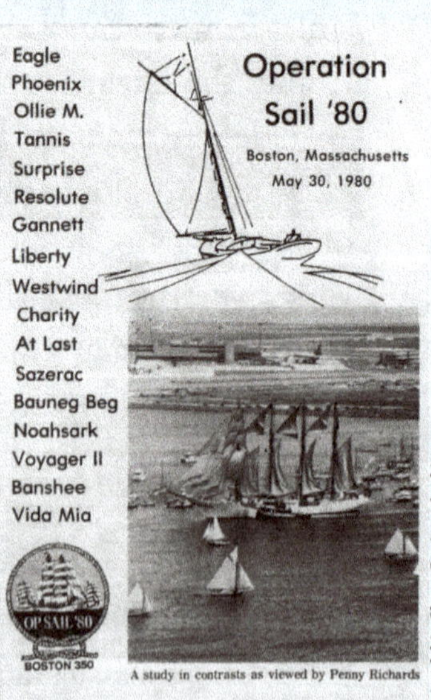

Friendship Sloop Society Archive

came to be known as the "Mass Bay Friends".

As the Friendship Sloop Society matured so did many individual and family friendships. It was only a matter of time before some members couldn't wait until summer to get together. Largely under the stewardship of Dick Salter, owner and skipper of LIBERTY #157, this informal group began meeting once a month during the winter to continue the good cheer and friendship. Dick organized different venues, including his own shop and barn. He set up occasional guest speakers and tours of boatbuilder's shops, and even arranged a private tour of the U.S.S. CONSTITUTION. As the decade progressed, this group did more than meet socially, they passed the hat to raise money for causes that the Society supported. They took on projects, maintained a mailing list, and in many ways extended the word "friendship" in the Friendship Sloop Society to mean more than a town in Maine.

While the Mass Bay Friends were meeting in the winter months, Friendship sloop racing found footing in Massachusetts during the summer. The Marblehead Regatta had become a tradition dating back to 1963. Originally the sloops were guests of the Boston Yacht Club, and part of a larger racing event, but Linc Ridgway worked hard to develop a Friendship division. Once established, the races blossomed, mostly because of the work of David Graham, who coordinated and promoted them. David also nurtured a relationship with the Corinthian Yacht Club, which took over as hosts of the races. Regular attendance of Friendships to Marblehead became another extension of the Society through the 1960s.

In the mid eighties, Holt "Jack" Vibber, at the time owner and skipper of TERN #24, organized a Friendship race as part of the New London Sailfest. What emerged out of this first gathering in Connecticut became the New

Friendship sloop members aboard U.S.S. CONSTITUTION.

The Corinthian Yacht Club.

Jack Vibber

London Rendezvous, which has continued on, although in recent years it has become more of a social network for owners than a racing group. It has allowed sloop owners from the Chesapeake Bay, New York, Connecticut, Rhode Island, and Massachusetts to get together and share stories and resources, and occasionally to race. At times the goings on that Jack promoted in New London even drew some of the owners and boats from Maine.

It seemed as though multiple chapters of the Society were springing up. It also must be said that times had changed. Fewer families could take several weeks to move their boat to and from Maine simply to race against the fleet, so the chapter development made sense. Another complication was that by 1990 there were a number of Friendships that were actively in use as charter boats. The reality of losing several weeks, or even a busy weekend of charter business in order to attend the gathering was simply not an option for these boats or owners.

A further extention of the chapters idea evolved in 1992. There were a number of boats based in the Mount Desert Island area, and the idea came about to have a single scratch race on one Saturday in July, followed by a cookout. Thus the Southwest Harbor Rendezvous was born. This event has become very popular in recent years. One reason is that a number of sloops use the event as a cruising destination. Another may be the relaxed nature of the event which feels more like an improvised race—no trophies, no handicaps, and the same basic round-the-island course each year. Still another is that the charter boats in the area can take one day to meet up with other sloop owners to socialize as well as show off their sailing skills. Some even bring charter customers as crew.

Miff Lauriat takes over the story:

After several years' hiatus from racing, I brought my Newman built Pemaquid, SALATIA #90 for the first time to the races in Boothbay Harbor in 1991. Lots had changed, but biggest among the changes was the race committee adopting a computer-based handicapping system. The first boat over the line, for whom the cannon was fired, was not necessarily the winner. The seconds-per-mile handicaps had to be crunched, and it wasn't until we all had returned to the yacht club that we saw the final results.

I started the Southwest Harbor Rendezvous for three reasons: 1) I live in Southwest Harbor, and know that this area offers some of the best sailing and scenery on the coast of Maine. 2) In a 10-mile radius of Southwest Harbor is the largest concentration of Friendship Sloops anywhere in the world. 3) I missed the old common sense protocols of the regattas in the town of Friendship and wanted to bring back a simpler way to have fun.

Planning the inaugural race in 1992, I got together with summer resident Alex Forbes, owner of the 19-foot Stanley-built BUCEPHALUS #251. We wanted to revive signaling on the committee boat, and not rely on radio communications. So we went through his family's ancient code flag set and matched flags up with government aids on the chart. Alex got his dad Peter to use their lobster boat the ANNIE T to be the committee boat, and Peter himself agreed to decide the course and fire off his signal cannon. For the start, the ANNIE T on her mooring off Sand Point, established one end of the line, the other end was an inflatable mark we could adjust for the wind direction.

We promoted the event by announcing that there were no entry fees, no handicaps, no trophies: only the great fun of sailing Friendships plus the glorious sound of cannon fire for the winner. We planned it for the Saturday before the Homecoming Regatta, to give boats time to sail from one venue to the other.

We were all very excited in planning that first race and we enjoyed great publicity. I invited Peter Travers, an award-winning sports photographer working for the *Bar Harbor Times*, to shoot the event from the ANNIE T. Noted scenic Maine photographer, Ed Elvidge showed up on his own. Photos from that day graced many a publication and calendar for many years.

In 2001, Don Ellis aboard his boat ELLIS 36 served as

race committee, with Jonny Mullins as cannoneer. Following that, and ever since, Ralph Stanley stepped in with his boat SEVEN GIRLS; he's been ably assisted by Rodney Flora and Jill Schoof (owners of Roger Morse-built WINGS OF THE MORNING #70) as cannoneer, statistician and timekeeper.

After the first few years, my wife Marge Russakoff and I decided we would hold an after-race party at our home. This began a wonderful tradition for us: one day each year, our deck and home were filled with Friendship Sloop enthusiasts until well after dark. In 2012, Steve and Kate Hughes (owners of the Newman-built Pemaquid OSPREY #139) graciously offered their Manset shore home and dock as the party site. At the same time, Shane Dowsland, skipper of ADDY CLAIR #217, generously arranged for his workplace Hinckley Company to offer free dockage and facilities which are a stone's throw from the Hughes place.

We've been delighted to see our race grow from a few vessels that inaugural year to a fleet of thirteen. Sometimes as many as four local charter boats participate. Seeing all those sloops sailing around together in "my back yard" is like stepping back in time 100 years, when gaff-rigged vessels populated the coast against the dramatic background of the mountains and cliffs of Acadia and Mount Desert Island.

Back in Boothbay Harbor, Bruce Morang pushed himself to find new twists that might appeal to the membership. There was the famous scavenger hunt where skippers were sent off to accomplish tasks. Dick Salter recalled that his task was to sail out of the harbor, through the swing bridge in Townsend Gut, to the waterfront cottage of the Commodore of the Boothbay Harbor Yacht Club (the hosts of the Friendship gathering) and kidnap the wife of the commodore! "I wasn't so sure I could pull it off," recalled Dick, "especially when I arrived at the house and found she was giving a cocktail party! She was a pretty good sport about it though, and just announced to her guests that she had to go."

In 1989 John Wojcik, owner and skipper of BANSHEE #180 and commodore in 1989-90, started the Friendship Sloop Society newsletter *Friendships* to keep the membership

Southwest Harbor Rendezvous.

Sloops in Boothbay Harbor.

Bruce Morang.

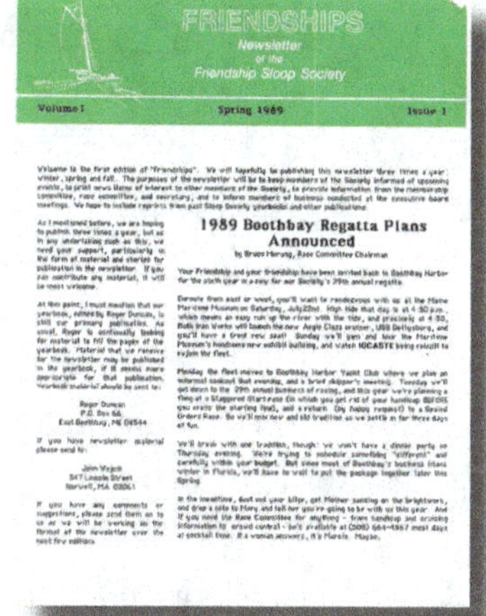

Sail '92

Adapted from the 1993 FSS yearbook.

Friendship sloops at Sail '92

by Andrea L. Wilson

Aboard Dick Salter's MESSING ABOUT

The Friendship sloops rendezvoused in Hull at 5:30 a.m., and in the thick of fog Jim and I boarded MESSING ABOUT. With one click of the VHF mike, Dick gathered the sloops together and herded them out toward the harbor. It was a good-sized group of Friendships, some 22 in all, including TANNIS #7, EAGLE #87, SECRET #112, AMICITIA #64, COAST O'MAINE #69, PERSEVERANCE #83, VOYAGER #96, AT LAST #105, RESOLUTE #123, NOAHSARK #131, OLLIE M. #152, KIM #258, DEFIANCE #169, BANSHEE #180, GAIVOTA #214, WILLIAM M. RAND #218, COMPROMISE #232, CHEBACCO #239, BUCEPHALUS #251, and SALATIA #90. As we made our way through the fog, each sloop kept a watchful eye on the others to be sure we stayed together.

We reached our positions to begin the festivities at the appointed hour. The Friendship sloops' sails filled as they fell in line to lead the U.S.S. CONSTITUTION up the harbor. While the sun glistened on the quiet waters in the morning sunlight, the Coast Guard managed the near impossible - keeping the harbor calm and under complete control.

As the sloops marched up the harbor toward Castle Island, we saw enormous crowds all along the shore.

The mass of humanity looked like a sea of balloons lining the shore with all their brightly colored shirts. The Friendships responded in party-like style, sailing up to the crowds as close as they dared and giving a congratulatory cannon blast as they came abreast of the spectators. The sloops' traditional gaff rigs against the Boston skyline presented an unusual mixture of the past and the present.

We neared our destination, and to our surprise found a number of suitable openings in the mooring field in choice locations to observe the rest of the show. One by one the sloops dropped their sails, dropped their anchors, and settled in to enjoy the impressive display.

It is hard to imagine the greatness of these fine ships that made their way into Boston Harbor that day. Yet, the boat that gave me the most cause for thought was the lateen-rigged replica of the NINA, one of Columbus' boats. It was so small compared to the other ships in the harbor that day. I sat in amazement as I thought about how difficult the journey must have been in 1492. Politics aside, our voyage to get to this celebration wasn't nearly as difficult as the journey sailed by Columbus.

informed about Society activities. It also gave Roger Duncan space for material that didn't fit into the yearbook. Twenty-five years later John is still publishing *Friendships* two or three times a year (although Laurie Raymond has taken over as editor). *Friendships* has proven invaluable to the Society because it not only gives the membership a better way to share information, it also provides a historical record of many of the decisions made and the challenges faced over the years.

In 1990 the Society started a model division. Several years of Friendship sloop races for remote-controlled models followed, which helped boost attendance and broaden the membership.

One event that cannot go without mention was the Society's participation in Sail Boston '92, organized by Dick Salter, David Cashman, and David Graham of the Marblehead race committee. Applications were sent in to have 26 Friendships participate in the Parade of Sail. The organizers' response was that they would allow only six sloops to participate. Dick and the two Davids persuasively argued their case, and in the end all 26 sloops were granted the right to participate. The sloops preceeded the U.S.S. CONSTITUTION in the Parade of Sail, and then anchored in their designated area—a prime viewing spot—which may well have irritated some spectator boats because the Coast Guard had expressly forbidden them to anchor in the same area.

After more than a decade of gathering in Boothbay Harbor, there was a sense among many attendees that a change of venue might be in order. Despite heroic efforts made by Bruce Morang and the rest of the race committee, the organization of the event was becoming more challenging by the year. Part of the reason for this had to do with the tradition that had been established in Friendship that the race committee was responsible for arranging dockage, moorings, anchorage, the skippers' meetings, permits, and to some extent, places to stay. They also had to keep track of sloops, handicaps, results, award trophies, and if weather permitted, set up and run three races. This long practice of putting so much on the shoulders of the race committee had two origins. One was that as commodores (originally called presidents) only served two-year terms, it was thought that to have them take over logistics would leave the Society without organizational continuity. The other was, once again, the extraordinary nature of the people who had stepped forward to put their talents at the disposal of the Society. Bruce Morang inherited a tradition started by Bill Danforth, Carlton Simmons, and Elbert Pratt of selfless service and commitment. However, the nature of the Society had changed. Bruce found himself sought after by organizers of the multiple events, and the logistics in Boothbay Harbor were far more challenging than they had been in Friendship. By the late 1980s it was clear that some sort of restructuring needed to happen.

Race committee burn-out was not the only concern. There were other issues. Whereas in Friendship people mostly anchored their boats, in Boothbay Harbor if you wanted to be near the yacht club, you needed a mooring, which could be a logistical challenge. In order to socialize one needed to go to the yacht club float, which had a somewhat different dress code than Robert's wharf in Friendship. Despite huge efforts on the part of the organizers, the banquet was a bone of contention for some. Everything from elaborately catered meals in inns to cookouts had been tried, but the venue never seemed to quite fit. Another problem was that the accommodations in Boothbay Harbor were spread out, making it difficult for those

Phil Nichols
of Round Pond

Adapted from the 1976 FSS Yearbook.

At 82, Philip Nichols of Round Pond says he's "slowed some," but in mid-April he seemed to have wintered well, and his dooryard was literally littered with fitted firewood ready for the shed and next fall. He said he hadn't started all his wood yet, because his Model-A tractor needed a valve job, and he'd been doing the job up in the woods rather than bring it to the shop. He hoped to get it running that afternoon.

Philip Nichols has built five Friendship Sloops, alone and from scratch, and they have been as pretty as any and prettier than some. The fifth, unnamed, is "all set and ready to go 'cept for puttin' overboard," and when asked if she is for sale Philip said, "I don't know."

A very shrewd a-la-Nichols guess might be that she will come forth some day as I DUNNO. His first was the RESULT of his inexperience; the second was built under PRESSURE; the name of the third was to be a SURPRISE; and the fourth's name was a well-kept SECRET. When Phil talks to you, there's a twinkling to his eyes that suggests he is always amused at some little thing nobody else knows about

who could not stay on their boats or chose not to. Perhaps the biggest issue was that the number of sloops attending was dropping.

Boothbay Harbor, while a terrific sailing venue, was a less-than-perfect spectator venue. Unless you could get on a boat, it was difficult to see the races. Members attending usually had no difficulty getting a lift out to watch the races, but there was no real opportunity to interest the public or the tourists who flock to Boothbay Harbor.

In 1992 Bill Rand undertook the onerous job of updating the Friendship Sloop Society Constitution to have it better reflect changes within the Society. That same year Bruce Morang stepped down as chairman of the race committee and Bob Rex, who took over, found he had enormous shoes to fill. Bob did a fantastic job, but when Bruce stepped down it definitely signaled the end of an era.

Concerns came to a head when Jim and Andrea Wilson (then owners of OLD BALDY #57) shared the position of commodore, and

Rich and Beth Langton 1991.

while Rich and Beth Langton (then owners of CONTENT #5, now owners of QUEEQUEG #155) shared the position of vice commodore. After serious discussion and investigation, and what was a difficult personal choice for the Langtons, who lived in Boothbay Harbor, the decision was made to move the 1995 homecoming to Rockland.

Rockland had a number of advantages over Boothbay Harbor. There were several hotels and B&Bs within an easy walk from the waterfront, and the large open harbor had a mile-long breakwater for spectators. The biggest attraction was that the town was very interested in being host to the homecoming, and offered the use of the town docks for gathering and rafting up. For the first time, all the sloops could tie up together, and skippers, crews, spectators, and friends could wander around on foot and visit without the restrictions of a yacht club or the necessity to row from boat to boat. Further cinching the deal was the town green and park adjacent to the town landing that could accomodate a large tent for skippers' meetings, displays, and the awards dinner. It presented a more comfortable setting than either Boothbay Harbor or Friendship.

The town of Rockland actively courted the Society, sending representatives to an executive board meeting to sell the idea of Rockland for the homecoming. Even so, there was concern about moving. Roger Duncan was concerned that being further east might result in fewer boats attending. Once again volunteers stepped forward. Jack Cronin (owner of TANNIS #7 and commodore in 1977-78) did an exhaustive phone poll of members for their opinions about the move to Rockland, and the results were overwhelmingly positive. In 1995 under the leadership of the Langtons, the Society held it's first Friendship Sloop Gathering in Rockland.

Rockland has proven to be family friendly. The harbor master Ed Glaser has been welcoming and accommodating, and Rockland's Share the Pride organization and the Chamber of Commerce have made us feel welcome. Rockland offers many things to do: museums,

Sloops gathered at the dock in Rockland.

GLADIATOR #71 and GAIL O. #44 at the dock in Rockland.

At the dock in Rockland.

Lasting Friendships: Ralph, Albie &
"Pantoosy"

Adapted from the 1987 FSS yearbook.

by Robert C. Brooks

Two young Southwest Harbor teenagers in a Friendship Sloop: one a local lad, the other summer folk—thus more than forty years ago begins the tale of lasting friendships.

As a result of gas rationing during the second World War, in 1944 Albie Neilson's grandmother chartered Jake Lunt's old Friendship-type sloop RELIANCE out of East Blue Hill Bay and hired Ralph Stanley's father to captain the sloop and to refine Albie and his brothers' sailing skills. The RELIANCE was built just after the middle of the first decade of the century by Swans Island boatbuilder George Tainter (1863-1949) for his son Blanchard, who kept her until about 1915. A 1909 Custom House record rates her at 7 tons. Ralph remembers her as being about 32' long, but Albie recalls about 36'. She was a bit narrower and a lot deeper than the traditional Morse model and had been modernized by the addition of a make'n'break engine driving an off-center prop. Most notable was the RELIANCE'S reputation of leaking "ten buckets a day!" If one tried to bail her dry she'd just fill back up to the same level, so one bailed ten buckets out of her well and that would hold her for the day.

Ah, the memories of a summer as teenagers! But with time, these young teenagers passed to maturity and each followed his calling: Reverend Albert P. Neilson into the ministry and Ralph W. Stanley into wooden boats. Yet the influence of that summer was to influence both their lives.

By 1961, Ralph had been building wooden working boats for nearly a decade. Albie had frequently discussed having Ralph build a Friendship sloop for him when the timing became right for the commission. Albie wanted a sloop that he could stand up in when down below. Ralph had yet to build a Friendship sloop, but for years had liked and studied the design, so he whittled a half-model of his proposed sloop. This he took to Thomaston for Roy Wallace (Newbert & Wallace) to critique. Roy "allowed it was alright" so the model was lofted, molds fabricated and the keel laid that fall. At that time, Ralph was building boats in the shed behind his mother's house on Main Street in Southwest Harbor. It was a quarter of a century ago this summer that a big beautiful black sloop, with cabin trunk brightwork glistening, was towed down the road on her skid to the water's edge near Hinckley's in Manset and launched by the rising tide. Displacing 17,000 pounds; she measures about 33' overall, 29' at the waterline, 11' on the beam and draws about 5'10" of water. In a search for more speed in light airs, her original bald rig was to be replaced with tops'ls about eight years later.

She was christened HIERONYMUS after the medieval Flemish painter, Hieronymus Bosch (c. 1460-1516). "Hieronymus" translates from the Latin as "Jerome." This led to the confusion perpetuated by *Enduring Friendships* that she was named for Sophronius Eusebius Hieronymus (c.347-c.419), sanctified as "Saint Jerome" for his Latin translation of the Bible. One time, while moored in Kennebecasis Bay (St. John, N.B.), a small boat came under HIERONYMUS' stern, read her name and hailed her. The hail acknowledged, the question was "Bosch?" This was the only occasion that a stranger properly identified the origin of her name.

One day in the 1960's, Chester Stanley (Ralph's father) absent-mindedly referred to HIERONYMUS as "Pantoosy" within the hearing range of the Neilsons. The comment was an obtuse reference to the old black sloop-rigged yacht PANTOOSET which used to ply the waters around Mt. Desert Island before World War I. Today "PANTOOSY" remains a nickname for HIERONYMUS.

It is easy to imagine the difficulties the name HIERONYMUS causes when trying to place a radiotelephone call. One must rapidly master the international phonetics; "Hotel, India, Echo, Romeo,..." Albie's son Will recalls an occasion he repeated the phonetics numerous times as the operator struggled to decipher the name. Much to Will's amusement, the operator finally acknowledged, "Oh, Albie's sloop!"

HIERONYMUS was registered with the Society in 1966 and the Neilsons actively campaigned her for about fifteen years until her crew scattered to various corners of the world. Older campaigners recall chasing HIERONYMUS during one regatta at Friendship when she bumped across a ledge. Apparently the incident looked far more dramatic from astern than it felt on her deck. More dramatic from the deck was the time that, coming out the back door at Friendship following a regatta, they snagged a ledge and ate lunch while awaiting the tide to float them off. HIERONYMUS' best placing in a Homecoming Regatta was in 1975, when the Neilsons won the Anjacaa Trophy (Class 'B' overall winner).

In the quarter of a century since the launching of HIERONYMUS, Ralph Stanley and Stanley-built sloops also have been active campaigners, and not infrequent winners, at the Society's regattas. Ralph skippered the AMOS SWAN to the Eda Lawry Trophy in 1975 and three times has skippered the MORNING STAR to the Jonah Morse Trophy (1984, 1985, and 1986).

Ralph Stanley, by vocation a master boatbuilder, by avocation a sailor-historian, and by nature a gentleman, has been a steadfast contributor to the continuance of the Friendship sloop and the Friendship Sloop Society. Besides being an active campaigner, Ralph has built at least four half models for presentation by the Society. The most prominently displayed is the one on the wall in the trophy room of the Corinthian Yacht Club, the Society's host for the annual Marblehead regatta. Ralph has been a frequent contributor of articles for the yearbook. And, of course, Ralph's entertaining the membership with his fiddle has become legendary.

Many sloop owners know what Ralph has contributed to their own sloops, but few (and certainly not this writer) know of all the sloops which Ralph has built, restored, repaired, sparred, rigged or rerigged, or otherwise contributed to. In addition to HIERONYMUS #67, a partial roll call includes: DICTATOR #2, AMITY #9, VIGOR #14 (now SADIE M.), GYPSY #43, SURPRISE #49, WINDWARD #61, VENTURE #66, MORNING STAR #82, EAGLE #87 (now STELLA MARIS), MAGI #107 (now MAGIC), AMOS SWAN #111 (now lost), LIBERTY #157, FREEDOM #167, BANSHEE #180, PEREGRINE #187, and two ENDEAVORS #196 & #201. Every Dictator-model hull and those with fiberglass decks and cabins are replicas of Ralph Stanley's work.

When asked which is his favorite sloop, Ralph diplomatically avoids a direct answer. If the reader wants to test the water, just mention the name of ENDEAVOR #196 and watch the twinkle in Ralph's eye and the curve of his mouth. Years ago, the late Bill Pendleton (BLACKJACK #19) and Ralph discussed sloop ownership. When Ralph remarked that some day he hoped to see his way clear to own a sloop, Bill said, "If you want a sloop, have one even if you have to give up something! Give up something, but have that sloop!" Bill's philosophy gnawed on Ralph until 1978 when Ralph, in a spur of the moment decision, ordered the material for ENDEAVOR. Ralph designed ENDEAVOR on classic lines and Lowell Wentworth recorded Ralph building her in the video *The Friendship Sloop: A Heritage Retained*. The ENDEAVOR has been sold, but she remains in Ralph's care at his boathouse and her current owner graciously encourages Ralph's use of ENDEAVOR. Last September, Ralph and his wife Marion cruised Penobscot Bay in Ralph's favorite Friendship sloop.

PANTOOSY

shops, restaurants, and the third version of Lance Lee's Apprenticeshop school are within walking distance. If there is any drawback to Rockland as a location it would be the problem of a busy commercial harbor, and adding some unwelcome excitement for the ferryboat captains. (We really do apologize for the times when we've gotten in the way).

The move has not alleviated all of the Society's problems. There are still passionate conversations about how to attract more sloops. And with the death of several key officers who had connections in the media world, the Society has struggled lately with attaining the free publicity that it once enjoyed. On the other hand, Rockland has drawn sloops to the homecoming whose owners have no interest in racing, but who come for the socializing and as a destination for a cruise.

The discussion goes on about how to meet members' needs as the demographics and the interests of the members shift. The focus on racing has changed in recent years, not necessarily in those boats that keep returning to race in Rockland, but for many members, and in boat clubs across the country. Other forms of waterborne recreation, sea-kayaking, small boat "raids", and small boat cruising have captured more of the sailing community, and racing has felt the impact. In 2013 seminars were offered as part of the homecoming in Rockland to try to reach a broader audience. However, we as an organization sometimes lose track of the fact that a group with less passionate and committed members would have died out a long time ago. Stop by in Rockland and ask anyone there what the future holds for the Friendship Sloop Society and you will get an earful of enthusiasm and good ideas.

Part Two: an Expanding Fleet

The 1965 book *It's A Friendship* conveys a sense that the day may be coming, not too far in the future, when there might not be any Friendship sloops left. This sense of "the last of their kind" turned out to be completely off the mark, for the growth of the Friendship Sloop Society had another more tangible side. Not only were owners of sloops making a renewed effort to keep their venerable vessels sound, but new sloops were being built. As we have seen, the design made the transition to recreational craft in the 1920s. Boats had been built occasionally since then, but with the formation of the Friendship Sloop Society, a new generation of enthusiasts discovered Friendships, and new boats were taking shape. Some builders were amateurs, building vessels for the experience of building a boat as much as for the pleasure of owning the finished craft. Some builders were professionals who saw a revival of interest, particularly in the 1970s when a small funky publication originally called *The WoodenBoat* (the name was soon changed to just *WoodenBoat*) went from the it-will-never-work stage, to wildly-successful in just a few years. Some builders, like Phil Nichols of Round Pound, Maine, treaded a sort of middle ground, considered professionals by some and amateurs by others.

The extent to which the Friendship sloop went through a revival in the later half of the twentieth century is often completely overlooked. Just to look at some basic numbers: when the Society was founded in 1961 an exhaustive search was made to try to find and document as many remaining sloops as possible. While it seems unlikely that every sloop still in existence was found, the Society did manage to locate 51 sloops built before 1920, and 29 built between 1920 and 1960. In other words the

Society believed that there were about 80 sloops left, some in better shape than others. Given that base number, and the fact that these were all wooden vessels and some were over 60 years old, it is understandable that many people might think that the fleet was dying. No one realized that the renewed interest in the Friendship sloop would result in a veritable building boom. In the decade of the 1960s, 39 new sloops were built and added to the fleet. That number is impressive enough, but it was the decade of the 70s that is most impressive when a staggering 95 new boats were built. In short, in the two decades following the foundation of the Friendship Sloop Society, the number of Friendships had more than doubled.

Some of the boatbuilders were simply continuing to do what they had always done. The Lash Brothers were still building boats in the town of Friendship, and it is hardly surprising that they would add at least four more sloops to the fleet in the 1960s. Another obvious example of continuity is Ralph W. Stanley, whose family had fished in Friendships and had grown up in a world where the Friendship sloop was greatly admired. Ralph would not only add significantly to the fleet with boats that are the gold standard of construction and beauty, but just as important, his son Richard continues that tradition of building today. In 1999 Ralph won a National Heritage Fellowship, recognizing him as a Master Artist. Many members of the Friendship Sloop Society have long considered Ralph a national treasure. Excellent examples of Ralph's work include HIERNOYMUS #67, FREEDOM #167, PEREGRINE #187, ENDEAVOR #196, and ACADIA #269.

Other builders, like McKie W. Roth Jr., Phil Nichols, Charlie Burnham, and James Rockefeller would build multiple hulls. And, of course, there were numerous builders who only produced one sloop.

Courtesy of Noel March

The crew at Lash Brothers 1966.

Courtesy of Jeff Dobbs

Ralph W. Stanley

The late 1960s and early 1970s were extraordinary times. There was a wooden boat revival brought on to some degree by *WoodenBoat* magazine. Interest in this renaissance centered mostly on the Maine coast, and it is logical to expect that the building of Friendships would be part of that. However, a small number of boatbuilders were willing to take this icon of Yankee tradition and dabble with a new form of black magic called fiberglass—a development which caught many by surprise.

In 1969 two young men from Bristol, Rhode Island, Dick Bruno and Garry Filmore, launched PERSEVERANCE #83, a 30' fiberglass Friendship sloop. She was the first hull built by their company—Bruno and Stillman Yacht Company. Marbridge Associates in Massachusetts drew up the design, and the plug for the molds was built using plaster and balsa wood over a metal frame. Bruno and Stillman would go on to launch multiple Friendship 30s from their Newington, New Hampshire yard. PHOENIX#91, built for Al Beck, is an excellent example of Bruno and Stillman's work. She is still owned by the Becks, and Al's son Tad now runs her.

Meanwhile, boatbuilder Jarvis Newman, who lived in Manset on Mount Desert Island, was taking a different approach. Why not take a proven Friendship and use her as the plug for

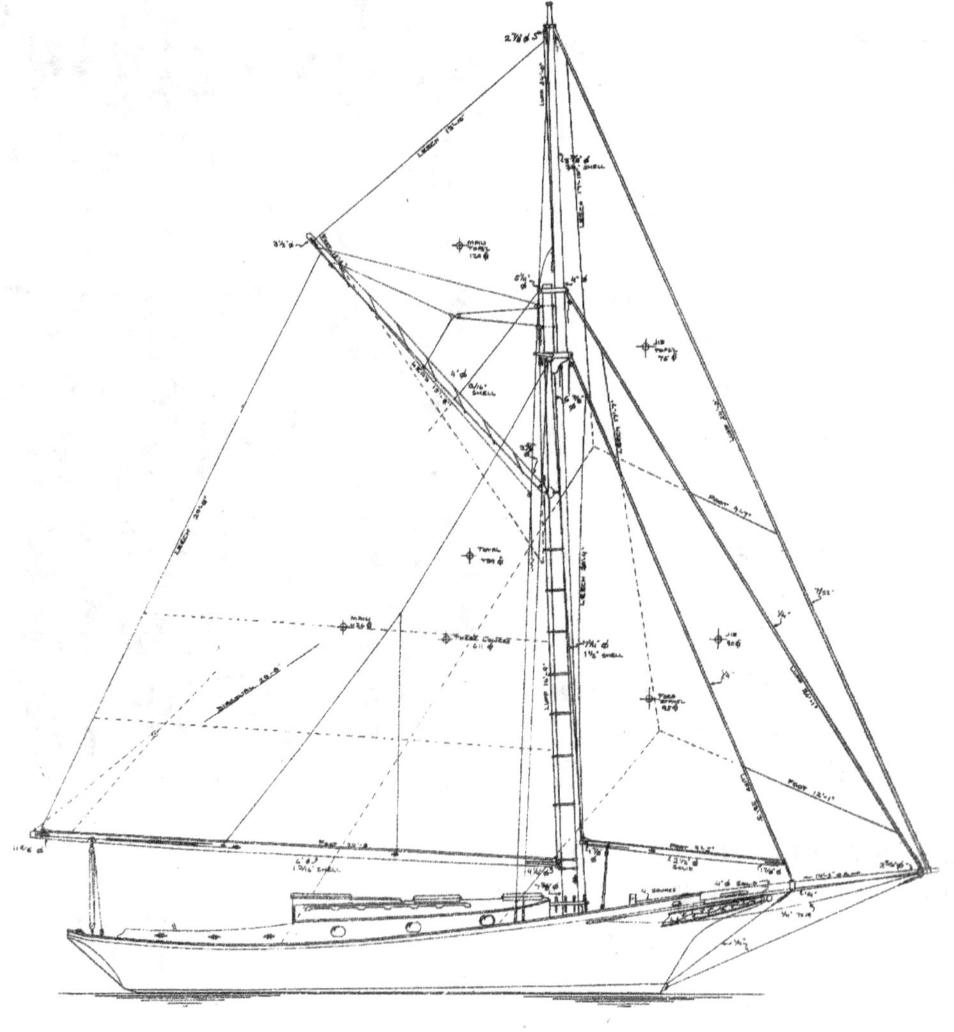

Bruno and Stillman sail plan for the Friendship 30

a mold? Have the resulting fiberglass boat match the exact displacement of the original and the result should be a high-performing fiberglass boat. Jarvis had some experience with fiberglass while at the Hinckley Company in Southwest Harbor. He was also educated as an engineer, so from the very first hull, the results were exceptional. In 1968 he borrowed OLD BALDY #57 from then owner Mahlon Hoagland. OLD BALDY was a new boat launched in 1965 and built by Jim Rockefeller of Bald Mountain Boatworks. Jim had chosen the design with care using the lines of a 1914 boat, PEMAQUID, ex FLORIDA, built by Abdon Carter on Bremen Long Island. The first hull out of the mold went to Jim's shop to be finished off at a later date. The second hull was brought in an unfinished state to the Friendship gathering in 1969. She went to George Lauriat of Southwest Harbor and was christened SALATIA. SALATIA #90 is still owned by the Lauriats, and George's son Miff Lauriat has her painted red. At 25 feet on deck, these sloops are known as Pemaquids, and Jarvis would go on to build at least 18 more. There has been some confusion as to which hull was the first, because SALATIA hit the water first, but was actually the second hull out of the mold. Part of the success that Jarvis enjoyed had to do with incredibly solid construction and excellent craftsmanship, but part of his success came from the fact that he preferred to build the hull and the deck components and then sell them to someone who could finish the boat off. This made the Pemaquids an excellent buy and allowed some people to purchase a new fiberglass boat who could not have otherwise done so. It was fitting that when OLD BALDY needed a complete rebuild in 2010, Jarvis bought her and brought her back to life, demonstrating that he had not lost his touch for wood construction either.

The first Pemiquid hull by Jarvis Newman.

Pemaquid hull number 2 which would become SALATIA #90, seen here at the Friendship Homecoming 1969.

Deck assembly and hull of what would become HOLD TIGHT #106. Picture taken in 1970.

On Friendship Sloop Construction
By OLD BALDY #57

Adapted from the 1969 FSS yearbook.

Time and tide wait for no man, not even the devil, so when OLD BALDY'S Mahlon Hoagland hailed me on Al Robert's wharf and asked if I knew a guy called Jarvis Newman, the plot was patently apparent.

"Jarvis of the lovely glass dinghys? Fine Fellow!" I enthused. "Good eye for the traditional. Marvelous craftsman in his material. His father-in-law is Raymond Bunker—one of the best wooden boat builders on the coast. Teases Jarvis …."

The good doctor cut me short. "He's offered me a proposition."

From the corner of my eye I watched Phil Nichols tack SURPRISE up the harbor, thinking how of all the Friendships here she looked the most authentic, right down to the builder-owner.

"I said he's offered me a proposition." Mahlon glanced furtively up and down the dock and lowered his voice. "He wants to use OLD BALDY to make a mold for a glass one."

"Fiberglass Friendship!" The ballon was loosed. Heads swiveled. A venerable member of The Society reeled, crossed himself, making the sign of the gaff, and glared in our direction.

Hoagland hustled me around back of the bait house. "See!" he said, laying into my shins. "People are going to get the wild hair up. A glass Pemaquid — its like renouncing God, Motherhood, baked beans! Do you think they'd kick me out of the society?"

"Dammit!" I said, rubbing my leg. "Take in a little sail. The important thing about Friendship sloops isn't in how they are put together. The magic is in their past utility, their pleasing lines, and the people who sail them. Construction-wise, the originals are nothing to found a tradition on. Take one with a little age on her and all you've got is trailboards, dry rot, and a damn good pump. Wilbur Morse was a marvelous business man, not a patron saint of wood boat construction."

OLD BALDY'S owner looked nervous. I pressed on, "Boats are for fun. What difference if they are built of wood, cement, glass, melted down old chocolate-covered rubber heels, long as the material is used well and honestly and the result is pleasing to the eye and it does the job!"

"Whose side are you on, anyhow? I thought you were a wooden boat man?"

"The side of magic," I replied. "Whispering breezes, raging gales, and the gaff rig even though it's a bitch for chafe."

"Don't get frivolous. This is serious. Newman would put OLD BALDY in his shop this winter—sand her topsides mirror smooth. She'd come out looking a lot better than when you built her." "Golly! Wouldn't that puff the old girl up," I said, ignoring the slur. "The chance to found a dynasty isn't offered to just any old Friendship wallowing in the gunk hole. Good stock there, Hoagland. Fine background. Breeding always shows!"

"I hope Jarvis can fix those cracks in the deck," he said. "They look awful."

Out in the harbor Phil Nichols brought SURPRISE into the wind. His nephew, Bruce Cunningham, the fine boatbuilder from Round Pond, went forward and let go the hook. I knew Bruce was working on a 42' fiberglass hull in his modern shop, while across the cove Nichols, with no power tools, was building another wooden Friendship a little smaller than SURPRISE.

Glass and wood, the materials change but the people don't. I was happy Jarvis was going to make a glass PEMAQUID. I knew he would do a first-rate job for he was a craftsman and he was building it for the right reasons. He was nuts about Friendship sloops. His burning ambition was to own one. Later on others, no doubt, would jump in to catch the bandwagon with tasteless imitations. But this first fiberglass one by Jarvis, I knew it would be right.

And I couldn't help but muse what Friendships meant to me. It was Betty and Al Roberts giving unstintingly of their time. It was Jane and Skip Bracy sailing off across the bay in WINDWARD on their honeymoon. It was John Gould carving SAZERAC'S trailboards on the wrong side; the friendly rivalry between Malcolm Barter and Roger Duncan, George Merrill's bald head, Phil Nichols working on a new Friendship in the dead of winter in his unheated shop with his shirt open, and when asked why he did it at his age, replying, "Better than looking at TV." It's the sight of all those gaff rigs coming into harbor the last three days in July against a background of spruces and rock. It's a thousand little things—a magic brew of people, place, and time—and 'just messin' around in boats.'

Dr. Hoagland interrupted my thoughts. "If you were going to build another Friendship for yourself what would you use?" I answered without hesitation, "Old chocolate-covered rubber heels."

In 1972 Jarvis bought another sloop, DICTATOR #2, a 31-foot sloop built originally by Robert E. McLain in 1904. With help from Ralph Stanley, he rebuilt her and she became the family boat for the Newmans throughout the 1970s. As with OLD BALDY, Jarvis struck off a mold from DICTATOR, and in 1974, the first of the fiberglass Dictator class, #147, now named MARA E., was launched. As with the Pemaquids, Jarvis built bare hulls and deck structures and sold them to people who would then finish the boat. For that reason the builder of these boats is usually a double name: Newman followed by the name of the builder who finished off the boat. Jarvis regretted selling DICTATOR in the early eighties and bought her back in order to rebuild her in the early 90s.

While Bruno and Stillman and Jarvis Newman built their reputations on larger boats, others were doing the same with smaller models.

A builder named McKie Roth in Edgecomb, Maine, developed a 22-foot design, also based on the lines of PEMAQUID. He built at least three of these in wood. Then George and Chester Harris of Passamaquoddy Yachts used the design to build molds for a 22-foot fiberglass model and produced a dozen of these "Quoddy" boats—MAGIC #107, VOYAGER #134, ANGELUS #153, GHOTI #282 and ELLEN ANNE #215 to name a few. The molds were lost in a fire but Patrick Ahern, using a Quoddy as a plug, built new molds and built another ten glass boats, all of which can be traced through McKie Roth to the original PEMAQUID. SEAL #221, MERMAID #228, COMPROMISE #232, CHRISTINE #237, and VIKING #238 are all examples of Ahern boats. These prolific builders are a sampling of the innovative resurgence that characterized the revival of the Friendship sloop.

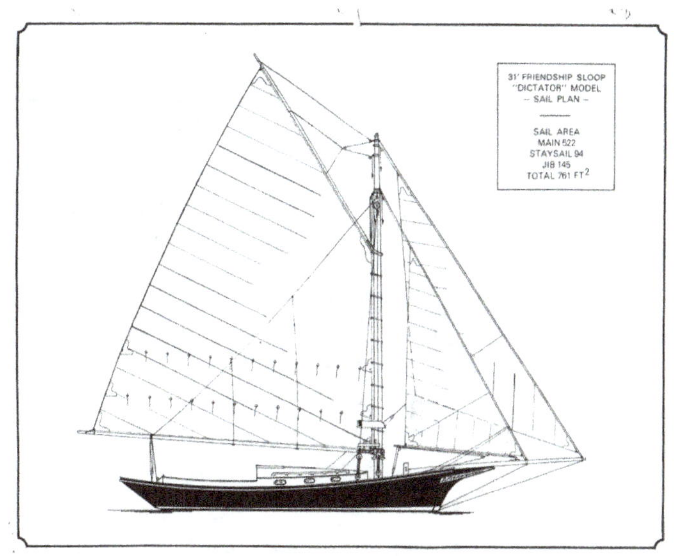

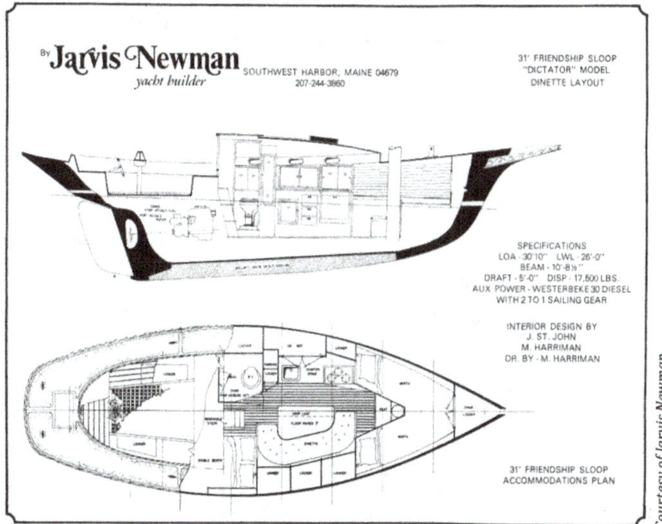

Jarvis Newman DICTATOR design based on the original DICTATOR #2 built in 1904.

HEGIRA #230 an example of a wooden McKie Roth sloop.

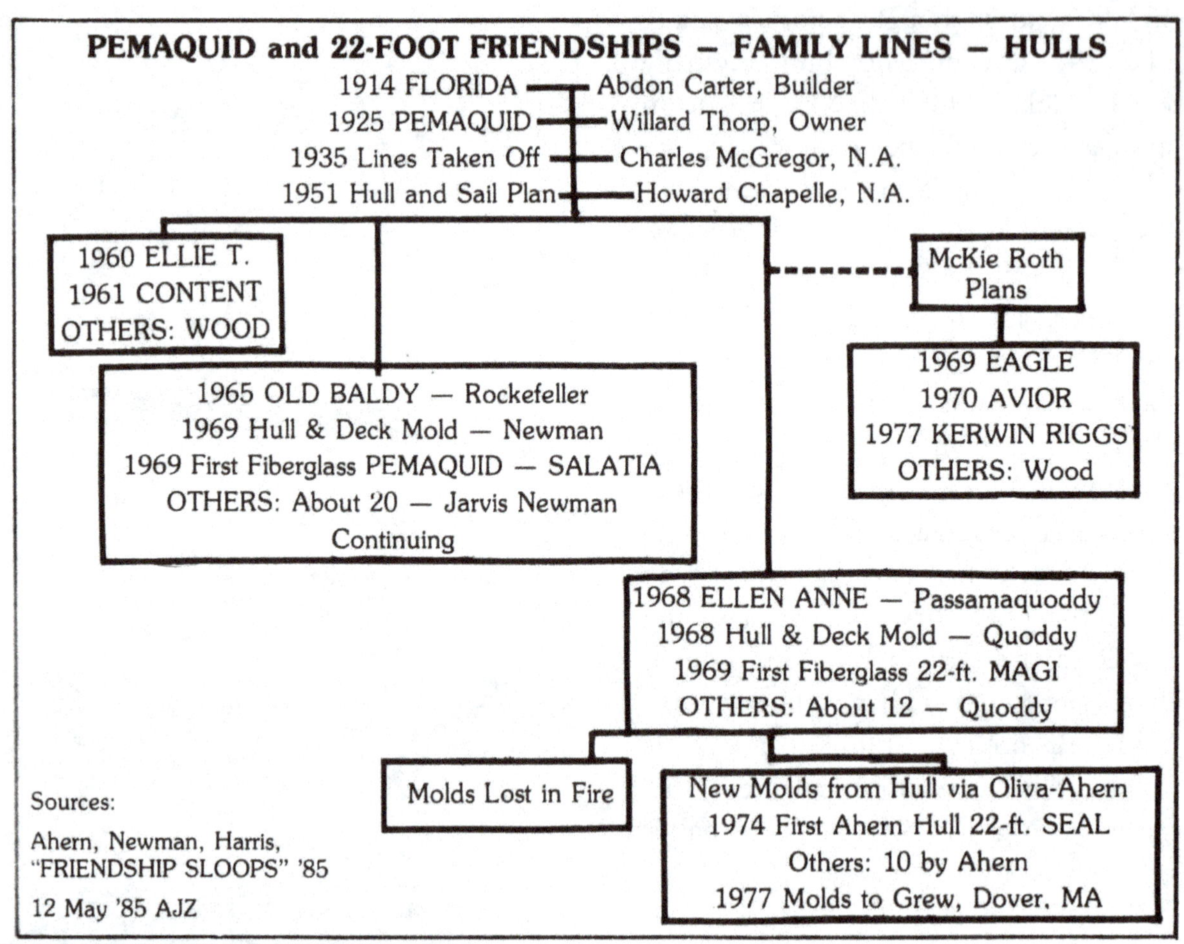

COMPROMISE #232 an example of an Ahern built boat.

On two occassions Friendships were built as tools for teaching. In 1987 the WoodenBoat School, which had developed out of the tremendous success of the magazine *WoodenBoat*, started a project that would occupy the shop for the next six years. The school wanted to recognize the contributions of local boat builder and teacher, Belford Gray, and decided to build a Friendship sloop in his honor. The sloop was built through a series of two-week summer courses, and many students returned year after year to contribute to the project. It was only the second large-scale project that the WoodenBoat School had undertaken, and it exposed students and visitors to the design and construction of a Friendship sloop. When it was launched in July of 1992, BELFORD GRAY #250 became a sailing classroom for the WoodenBoat School seamanship programs, a function she still fills today. The tie between *WoodenBoat* and the Friendship sloop was a strong one. Roger Duncan wrote occasionally for the magazine and had taught seamanship classes for the school aboard his own sloop, EASTWARD #6.

By 1988 Lance Lee had reorganized the Apprenticeshop and moved it to a new location in Rockport, Maine. At that time Frank Snyder who had owned the sloop RITA in the 1940s started discussions with Lance. In essence he wanted to build a new RITA, and he wanted the Apprenticeshop to do the building. By taking this approach, a number of apprentice boat builders would have an opportunity to learn their craft while working on a large Friendship sloop. Frank had the lines of the original RITA which had been taken by William Atkin in 1950. He had a local marine architect produce the building plans, and he hired a photographer to document progress. He kept meticulous notes on the construction process, which were later donated to Mystic Seaport. RITA II #247, now named BLACK STAR, was launched in 1989, and was loaned to the Apprenticeshop for part of several summers to be used as a classroom for teaching seamanship.

The building of these two sloops exposed many new people to the Friendship sloop while teaching traditional boat building and seamanship at the same time.

Whether it was individuals building sloops, like Charlie Burnham and Phil Nichols, or the influence of schools like the Apprenticeshop and the WoodenBoat School or the production methods employed by Bruno and Stillman, and Jarvis Newman, the Friendship sloop had gone through a revival in the 1970s and 80s that exceeded the wildest dreams of Bernie MacKenzie when he set out to found a society of Friendships. The Society itself had had

to grow and adapt to changing times to keep a more spread out membership informed and involved. The move of the homecoming to Rockland provided a better rallying point for the annual gathering, and the emergence of regional chapters involved more people outside of Maine waters. As the 1990s progressed, more changes were on the horizon.

BELFORD GRAY #250

Launching day for RITA II, now named BLACK STAR #247.

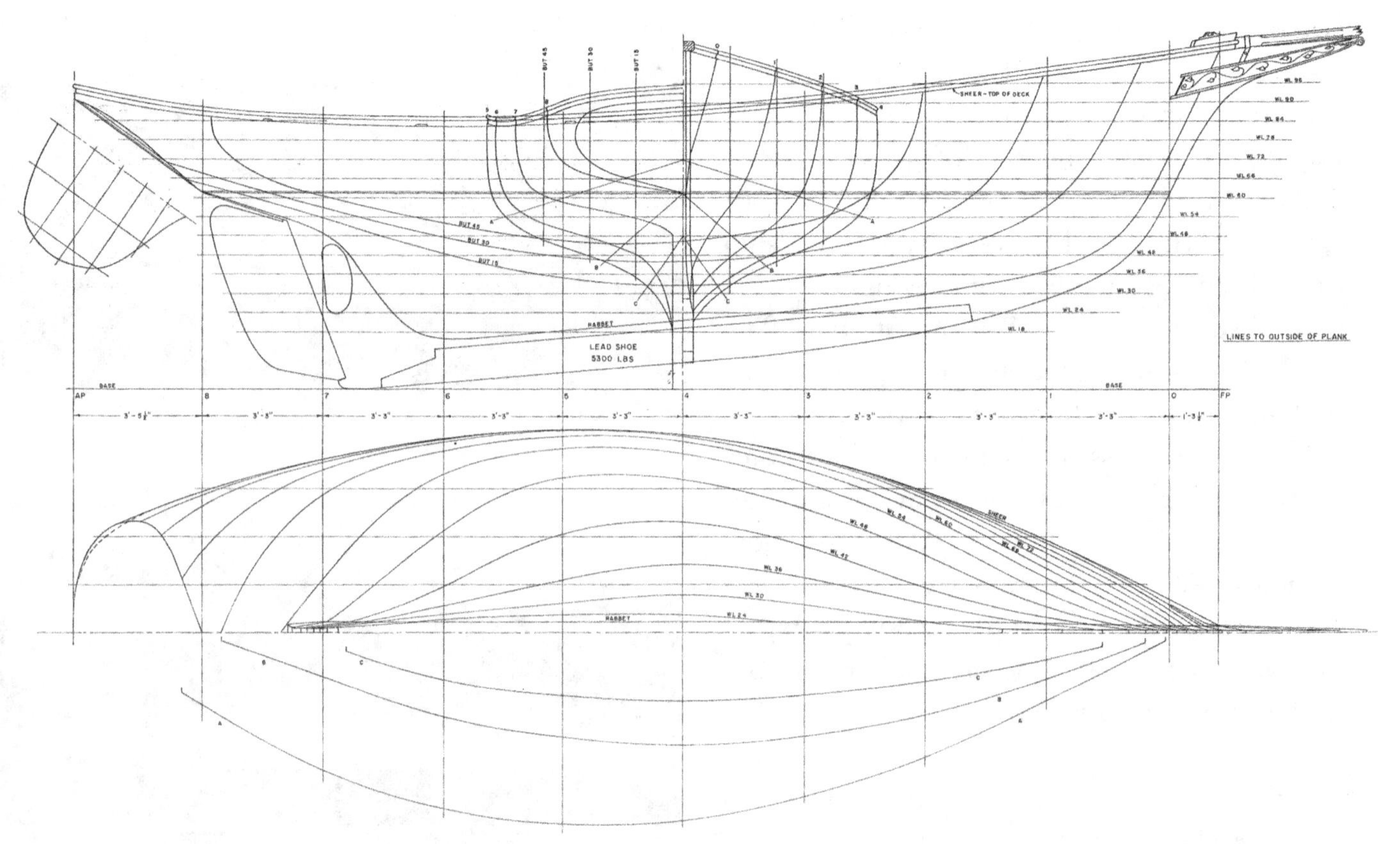

Lines for 31' Friendship sloop,
DICTATOR model.
Original built in 1904 by Robert McLain
Lines taken off by Ralph W. Stanley in 1972
for Jarvis Newman

Chapter Five: Fifty Years of Friendships

The last decade of the 20th century was one of transition for the Friendship Sloop Society. Ten more sloops would be added to the fleet. A sampling of some of the sloops built shows that the passion for Friendships had not moderated and that if anything, it had spread globally. Two sloops were built by Ralph W. Stanley, ACADIA #269, and the RALPH W. STANLEY #263, which was destined for the Mediterranean waters of Sardinia. DESIREÉ #226, built by Debby and Larry Plumer, would become the flagship by the end of the decade, as the Plumers shared the responsibilities of co-commodores of the Society. Harold Burnham built the sloop KIM #258, and one sloop, HAND OF FRIENDSHIP #279, was built in Australia.

Aside from new sloops being added to the fleet, there was also a changing of the guard. Harold Burnham inherited the boat-building gene from his father, Charlie, who built two Friendships in the 1970s, and from generations of Burnhams before that, who built boats in Essex, Massachusetts. Harold took on the reconstruction, some would say resurrection, of Ernie Wiegleb's old sloop CHRISSY #18. He gained recognition in the world of wooden boat builders and was featured in articles in *WoodenBoat* and *Messing About in Boats*. Some of that notoriety spilled over to the Friendship Sloop Society. Charlie Burnham, Harold's father, had long been an influence in the Society, and now Harold was becoming one, whether he was aware of it or not.

A small burst of attention came from an unexpected quarter—Hollywood. The 1998 movie *The Truman Show* takes place in an idealized world, and what is the most ideal sailing yacht for the main character to escape on? Why

RALPH W. STANLEY #263 in Sardinia.

HAND OF FRIENDSHIP #279 in Australia.

DESIREÉ #226

Roger and Mary Duncan
and EASTWARD #6

Adapted from the 1997 yearbook dedication.

Roger and Mary Duncan have been active contributors to the Friendship Sloop Society since its inception in 1961. Roger has served two terms as Commodore and many years as yearbook editor. Their dedication to the Society, participation in countless Society events, publication of key sailing books, and their quiet devotion to the cause of Friendship has given us all a legacy.

Roger and Mary met in 1938. From 1945-1981, Roger worked at Belmont Hill School as the head of the upper school. He was acting headmaster from 1978-79 and headmaster in 1981. He taught English and coached soccer, intramural hockey, crew and sailing. Mary worked as the school's librarian. By 1956, they had their sloop EASTWARD built and their Friendship legacy began.

EASTWARD was first to cross the line in the first sloop regatta held in Friendship in 1961. The following year, EASTWARD took home the Governor's Trophy. In the early years, boats would receive additional handicaps if they finished first in a previous race. Roger used to remark that EASTWARD'S handicap was so large, the race committee must want him to go pick blueberries before continuing the race.

EASTWARD has been recognized at each regatta as a formidable competitor with a prepared crew and rigorous captain. Roger and Mary have never tired of sharing the magic of EASTWARD. From their apprentice cruises - to introduce youngsters to the wonder of sailing - through the WoodenBoat School and their own charter business, they have shown hundreds of people the wonder and delight of sailing.

Roger has combined his gift of writing with his love of sailing and become the esteemed author of many books, including: *EASTWARD, Friendship Sloops, Sailing in the Fog* and, a staple to all who cruise, *The Cruising Guide to the New England Coast.*

Roger and Mary are the epitome of what the FSS seeks for all members. They raised their three sons, Bob, Bill and John, sailing EASTWARD. Roger is extremely curious, loves history, loves to build things, and never stops moving - even for a swing in a hammock. Mary has a love for the time spent on the water.

She is an avid fisherwoman and is in her glory while catching mackerel. She even claims that hoisting the sails on EASTWARD is a sure cure for arthritis!

The word "friendship" permeates everything about the FSS. Besides racing, trophies and awards, there is a deeply rooted tradition which binds all the members of the Society. Fun-filled, family-oriented activities are held annually to honor the beauty of the Friendship Sloop. Roger and Mary Duncan have been part of that legacy from the beginning. Generations of new families and their children continue to be welcomed into the Society. It is through the wonderful, continuous contributions of members such as Roger and Mary Duncan that we continue to gather and enjoy life the way it should be for all.

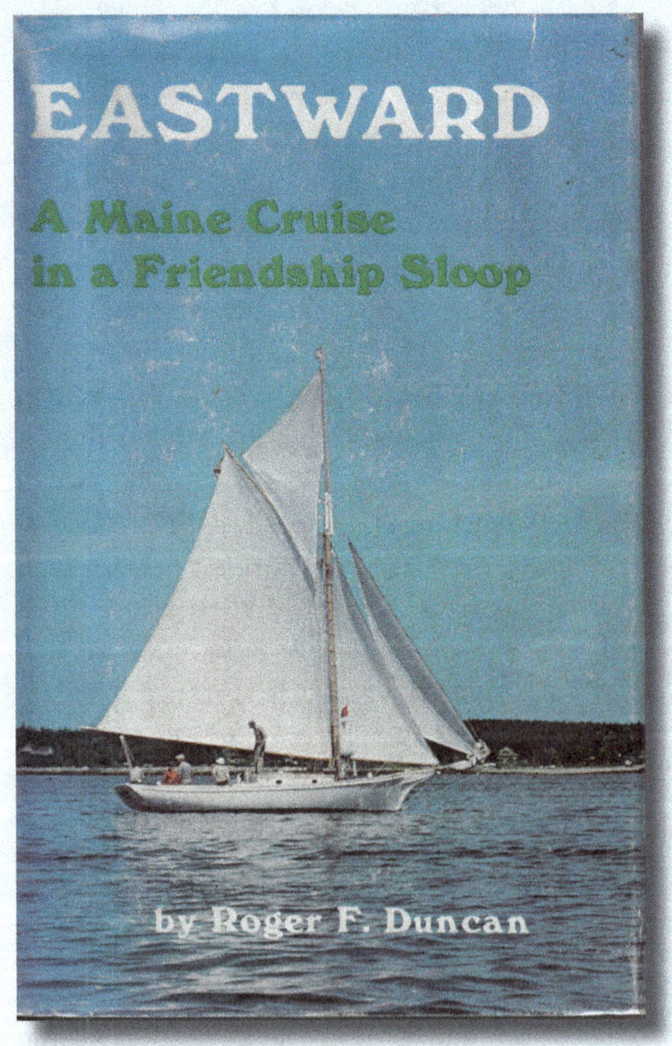

a Friendship sloop of course. Two sloops were used in the making of the movie, OSPREY #139, now owned by Steve Hughes, and HATSEY #135. OSPREY survived her brush with Hollywood special effects, but HATSEY did not.

In the mid-90s a milestone was reached with the creation of the Friendship Sloop Society website. John Wojcik set up the website, which included a forum for members, a listing of sloops, and a listing for sloops that were for sale. As might be expected, among any group of gaff-rig sailors there are a few luddites, so the importance of the website was not immediately realized, but for the first time members who did not live on the east coast of the U.S. could interact more easily with the group through the internet.

Just as some members were stepping forward, others were stepping back. Roger and Mary Duncan had long been foundation stones on which the Society relied, more than they perhaps realized. Roger and Mary had been a part of the Society since 1961. Roger had been commodore in 1965 and again in 1968. He had taken over the Friendship Sloop yearbook and had served as editor of that magazine for decades. As the author of the *Cruising Guide to the New England Coast*, he had enormous credibility. His books *Eastward* (1976 International Marine Publishing) and *Friendship Sloops* (1985 International Marine Publishing) had both brought renewed attention to the Friendship sloop. Roger was a charter captain, and he and Mary had introduced countless people to the joys of sailing a Friendship. A goodly number of their former clients caught the Friendship sloop bug and got sloops of their own.

In the late 1990s Roger and Mary felt it was time for a change. EASTWARD'S large mainsail was becoming hard to set and manage for two sailors starting their eighth decade

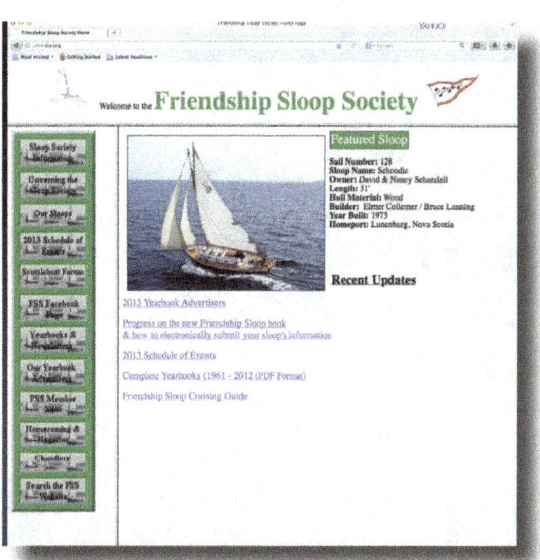

FSS website.

of life. They asked Ralph W. Stanley to build them a pocket schooner, smaller than EASTWARD and with smaller sails. They handed off their much-loved sloop to their son Robert and grandson Alex. In 1993 he passed the editorship of the yearbook to Beth and Rich Langton, and in doing so stepped back from a stewardship roll that he and Mary had maintained in the Friendship Sloop Society since its inception.

There were other important and influential people within the Society who took a more nuanced step back. Dick Salter, commodore in 1985-86, founder of Mass Bay Friends, and owner of LIBERTY #157, is a case in point. A change in health forced Dick to part with his lovely sloop in 1992, but he gracefully stepped into a different kind of stewardship as the official measurer for the Society. His work with the race committee and his gentle wisdom on the executive committee are felt to this day.

The transition made by Dick Salter was an important one. Since the term of commodore is only two years, the Society has had to depend on other forms of stewardship to provide continuity. People like Dick Salter, Marcia Morang, Jack and Mary Cronin, Bill and Caroline Zuber, and John and Carole Wojcik have

John Wojcik and Dick Salter

Caroline and Bill Zuber aboard FRIENDSHIP PATROL.

Carole and John Wojcik aboard BANSHEE #180.

repeatedly taken on responsibilities that provided that continuity.

Marcia was a constant support to her husband Bruce Morang when he was head of the race committee. After Bruce's death Marcia continued to keep track of trophies, arrange gifts for skippers at the gatherings, provide support to new members, and keep the commodores in line. Aided by her daughter and able lieutenant, Penny, she keeps order under the tent in Rockland and keeps a newspaperwoman's eye on the yearbook as well.

Bill Zuber moved from charter captain, commodore, and sloop owner, to the race committee. His common sense and safety consciousness are greatly valued commodities. Caroline Zuber managed the Pendleton Scholarship fund for many years and has been a key player in keeping the Friendship Museum alive. She and Bill have provided a consistent link between the Friendship Sloop Society and the town of Friendship. The two can still be found on GLADIATOR, but more in the role of mentors and caretakers since they wear so many other hats.

Jack and Mary Cronin have not only served the Society in the roles of commodore and secretary, and in Jack's case the race committee, but with eight children and fifteen grandchildren, have significantly increased the membership.

John and Carole Wojcik have repeatedly taken on roles of commodore, registrar, membership chair, publishers of the newsletter, *Friendships*, web masters, and the unofficial heads of the cruising division.

The list of passionate volunteers willing to take on the work to keep the Society and the Friendship sloop alive is a long one of which this is but a sampling. Without them the Society would not have survived.

As elder statesmen of the Friendship Sloop Society stepped back, a new generation stepped forward. In 1999 Tad Beck was elected commodore of the Society. Tad represented a true passing of the baton to a new generation. Tad's father, Alfred Beck, had owned PHOENIX #91 and was commodore in 1981-82. Tad became the owner of PHOENIX, and he too took his turn at the helm as commodore.

If the last decade of the 20th century represented change and growth, then the first decade of the 21st century represented change and challenges.

In July of 2001 Harold Burnham made the cover of *WoodenBoat* magazine. The cover story was titled, "The Virtues of the Friendship Sloop", and was great publicity. The cover shot of Harold hauling old-fashioned lath traps from the cockpit of his sloop CHRISSY #18 was a tonic to anyone who was a fan of Friendship sloops or lobstering or Harold. It certainly seemed like a good omen, but what no one could foresee was that both the Society and the nation were about to be shaken to the core.

Any discussion of the year 2001 has to include the impact made by the events of September 11th; most Americans would never see the world in the same way again. But for the Friendship Sloop Society, a change in perspective had come earlier that year, on July 24th, with the sinking of ENDEAVOR #196.

It was the first full day of the annual Homecoming in Rockland. NOAA had forecast afternoon winds, southwest, 12-15 knots—in essence a beautiful summer day. The race started without incident in steady winds as predicted, but by the time the sloops had rounded the first mark, the winds had built up to a steady 25 knots. Several sloops at this point withdrew from the race. SALATIA #90 radioed that she had broken her gaff. Ralph Stanley was on his

Al Beck and Tad Beck.

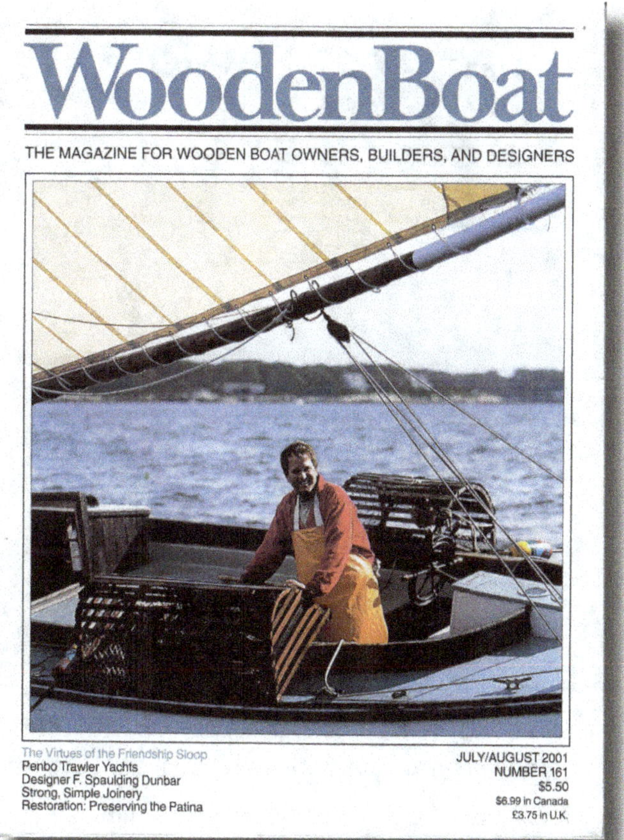

*Harold Burnham on the cover of **WoodenBoat**.*

Raising ENDEAVOR

By Ralph W. Stanley Adapted from the 2002 FSS Yearbook.

ENDEAVOR was on the bottom in about 65 feet of water. A diver could find nothing at the marks I took. He got a boat to look with a fish finder and a side-scan sonar. Another boat searched for two days with a side-scan sonar and found nothing. Then Jill Flora told me about Garry Kozak of Klein Associates, makers of side-scan sonars. He came to Rockland with two helpers and sonars, depth sounders, generators and a GPS. We searched all day over a big area and found nothing. Finally Richard suggested we go out to where I had picked them up and tow the sonar southwest, We did this and we found her. We checked with the depth

tom for several weeks. She went down again stern first as the air bag was still attached to the bow. The rudder struck bottom and was damaged while the tiller hit the coaming, cracking it and breaking the tiller. The boom went up and struck the spreader, breaking it and cracking the topmast. The gaff jaws were also broken.

I then got Doug Beal to come with his barge from Southwest Harbor to put straps around her and lift her with his derrick. In three hours she was on the deck of the barge on her way to Southwest Harbor. When we got home, we found the anchor we had

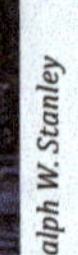

Ralph W. Stanley

Ralph W. Stanley

sounder, and to make sure, got a position with the GPS. We dropped an anchor with a buoy to mark the spot.

Next morning the diver went down and confirmed that it was ENDEAVOR and proceeded to lift her with air bags. The top of the mast came out of water when the air bags broke the surface, but the boat bounced and the strain pulled the traveler out of the deck. The oak was real soft from the pressure after being on the bot-

dropped still in the cockpit.

ENDEAVOR has been scraped to bare wood, dried out and repainted. The space under the deck in the cockpit has been sealed to create an airspace that will give her more buoyancy if she dips her coaming again. The engine has been replaced and necessary repairs made. She will be sailing again this summer.

boat, SEVEN GIRLS, as part of the race committee and was dispatched to see SALATIA safely back to her berth while the wind continued to build. Ralph saw SALATIA out of danger and was heading back out towards the sloops, which were reaching along the shore of Owls Head, when he saw what happened next. A big gust laid ENDEAVOR over, pushing her bow down and her coaming under while lifting her rudder clear out of the water so she could not steer. Ralph said later "When I saw her go over, I knew she was going to sink." In moments ENDEAVOR was gone.

Ralph was able to get to the scene of the sinking quickly. Thankfully the five people aboard the sloop had all gotten off safely, but getting them aboard SEVEN GIRLS in the wind and seas was a challenge. By the time everyone was aboard, the crew of ENDEAVOR had been in the cold waters of Penobscot Bay for ten minutes.

As might be expected, there was a great deal of reflection within the Society after the sinking, but in the final analysis no one had been badly hurt, and when needed, the boats of the race committee had been there to do their job and provide support and rescue. There is no way to guarantee the weather, and the forecast from NOAA was reasonable. There is always risk whenever any boat goes sailing; the best you can do is try to minimize the risks and prepare for when things do go wrong. In this perticular case, due to an oversight, the bilge pump on ENDEAVOR had been turned off, and she was much lower in the water than she otherwise would have been. As a result of that blustery July day, there was a reevaluation of safety procedures and radio protocols, and changes were made to required safety equipment for sloops that intended to race.

ENDEAVOR was found and successfully raised after a month on the bottom in 65

ENDEAVOR today sailing in the Southwest Harbor race 2013.

feet of water, and she is still sailing today, but it was a sobering beginning to the new century.

Predictably, the sinking got plenty of newspaper coverage, but the majority of that coverage was not negative. The media wanted to focus on the rescue and the fact that no one had been hurt. The discovery and raising of the sloop made a great story.

Within months of ENDEAVOR'S sinking, the nation was coming to terms with September 11th. What followed was a period of reexamination, assessment and questioning for many Americans: How did we get here? What should we do? Are we headed in the right direction? That some of those concerns would color the next few years of the Friendship Sloop Society was inevitable. There was so much happening within the Society at this time—sloops were changing hands, and new owners had new perspectives to share. At the same time the Society was saddened by the passing of two of its founders, Bernie MacKenzie in 2002, and John Gould in 2003.

The Friendship Sloop Society is a non-political organization, as clearly stated in its constitution. It is a place where members can escape the political wrangling and the daily discussion of terrorism and extremism. There is also the notion that the sloops themselves are a wonderful diversion from the "real world". After all, a working sailboat that has survived from the late 19th century, largely as a result of the sheer beauty of its design, is the very definition of escapism. One very positive attitude that came out of this time was an increased emphasis on being inclusive and welcoming to all new members and to anyone interested in Friendship sloops.

Even though there were new owners for many sloops and a great deal of expansion in the Society, with five boating events scheduled on the east coast, there were fewer members participating in each event. The same kinds of niggling questions that dominated the cultural landscape of the country infiltrated the discussions of the membership. How did we get here, are we going in the right direction, what should we do?

In 2003, the new commodore, John Rand, representing the new generation, stepped up to take a leadership roll. John's father, Bill Rand, had been commodore in 1991-92, so John had the advantage of perspective from the past, but he could also read the changing landscape. In January 2004, a survey was taken by the executive committee to find out what could be done differently to increase membership in general, and membership participation in specific activities, like the homecoming in Rockland. The results of that survey were printed as part of the commodore's message in the 2004 yearbook:

1.Include a non-racing venue at the regattas, such as a family sailing day.

2.Welcome and mentor new members to speed the process of feeling comfortable with the group.

3.Increase our publicity and invite the public to sail with us at regattas.

4.Encourage local sailing (and other year-round) events to make it easier for enthusiasts to participate and promote the history and traditions of Friendship sloops. Coordinate these events with other traditional sailing craft organizations to build momentum.

It is fair to say that we as an organization have been grappling with how to make these goals a reality ever since. This book is one tangible example of the ongoing effort made to meet those goals.

As the debate continues about how to enact the goals determined by the 2004 survey, it is important to realize the real focus of most members is on sailing, socializing, and messing around in sloops—not necessarily in that order. One need only to read the yearbooks from this decade to see that the real focus is on having fun.

Mixed with the fun and socializing is plenty of boat gossip: How was the rebuild of HERITAGE #50 by Steve and Dee Dunipace going? Did you hear the rumor of a new large sloop to be built by Ralph and Richard Stanley? Did you hear that DIANNA #94 has a new owner and a new name?

Charlie Burnham, builder of RESOLUTE #123, became commodore in 2005, full of fun and mischief. When the fleet was late leaving the dock for the races in Rockland, Charlie tried to make several announcements that we should all be getting underway. When this had little effect, he simply started casting off dock lines. As sloops began to drift away from the docks, crews had no choice but to scramble aboard and get underway. When a child celebrated her seventh birthday under the tent in Rockland and invited all the other children to share cake and ice-cream with her, Charlie was first in line.

Roger Lee became commodore after Charlie. Roger and Gail O' Donnell had been married on their boat SAZERAC #44 in 2000. Now, in his position as commodore, Roger tried to address some more of the goals outlined in the 2004 survey, such as more emphasis on the public getting to see the sloops, an open house on the dock for visitors, and a DVD made about the Society. These were little steps forward. Meanwhile Gail had a lasting effect on the celebratory dinner at the end of homecoming. Since the move to Rockland the dinner had been provided by a local organization for a fee. Gail returned it to its roots as an informal dinner provided by the membership. When Gail died suddenly in 2010, Roger changed the name SAZARAC to GAIL O. in her memory.

John Rand, family and friends aboard the WILLIAM M. RAND at the docks in Rockland.

Roger Lee on GAIL O. Her name has been since changed back to SAZERAC in hope of finding her a new owner.

Adapted from the 2011 FSS yearbook.

50th Anniversary Friendship Sloop Days

in Rockland, Maine and my first time in attendance at the annual gathering. It was wonderful, breathtaking, marvelous, remarkable, amazing, exciting…etched-in-stone memorable!

I'll start my story with the sail down West Penobscot Bay that Tuesday afternoon, bound for Pulpit Harbor. We were in fine company, with the schooner MARY DAY headed down the bay near us and EDEN #122 scudding along the shore of North Haven. She moved along light and smart, and we thought the boys were making a fine show of it. (I hadn't met EDEN or the boys yet, but that was about to change.) I sailed the Maine waters as crew on the schooner J&E RIGGIN in the 1980's but it had been 25 years, and I was very excited and happy to be headed to Pulpit, a place of more than one adventure for me. I was stunned as we entered the harbor, finding more than 65 boats anchored or moored there. There wouldn't have been more than 15 boats tops in that harbor, on a Friday evening no less, back then. It was nonetheless quite a thrill for me, with even my old schooner anchored there as well as so many Friendships. We decided to borrow a mooring, and slept quite well. We forgot to lash the halyards so I got up in the middle of that moonless night, and was rewarded with the crispy clear star-filled sky that always makes my grumbling thoughts fade quickly.

We motored to Rockland the next morning, and did the cruise ship shuffle along with everyone else. So many people to meet and so many wonderful sloops! The Cronins did a great job, even included an unscheduled "fireworks display" (a significant thunder storm), was that Wednesday night? We went below decks early that night with the wiser folks high and dry at a nearby restaurant. As we nodded off, we heard the impressive "POW!" as the strain of the cruise ship broke a dock I-plate, managed to say "Wow, wonder what that was?", then drifted off to sleep hearing strange underwater gurglings I could only imagine were being generated by the cruise ship. We apologize for sleeping through the rearranging of the docking lines that night; thank you to everyone who helped! We weren't ignoring you, just deeply asleep.

There is so much to say about Thursday. Our race crew that day was my 81-year-old Dad, my 76-year-

old Mom, and my 84-year-old aunt, as well as a friend from NY, who is an apprentice at the Apprenticeshop in Rockland. As planned, we kept to the back of the fleet initially, and took some stunning pictures of the first leg of the race. We had quite a few "ooohs" and "ahhhs" on board as we watched sloop after sloop execute some impressive jibes around the leeward mark. Things changed quite quickly when we got down to the first buoy, as I expect it did for a few others. In tending to the main sheet, at the last second I noticed there wasn't a stopper knot at the bitter end and quickly handed it to my aunt. Upon jibing, I gingerly managed the main sheet, with it just smokin' around the quarter bit. To this day I am grateful that I stayed on top of it, grabbed the end out of Muriel's hands, and took 2 wraps just as we got to the end of the line. I've had nightmares ever thus of my dear aunt getting yanked out of the cockpit. She's not a sailor, was having a ball, and would have had no idea what happened. (An aside, she has adored Friendship sloops ever since we rented a camp in Friendship when I was a kid, in the '60's.)

Back to rounding that mark… As many of you recall, the next leg of the race was handicap alley. We came around that mark to a wall of Friendships headed straight at us, bound for the alley. I counted 5 boats side-by-side, in that spankin' northerly, and there probably were more to weather, all going in exactly the opposite direction of us. Ted first headed below everyone (as we were on a port tack), but thought the leeward boat indicated going below us, so he then aimed to go between that one, PEREGRINE #187, and the next boat to weather. But that was a judgment made in a second, and in the next second PEREGRINE was headed up, all this with the boats sailing like race horses, and distances closing fast! Ted held his course, and thank you PEREGRINE for heading down, is all I can say. We threaded that needle, although our main boom did rake a bit of their rigging. That turned out to be just the beginning of too much excitement for PEREGRINE. When Ted spoke with Paul that evening and apologized, Paul had said so much happened afterwards that it was the least of his troubles. We did sail a bit more that day, but opted out of the remainder of the race, to the crew's relief. Meanwhile, EDEN was playing hide and seek with a ledge, PEREGRINE was clawing off a lee shore with an engine that wouldn't start while trying to fish a crewmember out of the water (RIGHTS OF MAN #52 graciously abandoned a favorable position in the race to pick Holly up out of the water), someone on TANNIS #7 was stuffing socks into geysers below decks, and everyone was wondering if they would make it back to the dock. I am confident there were numerous other wide-eyed moments for others as well.

You may have gathered, at this point, that while I am a sailor, I am not a racer, never have been and never care to be. I do have to say the gin and tonic I had that evening tasted especially good; perhaps this effect is part of the appeal of racing? I salute all of the racing folks in the crowd, hats off to you for all of your fun, it certainly is an exciting game! And while I do look forward to coastal cruising on BLACK STAR #247, I think I lean more towards the "feet up, binoculars at the ready" hubbub so well promoted by *Maine Boats, Homes and Harbors* contributor Peter Bass.

Friday we joined ECHO #54 and HEGIRA #230 for a lovely sail in a perfect southwesterly up the Mussel Ridge to Birch Island. GAIVOTA #214 had left ahead of everyone for the same destination...something about a beer on the beach! We arrived a bit late, and only had a brief walk on the beach before returning to the boat to get back to Rockland. It was a much appreciated alternative to racing for us, and we'll be looking to do more of that at future gatherings.

Saturday commenced rainy and somewhat foggy, but the parade of sail progressed quite nicely. The rain stopped, the fog lightened up and there was a nice light breeze, so people who still had some energy or fresh crew could set lowers and uppers. Our most exciting moment on this day was as we approached the breakwater, with boats all around (and probably a ferry approaching), in one very intense instant we realized we were in the line of fire of Charlie Burnham's cannon! I think Ted, Saxon, and I all would have had a heart attack if that cannon had gone off. Fortunately we saw the situation in time and spun a slow 360 to get us out of that close proximity. We had a wonderful time at the awards dinner. My parents are racers, so they felt quite at home at the dinner, having attended a plethora of awards dinners in years past.

I've added this amazing gathering to my duffle of fond memories. It was such a pleasure to attend, to meet so many people, and to see so many wonderful sloops. After nearly forgetting our dinghy, we sailed away (okay, we motored) on Sunday, in a delightful pocket of sunshine that lasted just long enough for us to pick up a mooring in Rockport before the fog closed in again. Fair winds and fair tides to all, hope to see you all next summer for the next memorable Friendship sloop gathering in Rockland!

Judy Heininger

Sloops rounding the first mark on the 50th.

Jarvis Newman rebuilding OLD BALDY in 2010.

First days race on the 50th

TAMARA #272 at the 50th.

At about this time another subtle development of the 21st century began influencing this group of traditional sailors—something called "Facebook". Just as the website had created a connecting point for the more far-flung members a decade earlier, Facebook allowed members to share pictures and stories and information through social media. Added to this, several members have their own websites or blogs, so the amount of sharing on the internet has been extensive.

Despite these technological developments, some patterns repeat themselves. In 2010 Jarvis Newman bought OLD BALDY #57, the boat he had used as a plug for his first fiberglass sloop in 1968. OLD BALDY needed a complete rebuild and Jarvis worked on her ten hours a day to make her ready for the Southwest Harbor rendezvous in 2011.

When Wayne and Kirsten Cronin took over as commodores, the buzz was all about the 50th Anniversary of the Friendship Sloop Society. Plans were made to attract the most sloops possible to the scheduled events. Twelve sloops participated in the Southwest Harbor gathering, and sailed by the Boathouse of the Claremont Hotel, putting on quite the show as the Obama family finished their lunch there. Twenty-eight sloops showed up at Rockland, including the brand new TAMARA #272, built by Ralph and Richard Stanley. WENONA #118, which came all the way from the Chesapeake, and TECUMSEH #242 took a year getting to the homecoming from Ontario Canada—by way of Florida.

The 50th Anniversary in Rockland was a terrific time, although not without drama, as the first race was held in very windy conditions complicated by a down-wind start. There were some close calls—a man overboard and a near grounding (it does not count as a grounding if you can push the sloop off the ledge). TANNIS #7

94

started her seams. Socks were collected from her crew to stem the leaks. She made it back to the docks safely, but had to retire from racing. Jack Cronin was heard to remark, "This is what happens when you give the kids a perfectly good 72-year-old sloop!"

These incidents raised concerns about safety, and about making the racing less complicated and easier for newcomers to participate in. Still the prevailing mood was one of celebration, despite the sock-caulking in the seams of TANNIS.

TANNIS #7 would be completely rebuilt by the Cronins over the next two years, and has emerged from the rebuild ready for another lifetime of sailing.

As the first decade of the 21st century came to a close, it was a time to remember those who had passed over the bar. Betty Roberts, former secretary and historian who had done so much to make those early days in Friendship a success, died in 2006. Jack Vibber, founder of the New London rendezvous, passed away in December 2008. Then in 2010, the same month that Gail O' Donnell died, Roger Duncan passed away. That same year Bob Phaneuf, former owner of SURPRISE #49, also died. As the Society celebrated the start of the next half-century, it marked the end of an era and the loss of old friends.

As things began to wind down from the 50th celebration, Peter and Nancy Toppan took over as commodores, and continued to emphasize the goals set out by John Rand.

A half century after Bernie MacKenzie had the idea to form a group of Friendship sloopers, the work goes on. Raymond Covey is building a 25' sloop, yet to be named. And while it is not exactly new, Jim Sharp at the Sail, Power, and Steam Museum in Rockland, is completing a sloop started by Carlton Simmons in the 1960s. A team of volunteers is

Sloops gathered for the 50th with WENONA #118 in the foreground.

TANNIS #7

Rebuilding TANNIS #7

The first day of racing in Rockland fifty years after the founding of the Society was a day of high winds and a down-wind start (see page 92). On TANNIS, partway through the race, the cry came for crew to remove shoes and socks and pass the socks below. For those readers who are not Friendship sloop sailors, this is not a regular command. The socks were to be used as emergency caulking for seams that appeared to be opening up in the 72-year-old hull as multiple leaks appeared. #7 had to drop out of the races and return to the dock to scope out the extent of the problem. After closer inspection, it became clear that TANNIS had some significant problems below the waterline and needed immediate attention. She limped to her home waters and was more thoroughly examined where it became apparent that what she really needed was a complete rebuild.

For most sloop owners this would have been the end of the road, but when you have a family of boat builders and cabinetmakers, and some down time at the family business, it is only a minor setback.

Dropping the Keel.

The Cronin family put the 38' TANNIS in the shop and proceeded to gut her, drop the keel, remove the rotten frames, replace the rot in the keel and deadwood, reframe, replace the planking, replace the ceilings, replace the deck beams, give her a new deck, cabin house, interior, and cockpit. Other than that she was in good shape.

Reframing.

The work was done in two years and TANNIS was back in the water, a little light on ballast aft (nice looking propeller Jeff!), but good as new.

Jack Cronin looks over the first stages of deconstruction of TANNIS.

TANNIS being gutted.

New frames and new planking going on.

Replanking.

New deckbeams.

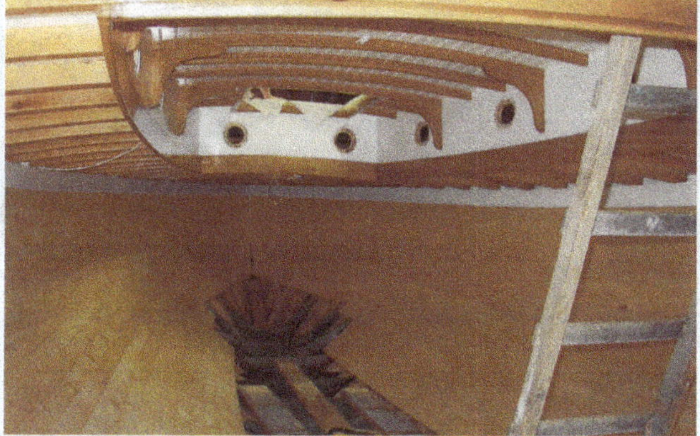

New ceilings and cabin.

TANNIS leaving the shop, good as new!

completing the 28' PERSISTENCE #120 to be part of the Museum. Bruce Brown is rebuilding the 30' LOON #168, and the 25' SEA DOG #141 is undergoing a complete rebuild by Walter Hines. And 30' PATIENCE #74 is being rebuilt by Chris Gerardi. It is clear that the spell these sloops cast has lost none of its potency.

The Friendship sloop still evokes a sense of wonder and beauty that is undeniable. The sheer "wow" factor still holds the attention of anyone lucky enough to see one of these vessels venturing out to sea, or riding composed at her mooring. More are being built, and the passion for these beautiful vessels is just as intense as it has ever been. Yes, we as a Society still look back longingly at the time in the early 1960s when there were fifty Friendships racing in Muscongus Bay and thousands of spectators showed up for the race, but we also tend to overlook that between our website, blogs, and Facebook, more people are engaged with the Friendship sloop than ever before. And ultimately the questioning and the concern for the future are good things, typical of the passionate people that these boats attract. The ongoing discussions about what should come next are in many ways the very best indicator that these sloops will indeed be lasting Friendships.

Raymond Covey working on the sloop he is building.

WEST WIND #95
A 32-year love story

By John and Diane Huston Fassak

"Every deep cove on the coast once had its resident sloop lying at mooring or grounded beside a wharf. If you came as a stranger, groping in through foggy or dusky channels, you expected her; you at once looked for her as the local guardian or divinity, and even in the gathering darkness you saw the distinctive profile that has remained one of the classic strokes of boat design. How many times in my youth has the white form taken shape against a dusky shore, the low freeboard aft sweeping upward in a noble curve toward the clipper bow and then subtly reversing itself and running out to the long bowsprit—a line of beauty, as old Hogarth would have called it, so delicate that sketchers and painters never quite get it: the Maine sloop, the Friendship sloop (not always built in Friendship), came as near sharing man's spirit as anything ever built of oak and pine and galvanized nails. She gave new character to the loneliest waters. She was always a reassurance, a message that a good man had conceived and made her, a triumph of function and elegance in a world of fog and storm....She was the emblem of the old coast life."

From: *Between Wind And Water*
By Gerald Warner Brace

WEST WIND is sloop #95; LOD is 40 feet, beam is 13½ feet, draft 5 feet; built in 1902 by Charles Morse in Friendship, Maine. Richard and Lorraine Stanley have recently found some evidence that Westwind was rebuilt around 1927 by Wilber Morse. Morse had taken the boat back in trade after it was used for 25 years in the lobster and herring fisheries around Gouldsboro, Maine.

We took ownership in 1982, purchasing WEST WIND from Herb Crocker from Wakefield, Massachusetts. Diane Huston (now my wife) and I saw WEST WIND in a yard in Newburyport, MA off Route 1 in the winter of 1980. We went back a

WESTWIND with three of her owners: Herb Crocker in the fishermans cap, Don Huston (left lighting a cigar) and Diane Huston Fassak.

year later and saw her there, full of fresh water. We found the Crockers through the yard.

I lived in Ohio when I went to buy the boat in 1982. Herb was reluctant to take an out-of-town check. Don Huston (former owner of EAGLE #53) bought the boat (by delaying payment of his home mortgage) and owned it for a few days until my check cleared. So Don owned a boat owned by both Morse brothers; like they say, "life is a circle."

Prior to the Crocker's we understand the boat was owned for three generations by the Matheson family, who kept it in Gloucester and Salem. I have

Replacing the keel and deadwood.

been in touch with Bill Matheson, who sailed on her for summers as a boy. Bill recalls her name being "VELOCITY."

Bill is first of the three generations. He sailed on VELOCITY with his grandparents, and now lives in Middleboro, Massachusetts. We are trying to connect with Bill to better document the WEST WIND'S history, and to show Bill and his family that she has been restored for the next hundred years of service.

Lorraine and Richard Stanley have heard from

Replacing deck beams

Bill's granddaughter, Sunny, in the past month. We are trying to share our WEST WIND history with her, as she tells Lorraine that she has heard about the boat for her entire life.

We have been rebuilding WEST WIND for the past 31 years. We have moved her from Newburyport to Lynn, Massachusetts in 1982, then to Mansfield, Massachusetts around 1987, and again across town within Mansfield in 1995. We then moved her to Southwest Harbor to Ralph and Richard Stanley's shop in 2008. WEST WIND was the last Friendship to come

out of Ralph's shop. He put the business and property up for sale in 2011.

To get to the Stanley shop, in a state of rebuilding where there were just a few planks on either side of the hull holding her shape, Jocelyn Trucking (who had moved her from Newburyport to Lynn and to Mansfield- we have good karma and dharma with Jocelyn's Clayton Crabtree and Andrew) moved WEST WIND from Mansfield to Southwest Harbor. She was then launched while supported by a barge and derrick, and floated from Manset across the harbor to Ralph's railway and hauled into Ralph's shop using a winch and deadman.

After extensive repairs at Ralph's shop by Richard Stanley and his associate David Norwood (more appropriately a "resurrection" than a "rebuild") we launched WEST WIND down the Stanley's railway and towed her across the harbor. We hauled her on the Manset side and brought her to Richard Stanley's Great Harbor Boatworks shop in Manset.

Nomenclature of a friendship

1 — Mainsail
2 — Staysail
3 — Jib
4 — Jib or Headstay
5 — Forestay
6 — Bobstay
7 — Lazy Jacks
8 — Topping Lift
9 — Peak Halyard
10 — Throat Halyard
11 — Main Sheet
12 — Reef Points
13 — Shrouds with Deadeyes
     and Lanyards
14 — Bowsprit Shrouds

a — Hull
wl — Waterline
b — Topsides
c — Cuddy Cabin
d — Cockpit
e — Elliptical Transom
f — Bitt
g — Trailboard
l — Clipper Bow
i — Knight Head
j — Bowsprit
k — Toerail or Bulwark
m — Staysail Boom
n — Mast
o — Mast Hoops
p — Gaff Jaws
r — Gaff
s — Pinrail
t — Main Boom Jaws

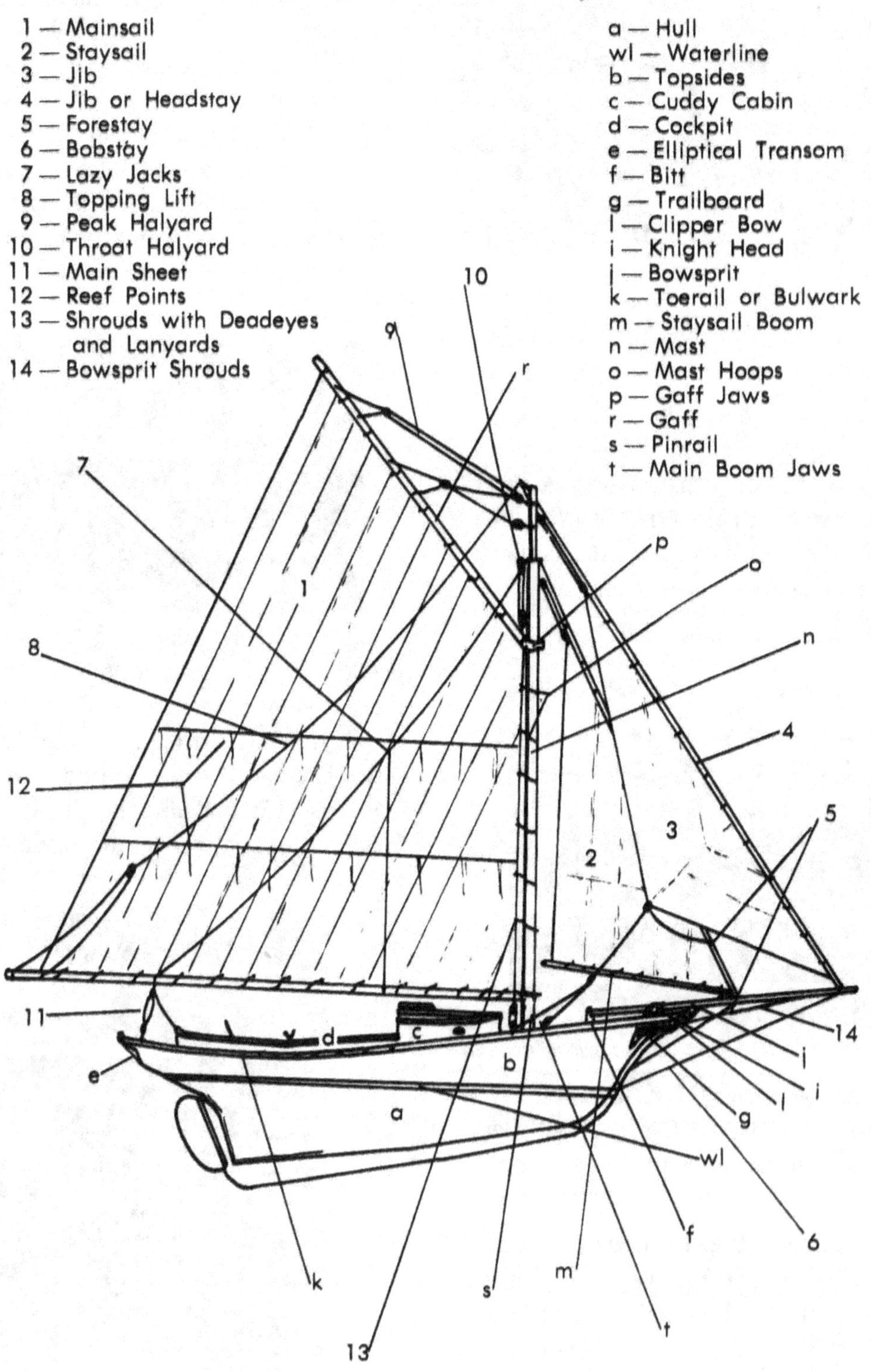

Catalog of Sloops

Notes on the Catalog of Sloops:

The sloops listed here are vessels that have been registered with the Friendship Sloop Society and assigned a sail number, and to the best of our knowledge, are still in existence. The sloops are presented chronologically by sail number and, to avoid confusion, the reader should note that sail numbers were issued whenever an owner chose to register with the Friendship Sloop Society and bear no relationship to the age of the sloop.

The Editors spent much of 2013 trying to contact owners of sloops to verify the information we have on record. Many sloop owners sent us information, for which we are very grateful. There are also sloops represented in this catalog that we are confident our records represent accurately, but where we did not receive a response from the current owner. In those cases we have listed the limited information we have and have noted that our source is our own records.

This catalog also lists sloops that we have reasons to believe are still in existence, but which have been sold to parties unknown, or the last known owner has moved and the Friendship Sloop Society no longer has contact information. In those cases, we have indicated that the whereabouts of the sloop is unknown. We include these sloops because we do still believe that they are in existence and in the hope that by listing them in this book, it may allow us to relocate as many as possible.

There are undoubtedly Friendship sloops that are in existence that we are unaware of, and we would encourage any owners of such sloops to register with the Friendship Sloop Society. There is no cost to register and owners do not need to be members of the Society to register.

If we have listed a sloop as "whereabouts unknown" and you know where the sloop in question is, or what has happened to it, the Friendship Sloop Society would welcome updated information. To contact the Society, please go to our website: www.fss.org.

1 *Voyager*

LOD: 30'
Homeport: Warren, ME
Builder: Charles A. Morse
Launched: 1906 Friendship, ME
Owner(s): Jim Salafia
Year boat took possession of
   current owner: 2003

The VOYAGER (original C. Morse 1901) has a long history of being shuffled around as a potential rebuild/derelict. Eventually she ended up in the now gone "Thomaston Museum" or similar name. When Lyman-Morse started expanding, the defunct museum and associated craft in the area were getting demolished. Jeff and I had been watching the sloop for quite awhile and, when the bulldozer was getting active, I paid Drinkwater to move her to my back yard in Warren. We then got Art Crane to lift her over a tree and into a more suitable area with thoughts of a rebuild.

Many years later, she is still a nice sculpture in need of everything. Her shape is still there and she is covered and in need of a benefactor, like many old boats that eventually get cut up.

Realistically, I will never get to rebuilding her, but we sit in the cockpit and have cocktails.

Perhaps someone out there is interested in her. She is a boat for free and has a mast, bowsprit and mainsail that may be of use.

(See pages 37, 41, 51, and Preface)

2 *Dictator*

LOD: 31' Beam:11' Draft: 5'8"
Homeport: Sylvesters Cove, Deer Isle, ME
Builder: Robert McLain
Launched: 1904 Bremen Long Is., ME
Owner(s): Peter M. Chesney
Year boat took possession of
   current owner: 1991

In 1924, my Grandfather, Dr. Alan Chesney, dean of John Hopkins Medical School, bought DICTATOR from Fred Torrey of Stonington, Maine. Three generations of Chesneys grew up using "boat braille" to feel for Penobscot Bay's rocks and ledges. She was also fitted with no engine to improve the family skills sailing a six and a half ton wood boat - learn by desperation. Granddad was a thrifty captain who enjoyed the family's slave labor.

We discovered DICTATOR was very sick following Granddad's passing in '69. The sloop had multiple failing ribs, many rotting keel parts; so sadly, she was sold to Jarvis Newman for her sixth rebuild. Twenty years and twenty fiberglass copies later, I bought her back from Mr. Newman, who had just rescued her as salvage from the last owner, who neglected her, had allowed her to sink twice at a mooring. According to one report, she suffered six weeks on the bottom at a backwater marina somewhere off the Hudson River.

After yet another rebuild, we had a big four-generation homecoming for DICTATOR in 1991. We sailed happily away until 1995 when the 1934 mast broke (see the 1997 FSS yearbook for the Hollywood The Truman Show *connection). It was then we discovered that much more than the mast was broken; the horn timber was completely rotted and the non-traditional laminated fir deck beams and fiberglass-lined cockpit were both disintegrating.*

In the great 1938 Un-named New England hurricane that killed 650, Granddad was out on Penobscot Bay for a day sail. On this little outing, Granddad took along a professor friend, my (then) 15-year old uncle, and my 13-year old father. Fortunately, sea room and DICTATOR lasted longer than the great storm... so by "proxy"... I survived. Thanks to her, I'm still around all these years later. To me, she is more than a boat; she is a relative, nearly an ancestor, and like a frail elderly family member, you simply have to keep caring for them.

She got her own work shed in 2003. For 2004 (DICTATOR'S 100th birthday!), her hull was finished, she was launched, and we celebrated with a good four-day soak in Stonington harbor. 2007 saw her 3D "digital" restoration to her lines and original big cockpit layout (see 2008 yearbook cover).

Meanwhile, this past summer of 2013, I chain-sawed through the old deck and installed the first of her beautiful new oak deck beams.

The journey continues....   *(See pages 4, 60, 73, 79, 82)*

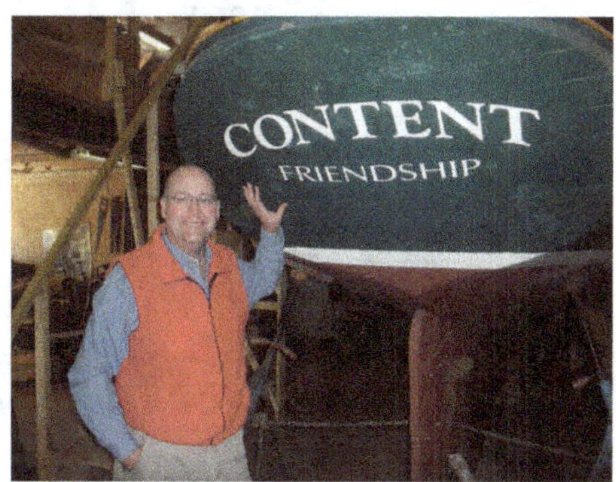

Content

LOD: 25'
Homeport: Rockland, ME
Builder: Stuart M. Ford
Launched: 1961   Bailey's Island, ME
Owner(s): Noel & Laurie March
Year boat took possession of
current owner: 2000

CONTENT was the final project of builder Stuart Ford (from Howard I. Chappelle's Pemaquid design), as he was finally content with his handiwork. From Boothbay Harbor to Friendship Harbor, to Rockland Harbor she is a well-known and welcomed sight. One of the earliest member sloops of the Friendship Sloop Society, she has always sported the #5.

(See pages 59, 70)

Eastward

LOD: 32' Beam: 10' Draft: 5'6"
Homeport: Basin Harbor, VT
Builder: James Chadwick
Launched: 1956 Pemaquid, ME
Owner(s): Doug Riley
Year boat took possession of
 current owner: 2013

EASTWARD was designed by Murray Peterson for sailing writer Roger Duncan, a former President of the FSS.   Roger wrote a book about some of his adventures, entitled simply EASTWARD. The Duncan family owned her for 56 years. She then passed through the hands of two successor owners, who each did some restoration work in Maine before electing to sell her. Work has now resumed in Vermont with the help of the Lake Champlain Maritime Museum. Re-launching is planned for summer 2014.

(See pages 49, 53, 81, 85, and sidebar page 84)

Tannis

LOD: 38'
Homeport: Salem Willows, MA
Builder: W. Scott Carter
Launched: 1937 Friendship, ME
Owner(s): Jack & Mary Cronin
Former name(s): Tannis II,
 Monkey Wench
Year boat took possession of
 current owner: 1968

TANNIS has been owned by the Cronins for 45 years. In 1976 we donated her mast for a memorial to the town of Friendship; once in place it served to help mark the finish line for the homecoming races. We have sailed her to the rendezvous since 1969, missing only the year 2011 due to the rebuild that was underway at the time. She received a complete rebuild in 2010-2011. All eight Cronin children enjoyed sailing on her. Now our 15 grandchildren sail frequently with us as well.

(See pages 32, 33, 34, 64, 68, 71, 93, 94, 95 and sidebars on pages 58 and 96).

Amity

LOD: 30'
Homeport: Belfast, ME
Builder: Wilbur A. Morse
Launched: 1901 Friendship, ME
Owner(s): Patrick Reilly
Former name(s): Edmar
Year boat took possession of
current owner: 2012

AMITY, an original Wilber Morse Friendship sloop, has been meticulously maintained over the years. For over 50 years she was owned by J. Russell Wiggins, former editor of the <u>Washington Post</u> and United Nations ambassador. Under his ownership, a complete rebuild was performed by Ralph Stanley of Southwest Harbor. Today she runs private and shared charters out of Belfast, Maine. For more information, view www.belfastbaycompany.com.

(See pages 15, 55, 56, 73)

10

Mary Anne

LOD: 31′
Homeport: Damariscotta, ME
Builder: Lash Brothers
Launched: 1958 Friendship, ME
Owner(s): Joe Griffin

(See pages 49, 58)

12

Friendship

LOD: 29′
Builder: Wilbur A. Morse
Launched: 1902 Friendship, ME

Whereabouts unknown.
While we presume that this sloop is still in existence, we were unable to verify the location, condition, or the owner of the sloop.

13

Easting

LOD: 29' Beam: 9'6" Draft: 5'3"
Homeport: Benjamin River, ME
Builder: Charles Morse
Launched: 1920 Friendship, ME
Owner(s): Dain and Sarah Frank
Former name(s): Ruth L.
Year boat took possession of
current owner: 2013

When 'EASTING' took possession of us this year, she was named 'RUTH L' after her then owner's mother. We have returned her to her previous name of 'EASTING' which had been her name since the '50s. 'EASTING' will be available for private charters on Eggemoggin Reach.

14

Sadie M.

LOD: 30' Beam: 9'8" Draft: 4'6"
Homeport: Bass Harbor, ME
Builder: Wilbur Morse /nephew
Launched: 1946 Thomaston, ME
Owner(s): Richard & Lorraine Stanley
Former name(s): Patrick, Posh, Vigor
Year boat took possession of
current owner: 2008

Nick Kingsbury owned the boat prior to us and he gave it to us, on the premise that having a friend with a boat is even better than having a boat. We are in the process of finishing the fiberglassing Nick started, repairing the cockpit, and have made a new mast for the boat. Before Nick had owned SADIE M., it was run as a passenger boat out of Boothbay Harbor. In the 1970s, when the boat was called VIGOR, Ralph Stanley was commissioned to design and build a topsail rig.

(See page 73)

Vida Mia

LOD: 31'6" Beam: 10' Draft: 4'9"
Homeport: Cape May, NJ
Builder: Edward L. Stevens
Launched: 1942
Owner(s): George & Cindy Loos
Year boat took possession of
current owner: 1980

15

Ted Brown built VIDA MIA with E.L. Stevens from 1939 to 1942; this history is well documented in our yearbooks. Ted sold VIDA MIA to Dave King in 1975; we bought VIDA MIA in 1980. VIDA MIA has been in Cape May since 1980 and has been a proud ambassador for the State of Maine and the Friendship Sloop Society. VIDA MIA has inspired many to photograph and paint her at her mooring and under sail. When sailing a Friendship Sloop you can't help but make many friends, too many to mention. Our family album of VIDA MIA was used to help stop construction in Cape May Harbor, the land is now set aside as Green Acres.

Also VIDA MIA was inspiration to me to stop anchoring regulations in Cape May Harbor and keep the harbor free to all sailors. VIDA MIA has inspired me to start a local chapter of the Traditional Small Craft Association in South Jersey and now help with the creation of the Cape May Maritime Museum. We sail most frequently off the coast of Cape May and Delaware Bay, but have made many trips to Delaware, Philadelphia and the Chesapeake Bay. VIDA MIA is now home in my yard under cover to be rebuilt and sail another 75 years.

Thank you George, Cindy and daughter Brittany

16

Retriever

LOD: 22'
Homeport: Marshfield, MA.
Builder: W. Prescott Gannet
Launched: 1942
Owner(s): Phil Rotondo

(See pages 34, 37)

Roger Duncan

18

Chrissy

LOD: 29' Beam: 9'5" Draft: 5'
Homeport: Bar Harbor, ME
Builder: Charles A. Morse
Launched: 1912 Friendship, ME
Owner(s): Downeast
Windjammer Cruises
Former name(s): Sonny
Year boat took possession of
current owner: 2012

CHRISSY was rescued & restored by boat builder & sailor Harold Burnham of Essex, MA. Capt. Harold sailed CHRISSY on day sails including hauling lobster traps under sail. CHRISSY& Harold made the front cover of WoodenBoat *magazine (see page 87) demonstrating a working lobster sloop hauling a trap under sail. Harold sold 'CHRISSY' to Captain Ed Zimmerman who brought her back to Maine and sailed parties (including hauling wood traps under sail) from Bar Harbor, Maine . Capt. Steve Pagels bought CHRISSY from Ed in 2012 .*

CHRISSY continues to sail the Maine coast from Bar Harbor .

(See pages 59, 83, 87 and fronticepiece)

19

Blackjack

LOD: 33' Beam 10'8" Draft 5'0"
Homeport: Bristol, RI
Builder: Wilbur A. Morse
Launched: 1900 Friendship, ME
Owner(s): Downeast
Windjammer Cruises
Year boat took possession of
current owner: 2014

BLACKJACK has a long Maine history. She was sailed out of Bar Harbor for many years by her previous owner Wilson Fletcher who would take passengers on public tours off Mount Desert Island. Prior to that she was owned by William Pendleton, Friendship Sloop Society President from 1971-72. The Pendleton Memorial Scholarship Fund was set up to provide scholarships to the students of Friendship, Maine. BLACKJACK was pictured in the Yankee Magazine *book "*Yankees Under Sail*" published in 1968 for the story "The Enduring Friendship."*

(See pages 15, 61, 73 and fronticepiece)

Roger Duncan

Wilbur A. Morse

21

LOD: 30'
Builder: Carlton Simmons
Launched: 1946 Friendship, ME

Whereabouts unknown.
While we presume that this sloop is still in existence, we were unable to verify the location, condition, or the owner of the sloop.

I was in my early twenties and living in Cundy's Harbor, Maine, when I became friends with Karl Heiser, a retired psychologist from Ohio, who had recently moved to Maine with his wife Ruth. He apparently had always dreamed of owning a Friendship sloop, carving sloops out of wood when he was young. He fulfilled his childhood dream when he bought the WILBUR A. MORSE in the mid-seventies. He hired a friend and me to help him work on her, even though none of us knew anything about Friendship sloops. She looked more than a bit rough and much neglected sitting in the bushes somewhere in Friendship when we first set eyes on her, but Karl's enthusiasm and commitment carried us through. We made many runs to Friendship in his Fiat 500 and worked at scraping, painting, caulking, etc. until she was finally ready to hit the water and make the voyage to her new homeport of Cundy's Harbor. Once there, he proudly sailed her and shared many a sail with locals and "highlanders" alike. At one point, he hired a couple of locals to replace her mast, one half at a time, while the mast was still in place! He invited loads of people to sail in the races in Friendship in the mid-1970s into the 1980s. His quite proper wife, Ruth, would serve the crew delicate tea sandwiches, which we politely ate while wishing for heartier fare. Karl owned the WILBUR A. MORSE until sometime after 1983, which was the last time I sailed on her with my husband, David, and a friend to deliver her to Friendship for the races.

According to the 1987 Yearbook, she was owned by Steven Marsella of Cranston, Rhode Island. The sloop's name was changed to MAINE ISSUE.

In 1989, the sloop was bought by Duncan and Susan Blair of Los Alamos, California, who changed the name back to the WILBUR A. MORSE. Homeport was Ventura, California.

Submitted by Julie O'Brien-Merrill (Crew on #227 Celebration since 1986)

22

Ellie T.

LOD: 25'
Homeport: , New London, CT
Builder: John Thorpe
Launched: 1961 Christmas Cove, ME
Owner(s): Greg & Daneen Roth

ELLIE T. is undergoing a long term restoration.
(See page 49)

23

Alice E.

LOD: 33' Beam: 10' Draft: 5'
Homeport: Southwest Harbor, ME
Builder: Unknown
Launched: 1899
Owner(s): Karl Brunner
Former name(s): Depression, Gladys
Year boat took possession of
current owner: 2005

ALICE E. is the oldest known Friendship sloop still sailing. In the early 1930s she was bought by a doctor who renamed her DEPRESSION. When I found her in 2005, I was delighted to find out her original name was ALICE E. and renamed her as such. She was rebuilt by David Nutt in East Boothbay, Maine in 1984, but her original builder is still a mystery. Anyone with information on her original builder, or an ALICE E. in the midcoast of Maine in the late 1800s is highly encouraged to contact the current owner, Karl Brunner. She sails daily from Southwest Harbor, offering shared and private charters under the business name Sail Acadia.

(See pages 32, 50, 53, 59 and Preface)

24

Tern

LOD: 25'
Homeport: New London, CT
Builder: Wilbur A. Morse
Launched: 1900 Friendship, ME
Owner(s): Jaxon L. Vibber
Former name(s): Ancient Mariner

Information provided from Friendship Sloop Society records, believed to be correct, but we were unable to get verification from the owner.

(See pages 15, 65)

Whereabouts unknown.
While we presume that this sloop is still in existence, we were unable to verify the location, condition, or the owner of the sloop.

Sea Duck

25

LOD: 35'
Builder: Charles A. Morse
Launched: 1901
Owner(s): Unknown
Former name(s): Freyea

Whereabouts unknown.
While we presume that this sloop is still in existence, we were unable to verify the location, condition, or the owner of the sloop.

Kidnapped

30

LOD: 21'
Builder: Unknown
Launched: 1921
Former name(s): Flyaway

(See pages 15, 59)

White Eagle

31

LOD: 28'
Homeport: Rebuilding, MA
Builder: Wilbur A. Morse
Launched: 1915 Friendship, ME
Owner(s): William A. Cronin & Cynthia Pendleton
Year boat took possession of
current owner: 1988

Information provided from Friendship Sloop Society records, believed to be correct, but we were unable to get verification from the owner.

(See page 15)

Nomad

32

LOD: 33'
Homeport: Rebuilding, MA
Builder: Wilbur A. Morse
Launched: 1906 Friendship, ME
Owner(s): Tom Ash

33
Smuggler

LOD: 28'
Homeport: Rebuilding, RI
Builder: Philip J. Nichols
Launched: 1942 Round Pound, ME
Owner(s): Mike Mulroney
Former name(s): Cyrano, Pressure, Suchel

Information provided from Friendship Sloop Society records, believed to be correct, but we were unable to get verification from the owner.

34

Pal O'Mine

LOD: 27' Beam: 8' Draft: 4'
Homeport: Essex, MA
Builder: W. Prescott Gannet
Launched: 1947 Scituate, MA
Owner(s): Jim Lane

Information provided from Friendship Sloop Society records, believed to be correct, but we were unable to get verification from the owner.

(See page 34)

Mary C.

35

LOD: 20'
Homeport: Islesboro, ME
Builder: Nathaniel D. Clapp
Launched: 1962 Prides Crossing, MA
Owner(s): Roger & Mary Burke

Information provided from Friendship Sloop Society records, believed to be correct, but we were unable to get verification from the owner.

Chance

37

LOD: 31' Beam: 10'2" Draft: 5'2"
Homeport: Bath, ME
Builder: Wilbur A. Morse
Launched: 1916 Friendship, ME
Owner(s): Maine Maritime Museum Library
Year boat took possession of
current owner: 1982

Roger Duncan

Official no. 651199 Boat is in storage and not in use. Was raced and chartered by the Museum for ten years. Museum accession number 82.86 donated by Alan Goldstein of Winter Harbor, ME.

(See Pages 15, 62, front cover, and side bar page 62)

Eleazar

38

LOD: 38'
Homeport: Rochester, NY
Builder: W. Scott Carter
Launched: 1938 Friendship, ME
Owner(s): David Schuler
Former name(s): Gold Ivy

Information provided from Friendship Sloop Society records, believed to be correct, but we were unable to get verification from the owner.

(See pages 32, 33)

39

Goblin

LOD: 30' Beam: 9'5" Draft: 5'
Homeport: Great Cove, Brooklin, ME
Builder: Lash Brothers
Launched: 1963 Friendship, ME
Owner(s): Christopher Eckelt
Former name(s): Dancing Bear, Downeaster
Year boat took possession of
current owner: 2006

Oh, many a story could be told. However, the one worth telling most is, GOBLIN was gifted to me by none other than the owner/captain of JABBERWOCKY, sail # 189, Dr. Brad Wilkinson. He had loved and sailed her for 9 years.

40

Comesin

LOD: 32'
Homeport: Jacksonville, FL
Builder: J. Ervin Jones
Launched: 1962 East Boothbay, ME
Owner(s): John & Linda Livingston
Former name(s): Elicia III

Information provided from Friendship Sloop Society records, believed to be correct, but we were unable to get verification from the owner.

41

Snafu

LOD: 35'

Whereabouts unknown.
While we presume that this sloop is still in existence, we were unable to verify the location, condition, or the owner of the sloop.

Selkie

LOD: 26' Beam: 7'8" Draft: 3'8"
Homeport: Essex, CT
Builder: Carlton Simmons /J.P. Hennings
Launched: 1963
Owner(s): Russell and Linda Stone
Former name(s): Pam, Nancy
Year boat took possession of
 current owner: 2004

Gypsy

LOD: 23'
Homeport: Buck's Harbor, ME
Builder: Judson Crouse
Launched: 1939
Owner(s): Holly Lash
Year boat took possession of
current owner: 1999

Roger Duncan

Many people in the Society remember GYPSY in connection with Holly's father, Bob Lash. Bob was President of the Society in 1966-67. After surviving multiple missions as a bomber pilot during World War II, nothing ever seemed to phase him. He was known for sailing with a joy that approached reckless abandon.

His attitude about racing was best summed up by a phrase he used about whomever was ahead; "Let's go get-em."

(See page 73)

44 *Sazerac*

LOD: 35' Beam: 11'6" Draft: 5'
Homeport: Belfast, ME
Builder: Wilbur A. Morse
Launched: 1913 Friendship, ME
Owner(s): Roger Lee
Former name(s): Gail O., Cheryl Lynn, Ranger
Year boat took possession of
  current owner: 1993

Rebuilt 1967 by James Rockefeller at Bald Mountain Boat Works. Maintained most of the time since then by Paul Bryant of Riverside Boat Company, Newcastle, Maine.

At the time of this writing SAZERAC is looking for a new home.

(See pages 15, 78, 91)

45 *Flying Jib*

LOD: 30'
Homeport: Rebuilding Jefferson, ME
Builder: W. Scott Carter
Launched: 1936 Friendship, ME
Owner(s): Ryan Graham
Former name(s): Monique
Year boat took possession of
current owner: 2013

(See pages 32,33)

46

Momentum

LOD: 30'
Homeport: Erie, PA
Builder: Lash Brothers
Launched: 1964 Friendship, ME
Owner(s): Bayfront Center for
Maritime Studies
Former name(s): Dirigo

Information provided from Friendship Sloop Society records, believed to be correct, but we were unable to get verification from the owner.

47

Galatea

LOD: 30'
Homeport: Unknown
Builder: McKie W. Roth Jr.
Launched: 1964
Owner(s): (last known) Don Murray

Whereabouts unknown.
While we presume that this sloop is still in existence, we were unable to verify the location, condition, or the owner of the sloop.

49

Surprise

LOD: 33'
Homeport: Bar Harbor, ME
Builder: Philip J. Nichols
Launched: 1964 Round Pound, ME
Owner(s): Steve Keblinsky
Former name(s): Windhorse, Windrose

Information provided from Friendship Sloop Society records, believed to be correct, but we were unable to get verification from the owner.

(See pages 73, 78, 95)

50

Heritage

LOD: 29' Beam: 9'4" Draft: 4'11"
Homeport: Rockland, ME
Builder: Elmer Collemer
Launched: 1962 Camden, ME
Owner(s): Neal Parker
Year boat took possession of
  current owner: 2014

HERITAGE was custom built for an early President of the Friendship Sloop Society. Under her second owner, HERITAGE, unfortunately, went ashore because of the failure of a mooring and was written off as a loss by the insurance company. The third owner's family knew the boat's original owner and had sailed extensively on her when he was a boy. He had always wanted HERITAGE and was able to buy her and have her rebuilt by Paul and Nat Bryant at Riverside Boatyard - New Castle, ME. This rebuild included a new keel, floors, lower frames, horn timber, stem, lower planking, etc.

(See page 91)

52

Rights of Man

LOD: 30' Beam: 9' Draft: 5'
Homeport: Rockland, ME
Builder: Lash Brothers
Launched: 1965 Friendship, ME
Owner(s): Wayne & Kirsten Cronin
Year boat took possession of
current owner: 1996

Wayne purchased RIGHTS OF MAN in the winter of 1996. Rights underwent a significant rebuild by Wayne and the Cronin family in Charlton, Mass. They replaced the deck beams, the deck, cabin house and interior. Additionally they fitted new shear planks and transom quarter blocks. The original iron keel was replaced with new lead keel and a Westerbeke diesel engine was fitted. RIGHTS OF MAN was berthed in Charlton during the winters and moored in Salem, Mass, until 2001 when Wayne and his family moved to Rockland, Maine. She now sails the waters of Penobscot Bay during the summer. Wayne continues to maintain RIGHTS; he fitted new shear planks and started refastening her in 2011.

(See page 93)

54

Echo

LOD: 22'
Homeport: Delano Cove, ME
Builder: Lee Boatyard Rockland, ME
Launched: 1965
Owner(s): Randolph & Beverly Major,
Stephen & Adrienne Major,
 Seth & Sarah Major
Year boat took possession of
current owner: 2000

Every year, we gather at Riverside Boat Company on the Darmariscotta to get ECHO ready while the horseshoe crabs romance at the tides' edge. We sail down river and out to Monhegan to deliver our Vermont maple syrup to the stores and inns on the island. Somehow we always find the island in the fog and catch a following breeze for the run home to Friendship.

(See page 93 and side bar page 21)

57 *Old Baldy*

LOD: 25' Beam: 8'8" Draft: 4'3"
Homeport: Southwest Harbor, ME
Builder: James S. Rockefeller
Launched: 1965 Camden, ME
Owner(s): Jarvis & Sue Newman
Year boat took possession of
 current owner: 2010

Jarvis bought her in the fall of 2010, worked on her all winter, and launched her in July 2011 for the Southwest Harbor Friendship sloop race. At the end of 1968, she was the plug for the first Friendship sloop mold & subsequent hull.

(See pages 53, 70, 77, 80, 94, and sidebar page 78).

56 *Iocaste*

LOD: 33'
Builder: Charles A. Morse
Launched: 1907 Friendship, ME

Whereabouts unknown.
While we presume that this sloop is still in existence, we were unable to verify the location, condition, or the owner of the sloop.

58 *Cathy*

LOD: 21'
Homeport: New Harbor, ME
Builder: Jeremy D. Maxwell
Launched: 1969 Spruce Head, ME
Owner(s): Ted & Cathy Chase
Former name(s): Tern, Departure

Information provided from Friendship Sloop Society records, believed to be correct, but we were unable to get verification from the owner.

Sarah Mead 59

LOD: 30' Beam: 9'5" Draft: 4'
Homeport: Boothbay Harbor, ME
Builder: Newbert & Wallace
Launched: 1965 Thomaston, ME
Owner(s): Nate Jones
Year boat took possession of
current owner: 2005

SARAH MEAD was partially rebuilt and re-rigged by Nate and Randy Jones in 2005.
Sarah Mead White-Walsh, for whom the boat was named, still comes onboard at least once a year, usually with Hank "Doc" White, the original owner. SARAH MEAD currently works as a charter boat in Boothbay Harbor, and was repowered with an electric drive system in 2013.

61

Windward

LOD: 25' Beam: 8'8" Draft: 4'5"
Homeport: Gloucester, MA
Builder: James S. Rockefeller
Launched: 1966 Camden, ME
Owner(s): Doug Parsons
Year boat took possession of
current owner: 2011

WINDWARD actually caught my eye (as every Friendship does) around 2000. She had been sitting on a mooring, not moving for a few years. After I sold our schooner, TRUENT (named after the Friendship that was in Searsport, Maine) in 2004, I asked the owner if he wanted to sell WINDWARD. Finally persuaded him in 2011 and now I have a lot of work to do. I have all the necessary pieces to sail her; just need the time to put them together.
(See pages 73, 78)

62 *Columbia*

LOD: 23'
Builder: Lester Chadbourne
Launched: 1950
Last reported sold to owners in
   Boston in the early 1990s.

Whereabouts unknown.
While we presume that this sloop is still in existence, we were unable to verify the location, condition, or the owner of the sloop.

63 *Kochab*

LOD: 28'
Builder: Edward Speers
Launched: 1953 Black Rock, CT

Whereabouts unknown.
While we presume that this sloop is still in existence, we were unable to verify the location, condition, or the owner of the sloop.

64

Amicitia

LOD: 33'
Homeport: New Bedford, MA
Builder: Lash Brothers
Launched: 1965 Friendship, ME
Owner(s): Jeff & Diane Pontiff

Information provided from Friendship Sloop Society records, believed to be correct, but we were unable to get verification from the owner.

(See page 68)

65 *Gallant Lady*

LOD: 33'
Homeport: Prinyer Cove, CN
Builder: Morse
Launched: 1907
Owner(s): Jim Smith
Former name(s): Gay Gamble

Whereabouts unknown.
While we presume that this sloop is still in existence, we were unable to verify the location, condition, or the owner of the sloop.

Venture

66

LOD: 26'6" Beam: 9'4" Draft: 4'4"
Homeport: Beverly, MA
Builder: Wilbur A. Morse, rebuilt 1971
by Ralph Stanley and Jarvis Newman
Launched: 1912 Friendship, ME
Owner(s): William Finch & Carol Rose
Year boat took possession of
 current owner: 1996

VENTURE is listed by name and length on Wilbur A. Morse's list of boats he built. She was built for a client in Boothbay Harbor, ME in 1912.

Roger F. Duncan in his book Friendship Sloops *gives the following list: In 1944 V. A. Hicks of Boston sold her to Pane Wemmerwesser, who sold her to Emmet Carver. He owned her for many years and sold her to Robert Thing in 1954. He traded her to Jarvis Newman, who rebuilt her for John Porteous of Cape Elizabeth. In 1971, he gave her to the Penobscot Marine Museum, which sold her to Kleinschmidth in 1971.*

R. Stevens Klineschmidth of Pittsfield, MA, sold her to William A. Sauerbrey III of Mystic, CT, in 1988. Sauerbrey moved to Centerville, MA and sold her to the current owner William B. Finch of Beverly, MA, in 1996.

VENTURE appeared in the 1956 movie adaptation of the musical Carousel *staring Gordon MacRae and Shirley Jones.*

In 1978, VENTURE is pictured on the cover of Nautical Quarterly 5 *and numerous photos of her appear within this publication in the article entitled "Princess and All Her Kin."*   *(See pages 15, 73)*

Hieronymus

67

LOD: 33'
Homeport: Southwest Harbor, ME
Builder: Ralph W. Stanley
Launched: 1962 Southwest Harbor, ME
Owner(s): Albert P. Neilson
Built for current owner: 1962

The vessel was built specifically for me. The longest voyage made was to the Bras d'Or Lakes from Southwest Harbor, skippered by my sons, Will and Joe, in 1976.

(See page 75 and sidebar pages 72, 73)

69

Coast O' Maine

LOD: 30'
Homeport: Fairhaven, NY
Builder: Vernell Smith
Launched: 1967
Owner(s): William & Shawn Poole

Information provided from Friendship Sloop Society records, believed to be correct, but we were unable to get verification from the owner.

(See page 68)

70

Wings of the Morning

LOD: 30'
Homeport: Southwest Harbor, ME
Builder: Roger Morse
Launched: 1967 Thomaston, ME
Owner(s): Rodney Flora &
Jill Schoof
Former name(s): Symbolon, Spirit,
Margaret Motte, Grace O'Malley

This sloop is listed as for sale through a marine broker.

(See page 67)

# Gladiator

LOD: 32'
Homeport: Friendship, ME
Builder: Alexander McLain
Launched: 1902 Bremen Long Is., ME
Owner(s): Bill & Caroline Zuber, II
Former name(s): Nancy Jean, Downeaster
Year boat took possession of
current owner: 1966

Launched as GLADIATOR, she was renamed NANCY JEAN, then DOWNEASTER, and returned to original name and Documentation Number in 1967.

(See pages 18, 28, 32, 86, front cover, Preface, and sidebar on page 35)

West Indian

LOD: 26' Beam: 9'4"
Homeport: Kenora, Ontario, CN
Builder: Pamet Harbor Boat
Launched: 1951 Camden, ME
Owner(s): Christoff Skoczylas
Former name(s): Dauphine

Information provided from Friendship Sloop Society records, believed to be correct, but we were unable to get verification from the owner.

74
Patience

LOD: 30' Beam: 10' Draft: 5'
Homeport: Rebuilding, Pemaquid, ME
Builder: Malcolm Brewer
Launched: 1965 Camden, ME
Owner(s): Chris Gerardi
Year boat took possession of
current owner: 2010

I first met PATIENCE in 2010 on my way to the 50th Regatta in Rockland. I accepted stewardship that day, after admiring Friendship sloops for decades. Having been a commercial fisherman in my youth, these boats combined my working heritage and sailing nostalgia all in one. The more I learned about this boat, the more I came to appreciate her. She was made by arguably the most skilled boatwright in Maine's history. Encyclopedia Britannica's TV special, American Character, claimed "his craftsmanship was the finest in New England." In 1983, WoodenBoat magazine cover story proclaimed "The Masterful Work of Malcolm Brewer." She is a unique boat because Malcolm built her for himself and added a raised cabin for stand- up headroom. PATIENCE is undergoing the process of being rebuilt. White oaks logs are curing in a pond, waiting their new home as keel, ribs and rudder. I see why the Lord gave me a boat named PATIENCE. For it is said "All good things come to those who wait" and "patience is a virtue"; her day will come and it will be worth the wait. Hopefully all will be able to say once again, "by all accounts she's a real beauty." You can follow the progress at www.MaineMaritimeMinistry.org.

(See page 97)

75

Omaha

LOD: 35'3" Beam: 13'1" Draft: 6'5"
Homeport: Spruce Head Island, ME
Builder: Norris Carter
Launched: 1901 Friendship, ME
Owner(s): Adrian & Pamela Hooydonk
Year boat took possession of
current owner: 1998

This sloop was built for the mackerel fishing industry and continued to fish out of the Merrimac River until 1961. It would take on 20 hogs heads of mackerel to fill her up for the trip home.

Whereabouts unknown.
While we presume that this sloop is still in existence, we were unable to verify the location, condition, or the owner of the sloop.

Beagle

77

LOD: 28'
Builder: Charles A. Morse
Launched: 1905 Friendship, ME

Down East

80

LOD: 35'
Homeport: Edgewood Yacht Club, RI
Builder: Fred Buck / E.L. Adams Launched: 1941 Stonington, CT
Owner(s): William Anderson & Donna Grant
Former name(s): Sepoy, Headway, Sunshine, Dickie II, Gray Dawn

This sloop is listed as for sale through a marine broker.

Regardless

81

LOD:39'
Builder: Fred Dion
Launched: 1963 Salem, MA

Whereabouts unknown.
While we presume that this sloop is still in existence, we were unable to verify the location, condition, or the owner of the sloop.

82

Morning Star

LOD: 28'
Homeport: Southport, ME
Builder: Albion F. Morse
Launched: 1912 Cushing, ME
Owner(s): Terry McClinch
Former name(s): Wild Goose

Information provided from Friendship Sloop Society records, believed to be correct, but we were unable to get verification from the owner.

(See page 73)

83

Perseverance

LOD: 30'6" Beam: 10' Draft: 4'6"
Homeport: Yorktown, VA
Builder: Bruno & Stillman (01)
Launched: 1969 Newington, NH
Owner(s): David & Lauren Niebuhr
Year boat took possession of current owner: 1998

PERSEVERANCE is Bruno & Stillman's hull No. 01 of their fiberglass Friendship sloops. Built in 1969, the Niebuhr family are the fourth owners of the boat (including the manufacturer rep). We bought her, in 1998, from long-time FSS member Dr. Bob Jacobson who kept her at Deer Island, Maine, during his many summers of enjoying this beautiful boat. For many years, we sailed her around the lower Chesapeake Bay, before transporting her to Sarasota Bay, Florida, when I changed jobs. While we planned trips to the Keys, and even a journey up to Virginia, she remained close to shore, sailing in the Gulf, Tampa Bay and the waters around Sarasota. We returned to Virginia in 2008 and are refurbishing her for launch in late summer. We hope to begin sailing her this fall, before we pull her for the season (December, here on the Bay!).

(See pages 68, 76)

Whereabouts unknown.
While we presume that this sloop is still in existence, we were unable to verify the location, condition, or the owner of the sloop.

Philia

LOD: 22'
Builder: McKie W. Roth Jr.
Launched: 1969 Edgecomb, ME

Heidi Lee

LOD: 38' Beam: 12' Draft: 6'
Homeport: Dutch Harbor, RI
Builder: Jeremy D. Maxwell
Launched: 1974 Spruce Head, ME
Owner(s): Matthew & Heidi Gabrilowitz
Former name(s): Ann Frances, Tern
Year boat took possession of
 current owner: 1991

The sloop and I first sized each other up in the spring, 1991. We took her over from Jeremy D. Maxwell, the builder and a renaissance man. She had been in the barn for a decade. She was launched in Tenant's Harbor with a new white dress and name. We sailed her to Rhode Island with a stopover in Gloucester in late September 1991. We entered the West Passage of Narragansett Bay with a gentle four-foot swell and a healthy breeze behind us. Heidi Lee danced along at a steady pace. These were her new waters. She dipped her shoulders, and with a giant thrust upward, surveyed the lighthouse at Dutch Island and surrounding waters with favor. That would be the first of many trips past this way. Fair winds.

Allegiance

LOD: 24'
Homeport: Cape Porpoise, ME
Builder: Albert M. Harding
Launched: 1970 Kennebunkport, ME
Owner(s): Hale Whitehouse

Information provided from Friendship Sloop Society records, believed to be correct, but we were unable to get verification from the owner.

Roger Duncan

87

Stella Maris

LOD: 22'
Homeport: Scituate, MA
Builder: McKie W. Roth Jr.
Launched: 1969 ME
Owner(s): James Russell
Former name(s): Eagle

Information provided from Friendship Sloop Society records, believed to be correct, but we were unable to get verification from the owner.

(See pages 68, 73)

88

Apogee

LOD: 30'6" Beam: 10' Draft: 4'6"
Homeport: Wickford,RI
Builder: Bruno & Stillman (02)
Launched: 1969 Newington, NH
Owner(s): Tony and Chris Bourget
Year boat took possession of
current owner: 2012

(See page 59)

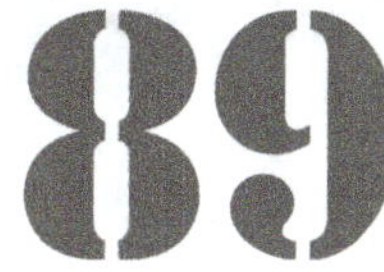

Erda

LOD: 22'
Homeport: Vineyard Haven, MA
Builder: McKie W. Roth Jr.
Launched: 1970 ME
Owner(s): Alexandra West
Former name(s): Avior

Information provided from Friendship Sloop Society records, believed to be correct, but we were unable to get verification from the owner.

Roger Duncan

Salatia

LOD: 25' Beam: 8'8" Draft: 4'3"
Homeport: Southwest Harbor, ME
Builder: Newman (P02)
Launched: 1969 Southwest Harbor, ME
Owner(s): Miff Lauriat & Marge Russakoff
Built for George B. Lauriat
 father of current owner: 1969

When built, SALATIA was white with red boot top and wale stripes. She had 12 foot sweeps instead of an auxiliary motor. For 20 years we rowed when the wind didn't blow. In 1976, I added topmast and topsails. In 1991, I painted the boat red, got the diesel motor, and put a taller topmast on. This one was cut from a tree that grew on Cranberry Isle in Muscongus Bay. The tree was over 90 years old when cut!
(See pages 59, 66, 68, 77, 80, 87, 89)

91

Phoenix

LOD: 30'6" Beam: 10' Draft: 4'6"
Homeport: Carvers Harbor, ME
Builder: Bruno & Stillman (04)
Launched: 1970 Newington, NH
Owner(s): Tad Beck
Year boat took possession of
current owner: 1970

My father had PHOENIX built in 1969 and it has been in the family ever since. I bought her from him in 1993. Her original home port was Kittery Point, ME and she has been on Vinalhaven since the early 1980s. The island seems to have adopted her. While the harbor does not really welcome most sailboats, the fact that she is a replica of an old fishing boat that used to fill the harbor seems to make all the difference. You can truly see her relationship to modern lobster boats when she is hauled out at the boatyard. She has sailed to Nova Scotia and as far south as Provincetown, MA. Over the years, five generations of Becks have sailed on her. Both my father and I have taken her to many Friendship Sloop Society gatherings with a huge variety of regular crew members. It's always been a pleasure to share her with others. She is a Friendship that has brought many wonderful friendships into our lives.

(See pages 76, 87)

92

Joyce Elaine

LOD: 25' Beam: 8'8" Draft: 4'6"
Homeport: Harve de Grace, MD
Builder: James Rockefeller/Basil Day
Launched: 1970
Owner(s): Charles "Rustamon" Geis III
Former name(s): Victory, Puffin
Year boat took possession of
current owner: 2008

93

Anna R.

LOD: 25' Beam: 8' Draft: 4'5"
Homeport: Rockland, ME
Builder: Kenneth Rich
 Launched: 1970 New London, NH
Owner(s): Aaron & Victoria Paolino
Year boat took possession of
current owner: 2013

Euphoria

94

LOD: 25' Beam: 8'8" Draft: 4'3"
Homeport: South Freeport, ME
Builder: Newman (P03) / Rockefeller
Launched: 1971 Camden, ME
Owner(s): Victor Trodella
Former name(s): Diana
Year boat took possession of
current owner: 2007

(See page 91)

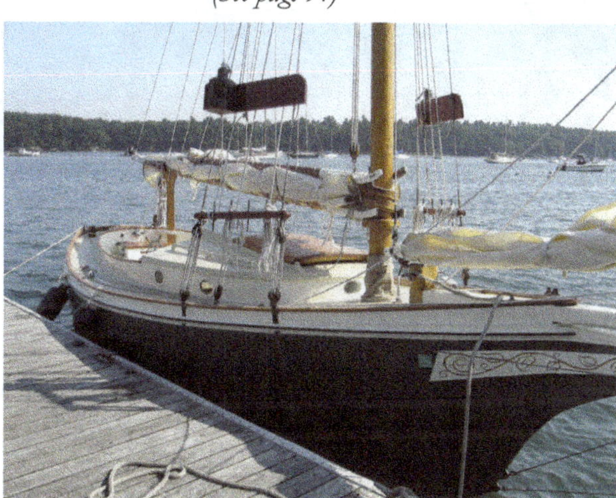

West Wind

LOD: 40' Beam: 13'6" Draft: 5'
Homeport: Rebuilding, ME
Builder: Charles A. Morse
Launched: 1902 Friendship, ME
Owner(s): John & Diane Fassak
Former name(s): Wanderer, Velocity
Year boat took possession of
 current owner: 1982

(See page 64, and sidebar pages 98, 99)

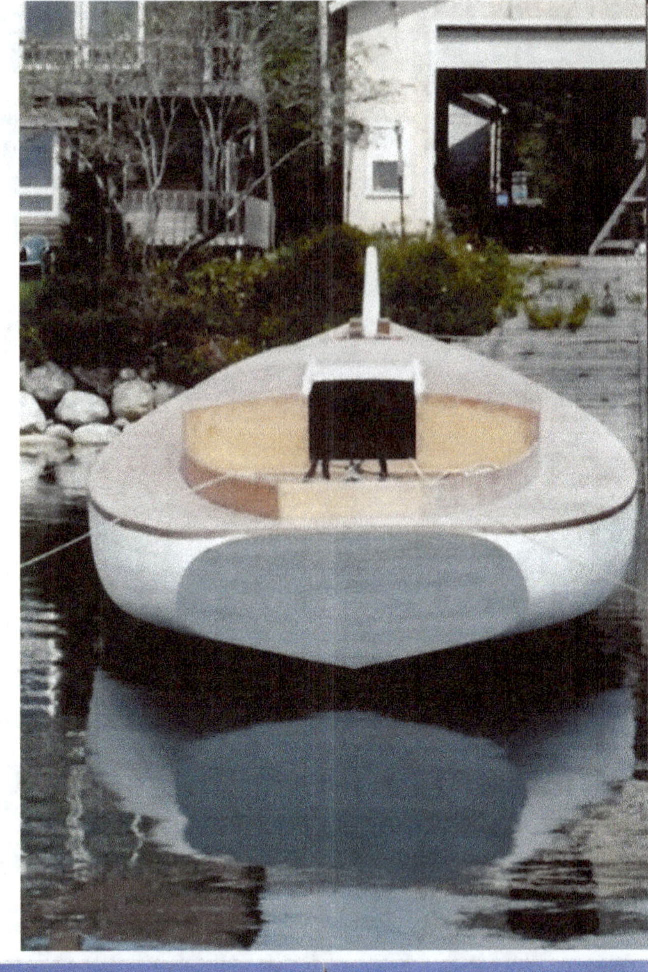

Voyager

LOD: 32'
Homeport: Plymouth, MA
Builder: Lash Brothers
Launched: 1965 Friendship, ME
Owner(s): Fred Perrone
Year boat took possession of
current owner: 2002

The original owner was Bernie MacKenzie who founded the Friendship Sloop Society. I was part of his crew and sailed with Bernie many years to Maine. I never anticipated owning VOYAGER and am thrilled to be her caretaker. The compliments come every time we take her out.

(See page 68)

Integrity

97

LOD: 27'
Homeport: Isle au Haut, ME
Builder: Wilbur A. Morse
Launched: 1903
Owner(s): Marshall Chapman
Former name(s): Gannett, Gay Gamble
Year boat took possession of
current owner: 2012

A major rebuild was undertaken in 2012 to bring her back to her original like new state. Impeccable work was done by Josh Howard at Northeast Boats in Belfast, Maine. She will be used to introduce the guests of the 1907 Keeper's House Lighthouse Inn to a boat that was fishing the waters when the Lighthouse and Keeper's House were built.

Defiance

98

LOD: 30'6" Beam: 10' Draft: 4'6"
Builder: Bruno & Stillman (06)
Launched: 1970 Newington, NH
Former name(s): Down East

Whereabouts unknown.
While we presume that this sloop is still in existence, we were unable to verify the location, condition, or the owner of the sloop.

Buccaneer

99

LOD: 29'
Builder: Wilbur A. Morse
Launched: 1911 Friendship, ME
Former name(s): Carolyn

Whereabouts unknown.
While we presume that this sloop is still in existence, we were unable to verify the location, condition, or the owner of the sloop.

100
Captain Tom

LOD: 26'
Builder: Bernard Backman
Launched: 1970 Beal's Island, ME
Owner(s): Matthew Vandevelde
Former name(s): Morning Star, Morning Watch

Whereabouts unknown.
While we presume that this sloop is still in existence, we were unable to verify the location, condition, or the owner of the sloop.

101
Good Hope

LOD: 30'6" Beam: 10' Draft: 4'6"
Homeport: Ipswich, MA
Builder: Bruno & Stillman (07)
Launched: 1970 Newington, NH
Owner(s): Lee & Barta Hathaway
Former name(s): Inverary, Minerva, Sea Fever, Patience
Year boat took possession of
current owner: 1988

In the twenty-five years of our ownership, GOOD HOPE has been moored in Marblehead, Newburyport, and Ipswich. She is currently part of the Ipswich Bay Yacht Club and sails most often in New Hampshire and Massachusetts Bay waters.

Toddy

LOD: 35' Beam: 11' Draft: 5'3"
Homeport: Caseville, MI
Builder: Lubbe Vosz
Launched: 1972 Aurich, W. Germany
Owner(s): Mary E. Morden, M.D.
Former name(s): Artios, Augustus
Year boat took possession
of current owner: 1991

TODDY is the only all steel Friendship. She was built in Aurich, Germany on commission from Tim Bliss and sailed across the Atlantic to be raced in the Miami area. Some of the stainless steel around the hauser holes was scavenged from German warships and plexiglass in the ports came from German subs. She was modified in the 1980s by Dave Westphal who put in her BMW diesel and beautiful wood with inlays below decks. She has sailed the Great Lakes since 1992 and is known in Canadian ports throughout the North Channel and Georgian Bay. She has sailed at the Friendship rendevous and is extremely fast. Unfortunately, she is also for sale because her owners are wearing out.

Solaster **103**

LOD: 25' Beam: 8'8" Draft: 4'3"
Homeport: Cranberry Island, ME
Builder: Newman (P04)
Launched: 1970 Southwest Harbor, ME
Owner(s): Chris Davis

Information provided from Friendship Sloop Society records, believed to be correct, but we were unable to get verification from the owner.

104

Cockle

LOD: 28'
Homeport: Mt. Sinai Harbor, NY
Builder: Elmer Collemer
Launched: 1950 Camden, ME
Owner(s): Rupert Hopkins
Former name(s): Lilanna

Information provided from Friendship Sloop Society records, believed to be correct, but we were unable to get verification from the owner.

105

Lady E.

LOD: 30'6" Beam: 10' Draft: 4'6"
Homeport: Annapolis, MD
Builder: Bruno & Stillman (05)
Launched: 1971 Newington, NH
Owner(s): Mike Johnson
Former name(s): Victory Chimes, At Last

Information provided from Friendship Sloop Society records, believed to be correct, but we were unable to get verification from the owner.

(See page 68)

106

Hold Tight

LOD: 25' Beam: 8'8" Draft: 4'3"
Homeport: Gloucester, MA
Builder: Newman (P05)
Launched: 1970 Southwest Harbor, ME
Owner(s): Chris and Alan Watkins
Former name(s): Lincoln D
Year boat took possession of
current owner: 2004

(See page 77)

107

Magic

LOD: 22' Beam: 7'3" Draft: 3'8"
Homeport: Rebuilding, MD
Builder: Passamaquoddy (01) / Johnson
Launched: 1970
Owner(s): Eric Applegarth
Former name(s): Magi

Information provided from Friendship Sloop Society records, believed to be correct, but we were unable to get verification from the owner.

(See pages 73, 79, 80)

109

Petrel

LOD: 31'
Homeport: Rebuilding,ME
Builder: G. Cooper
Launched: 1933

Whereabouts unknown.
While we presume that this sloop is still in existence, we were unable to verify the location, condition, or the owner of the sloop.

110

Amistad

LOD: 25'
Builder: Robert T. White / R.E. Lee
Launched: 1977 League City, TX

Whereabouts unknown.
While we presume that this sloop is still in existence, we were unable to verify the location, condition, or the owner of the sloop.

112

Secret

LOD: 27'
Homeport: Salem Willows, MA
Builder: Nichols, Philip J.
Launched: 1971 Round Pound, ME
Owner(s): Eddie & Lauren Good

Information provided from Friendship Sloop Society records, believed to be correct, but we were unable to get verification from the owner.

(See pages 68, 70)

Yankee Pride

LOD: 30'6" Beam: 10' Draft: 4'6"
Homeport: Keyport, NJ
Builder: Bruno & Stillman (14)
Launched: 1971 Newington, NH
Owner(s): James and Margaret Craig

Information provided from Friendship Sloop Society records, believed to be correct, but we were unable to get verification from the owner.

Helen Brooks

LOD: 30'6" Beam: 10' Draft: 4'6"
Homeport: Southwest Harbor, ME
Builder: Bruno & Stillman (08)
Launched: 1971 Newington, NH
Owner(s): Karl Brunner
Former name(s): Pearle, Baschert, Solaster
Year boat took possession of
current owner: 2001

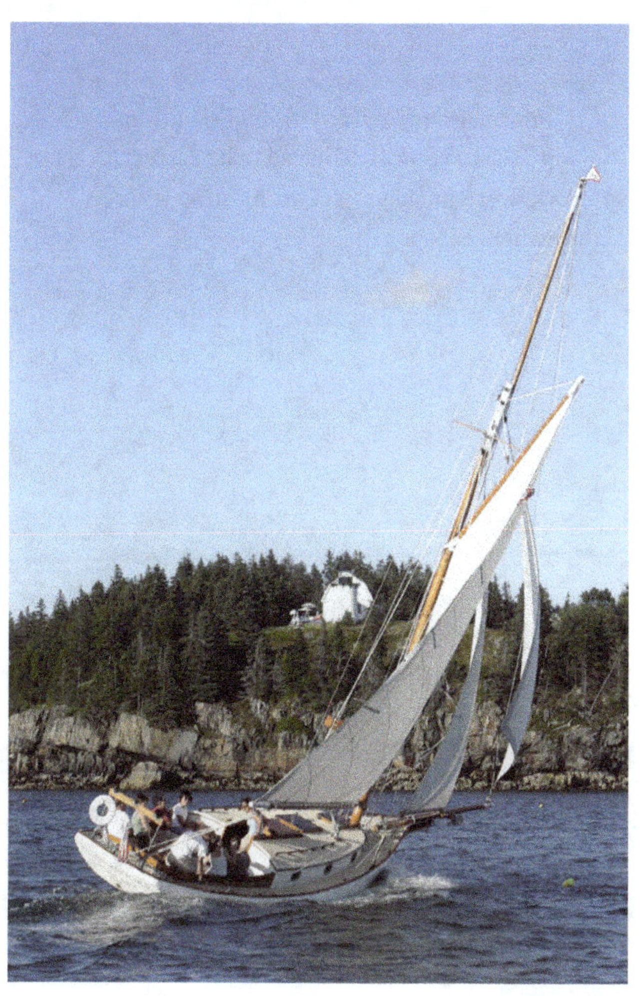

HELEN BROOKS was purchased by me in 2001 with the plan of living aboard and running a day sailing business from Southwest Harbor, Maine. When purchased, she was in Marathon Key, Florida, after her previous owner sailed her there from Massachussetts. She is named for my Grandmother Helen who kindly loaned me the start-up money to get my business off the ground. We originally sailed as Downeast Friendship Sloop Charters and now, 12 years later, operates as Sail Acadia and charter three different vessels in Acadia National Park. I believe she first was named SOLASTER, but soon it was changed to PEARL, then BASCHERT, and then HELEN BROOKS.

115

Celerity

LOD: 30'6" Beam: 10' Draft: 4'6"
Homeport: Long Cove, Chamberlain, ME
Builder: Bruno & Stillman (12)
Launched: 1971 Newington, NH
Owner(s): Anthony Cordasco and
Julie Gerow
Former name(s):Kittiwake, Good Friend,
Zephyros
Year boat took possession of
current owner: 2013

CELERITY is a well cared for Friendship sloop. Through the years, with the help of five owners, she has worked her way from Connecticut to Chamberlain, Maine, only ten miles from Friendship, her ancestral home.

Her current owners will be good stewards and plan on sailing with her for many happy years as she graces the Maine Coast.

117

Leading Light

LOD: 30'6" Beam: 10' Draft: 4'6"
Homeport: South Freeport, ME
Builder: Bruno & Stillman (10)
Launched: 1971 Newington, NH
Owner(s): John Crumpton, Jr.

Information provided from Friendship Sloop Society records, believed to be correct, but we were unable to get verification from the owner.

118

Wenonah

LOD: 30'6" Beam: 10' Draft: 4'6"
Homeport: Seabourne, TX
Builder: Bruno & Stillman (16)
Launched: 1971 Newington, NH
Owner(s): Steve Pytel

Information provided from Friendship Sloop Society records, believed to be correct, but we were unable to get verification from the owner.

(See page 94)

Valhalla

LOD: 30'6" Beam: 10' Draft: 4'6"
Homeport: Erie, PA
Builder: Bruno & Stillman (15)
Launched: 1971 Newington, NH
Owner(s): Bayfront Center for Maritime Studies

Information provided from Friendship Sloop Society records, believed to be correct, but we were unable to get verification from the owner.

Persistence

LOD: 28'
Homeport: Rockland, ME
Builder: Started by Carleton Simmons
Launched: TBL 2013
Owner(s): Sail, Power & Steam Museum, Contact Jim Sharp
Year boat took possession of current owner: 2011

PERSISTENCE was started in the 1950s by Carlton Simmons of Friendship, Maine. When Mr. Simmons' wife fell ill, the partially built boat sat in a field in Friendship for several years until the middle of the 1960s when it was purchased by a local contractor, who subsequently found he didn't have time for the project, and it sat untouched in his barn for over 40 years. Sail, Power and Steam Museum, of Rockland, Maine, convinced him to donate it to them for completion by volunteers. He had offered it to the Friendship Museum but they simply had no room for it or the capability to complete its construction.

(See page 97)

Clara

LOD: 27'
Builder: Elmer Collemer

Whereabouts unknown.
While we presume that this sloop is still in existence, we were unable to verify the location, condition, or the owner of the sloop.

122 *Eden (Ray of Hope)*

LOD: 25' Beam: 8'8" Draft: 4'5"
Homeport: Southwest Harbor, ME
Builder: Francis Nash & Ed Coffin
Launched: 1971 Owl's Head, ME
Owner(s): Scott Martin
Former name(s):,Ray of Hope
Year boat took possession of
   current owner: 1997

In 1983, RAY OF HOPE was bought by Peter Thompson in Camden, Maine and sailed to her new home port of Bar Harbor on Mount Desert Island. On the voyage with mate Scott Martin aboard, Thompson changed the vessel's name to EDEN, honoring her new anchorage. For the next few years EDEN was a charter boat; she was then sold to Doug Tarr, who continued using her to take paying guests out on Frenchmen's Bay. In 1990, EDEN was put on ground for the winter. But that winter turned into seven years. Finally, Doug reached out to Scott, EDEN'S former, but still loving, first mate. To save the boat from drying up in a boatyard, Martin bought EDEN in 1997.   With great joy, he had his grandmother officially re-christen her by cracking a bottle of champagne on her bow from a wheel-chair. Although he launched her on a shoe string budget , Martin experienced unbounded joy, gratitude and amazement that his dream had been fulfilled. EDEN was his! For the few years, he sailed EDEN out of Bar Harbor and then pulled anchor and came to her current home port of Southwest Harbor. Scott and his partner, Floyd Witham, along with their children, can be found sailing among EDEN'S sisters on the waters of Mount Desert Island. It is a common sight for a pirate flag to be raised up EDEN'S rigging, being sailed by Captain Monarch (aka Scott) with a water balloon throwing crew all dressed in their best pirate gear. For the last ten years, Scott has sailed in the Friendship sloop races and has moved up from finishing last in the fleet to being a competitive vessel, with the ever stern head-slapping navigation of Caroline Phillips and her boys on EDEN'S sheets. No matter if you're within ear shot of EDEN in a race or come upon her on a day sail, you will hear her crew singing and laughing from her rigging. But BEWARE, if you get too close, there is always a water balloon with your name on it. It was on the docks of Rockland, during a gathering of racing Friendships, that Scott miraculously met EDEN'S builder, Ed Coffin. Scott learned of Coffin's spiritual connection to EDEN and the significance of her original name, RAY OF HOPE. Coffin said that he had built the boat to bring hope to someone's life. Surely, she has fulfilled that quest by blessing Scott's life as they sail this voyage together. That is why Scott privately calls her EDEN'S RAY OF HOPE.

(See page 92)

123

Resolute

LOD: 28'
Homeport: Essex, MA
Builder: Charles A. Burnham
Launched: 1973 Essex, MA
Owner(s): Thomas Jarvis
Year boat took possession of
current owner: 2013

(See page 68, 91)

124

Callipygous
LOD: 30'6" Beam: 10' Draft: 4'6"
Homeport: Toronto,CN
Builder: Bruno & Stillman (17)
Launched: 1971 Newington, NH
Owner(s): Richard & Tina Sharabura

Information provided from Friendship Sloop Society records, believed to be correct, but we were unable to get verification from the owner.

125

Tiger Lilly
LOD: 25'
Builder: Al Paquette
Launched: 1970 Freetown, MA

Whereabouts unknown.
While we presume that this sloop is still in existence, we were unable to verify the location, condition, or the owner of the sloop.

126

Whim
LOD: 20'
Homeport: Rebuilding,NY
Builder: Chester Spear
Launched: 1939
Owner(s): Jack Manley

Information provided from Friendship Sloop Society records, believed to be correct, but we were unable to get verification from the owner.

127

Maria
LOD: 21'
Homeport: Essex,MA
Builder: Charles A. Burnham
Launched: 1971 Essex, MA
Former name(s): Lucy S., Aurora

Whereabouts unknown.
While we presume that this sloop is still in existence, we were unable to verify the location, condition, or the owner of the sloop.

128

Schoodic

LOD: 31′ Beam: 10′ Draft: 5′
Homeport: Lunenburg, NS
Builder: E. Collemer & B. Lanning
Launched: 1973 Camden/
Winter Harbor, ME
Owner(s): David & Nancy Schandall
Year boat took possession of
current owner: 2004

  Picture taken off Chockle Cap Island, near Lunenburg about 2008.
  SCHOODIC is still sailing and in excellent condition.

Leonie Drinan photo

129

Gisela R.

LOD: 25′
Homeport: Noyack, NY
Builder: Andrew P. Schafer
Launched: 1969 Rosedale Long Island, NY
Owner(s): James O'Hear

Information provided from Friendship Sloop Society records, believed to be correct, but we were unable to get verification from the owner.

Narwhal

LOD: 25' Beam: 8'8" Draft: 4'3"
Homeport: Chicago, IL
Builder: Newman (P06) / Morris, T.
Launched: 1972 Southwest Hrbr., ME
Owner(s): Kevin Murphy

Information provided from Friendship Sloop Society records, believed to be correct, but we were unable to get verification from the owner.

John Wojcik

Noahsark

LOD: 29'
Homeport: Cape Porpoise, ME
Builder: John Chase
Launched: 1972 Lynnfield, MA
Owner(s): Paul Werner

Information provided from Friendship Sloop Society records, believed to be correct, but we were unable to get verification from the owner.

(See page 68)

132

Vogel Frei
LOD: 30'
Builder: Wilbur A. Morse
Launched: 1910

Whereabouts unknown.
While we presume that this sloop is still in existence, we were unable to verify the location, condition, or the owner of the sloop.

133

Independence
LOD: 30'6" Beam: 10' Draft: 4'6"
Homeport: Rockport, ME
Builder: Bruno & Stillman (21)
Launched: 1973 Newington, NH
Owner(s): Ruth Schwarzmann
Year boat took possession of current owner: 1973

INDEPENDENCE has been part of our family since her beginning. We watched her being built. After launch, we stayed in Kennebunkport for the summer, sailing to Friendship for the 1973 homecoming. We sailed to Oxford, Maryland, and after stayed there and in Williamsburg, VA, INDEPENDENCE is again in Maine—Rockport with my son Mark; home where she belongs.

Voyager

LOD: 22' Beam: 7'3" Draft: 3'8"
Homeport: Hingham Harbor, MA
Builder: Quoddy / Collins
Launched: 1973 Bass River, MA
Owner(s): Charles Meyer
Former name(s): Four Sons,
Famous Bear, Bear, Angelus
Year boat took possession of
current owner: 2001

VOYAGER has brought many years of joy and adventure to the Meyer family and friends!
(See page 79)

134

Information provided from Friendship Sloop Society records, believed to be correct, but we were unable to get verification from the owner.

Ayesha

LOD: 35'
Homeport: Lake Ponchartrain, LA
Builder: Wilbur A. Morse
Launched: 1906 Friendship, ME
Owner(s): Larry Thomas
Former name(s): Friendship, Wild Dutchman, Snafu

137

Information provided from Friendship Sloop Society records, believed to be correct, but we were unable to get verification from the owner.

Gypsy Song

138

LOD: 31' Beam: 11' Draft: 5'
Homeport: Portland, ME
Builder: Robert P. Gardner
Launched: 1973 Rowley, MA
Owner(s): Shawn & Donna Teague
Former name(s): Red Jacket, Unicorn, Pua-Noa II

(See page 59)

139
Osprey

LOD: 25' Beam: 8'8" Draft: 4'3"
Homeport: Southwest Harbor, ME
Builder: Newman (P08) / Morris, T.
Launched: 1973 Southwest Harbor, ME
Owner(s): Steve & Kate Hughes
Former name(s): Covenant, Maristan,
Lynx, Tremolino, Santa Maria
Year boat took possession of
current owner: 1999

OSPREY *was one of two Friendship sloops appearing in the movie* The Truman Show *starring Jim Carrey. The second Friendship sloop was destroyed. Hollywood needed more visible "starter" buttons built into the bulkhead rather than under the wheel. Jim Carrey destroyed the bowsprit the day before filming so a second bowsprit was quickly assembled. Other than that,* OSPREY *was in pristine shape following the movie. We found her in Florida, having been nearly abandoned by Paramount Studios.*

(See pages 67, 85, and back cover)

140

Brandywine

LOD: 26'
Builder: McKie W. Roth Jr.
Launched: 1968 Marshall, CA

Whereabouts unknown.
While we presume that this sloop is still in existence, we were unable to verify the location, condition, or the owner of the sloop.

Sea Dog

LOD: 25' Beam: 8' Draft: 4'
Homeport: Michigan City, IN
Builder: James H. Hall
Launched: 1974 Rowley, MA
Owner(s): Walter M. Hines
Former name(s): Renaiscence,
The James Hall, Katie E, Recovery
Year boat took possession of
 current owner: 2009

141

SEA DOG is undergoing a major restoration. Shown here on the custom trailer designed and built specifically for SEA DOG and in a barrel-vaulted shed designed by her owner to keep her covered and dry during the restoration.

(See page 58, 97)

142

Audrey II

LOD: 21' Beam: 6' Draft: 5'
Homeport: Tiverton, RI
Builder: Peter Archbold
Launched: 1976 Pittsford, NY
Owner(s): John H. Moran
Former name(s): Psyche, Albatross

Information provided from Friendship Sloop Society records, believed to be correct, but we were unable to get verification from the owner.

143

Fair American

LOD: 25' Beam: 8'8" Draft: 4'3"
Homeport: Redondo Beach, CA
Builder: Newman (P10) / Morris T.
Launched: 1974 Southwest Harbor, ME
Owner(s): Jim Light
Former name(s): Matelot
Year boat took possession of
current owner: 2010

144

Petrel

LOD: 25' Beam: 8'8" Draft: 4'3"
Homeport: Cataumet, MA
Builder: Newman (P09) / Morris, T.
Launched: 1974 Southwest Harbor, ME
Owner(s): Bill Lundquist
Former name(s): Ribbit, Duffer, Josie
Year boat took possession of
current owner: 2011

Just finishing a major rehab/restoration that has taken the last three years. Major things included: all new bronze seacocks; all new hoses and hose adapters (instead of threaded pipe); replaced all DC and AC wiring and instruments; installed bronze opening portholes; replaced all lights with LEDs; installed custom fitted polypropylene holding tank; all inside and outside teak and wood trim taken down to wood and new varnish built up; repaired rot in mast and bowsprit; all blocks and deadeyes stripped and new varnish built up; all serving on rigging replaced and Stockholm tarred; cabin inside painted; bilge painted white; new ash mast hoops; all stainless or chrome plated hardware replaced with bronze; replaced side opening icebox with minimal insulation with custom top-opening vacuum panel box; refinished sole; installed roller furling staysail and jiffy reefing for main, etc.   With the work done by previous owners for cushions, sails, rigging, and topside paint, she will look better than new next spring. At 40, she still turns heads.

Sabrina

145

LOD: 31' Beam: 10'8" Draft: 5'
Homeport: South Portland, ME
Builder: Newman (D02) / Lanning, Bruce
Launched: 1974 Winter Harbor, ME
Owner(s): Don Zappone
Former name(s): Snow Goose, Yankee Lady,
Deliverance
Year boat took possession of
current owner: 2005

With her second owner SABRINA would venture to Antiqua for several winters and then she would sail to Chebegue Island, Maine for the summers and return to the Chesapeake for the winters; again another owner for several years. She does know how to sail and well.

Fiddlehead

146

LOD: 25' Beam: 8'8" Draft: 4'3"
Homeport: New London, CT
Builder: Newman (P01)
Launched: 1970 Southwest Harbor, ME
Owner(s): Greg & Daneen Roth
Year boat took possession of
current owner: 2003

FIDDLEHEAD was the first fiberglass sloop out of Jarvis Newman's shop- the start of a new class. While she was the first Pemaquid, she was not the first to be launched. That honor went to SALATIA (90), #2, in 1969. FIDDLEHEAD first got wet a year later, in 1970.

FIDDLEHEAD'S real story begins with Capt. Harry Jackson who brought the boat to Connecticut in the early 1980s. At that time, the sloop sailed the local waters out of Groton, CT. For well over 20 years, she graced eastern Long Island Sound and the Thames River estuary with Capt. Harry at the helm. A fine and fair and fast boat, she placed first in class five times in the 18 years of the New London Friendship Windezvous regattas.

She was rescued from a number of years of shed storage and brought back to form.

FIDDLEHEAD has been homeported in New London since 2003 at Crocker's Boat Yard and Thames Y.C. She sails primarily local waters but cruises regularly to New York, Long Island and Rhode Island. With a new set of sails in 2012 and upgraded power, the hope is to one day make the extended sail from Connecticut to the Friendship Homecoming in Maine.

147

Mara E.
LOD: 31' Beam: 10'8" Draft: 5'
Homeport: Satans Toe (Mamaroneck), NY
Builder: Newman (D01) / Jones, J.E.
Launched: 1973 East Boothbay, ME
Owner(s): Barrie & Mara Abrams
Former name(s): Anna B., Solace
Year boat took possession of
current owner: 2000

The MARA E. has traveled from Maine to Mamaroneck in some of the worst weather. She has survived hurricane Katrina and has a new mast as a result. She has survived a lightning hit and has new electrics as a result. The vessel is an example of successful survivability on the seas of Friendship sloops! She is always the most attractive and charming boat in the harbor.

(See page 79)

149

Fiddler's Green
LOD: 25'
Homeport: Yarmouth, ME
Builder: Roy O. Jenkins
Launched: 1978 Waterville, ME
Owner(s): Dick Leighton

Information provided from Friendship Sloop Society records, believed to be correct, but we were unable to get verification from the owner.

150

Woodchips
LOD: 25'
Homeport: Unfinished, MA
Builder: Deschenes & Willett
Launched: TBL Grafton/Holden, MA
Owner(s): Neil Allen

Information provided from Friendship Sloop Society records, believed to be correct, but we were unable to get verification from the owner.

Information provided from Friendship Sloop Society records, believed to be correct, but we were unable to get verification from the owner.

(See page 34)

Departure

LOD: 14'
Homeport: Alexandria, VA
Builder: W. Prescott Gannet
Launched: 1936
Owner(s): Llewellyn Bigelow

Ollie M.

LOD: 32'
Builder: Kent F. Murphy
Launched: 1977 Swampscott, MA

Whereabouts unknown.
While we presume that this sloop is still in existence, we were unable to verify the location, condition, or the owner of the sloop.

(See page 68)

Margaret Swanson

Angelus

LOD: 22' Beam: 7'3" Draft: 3'8"
Homeport: Bass River, MA
Builder: Quoddy / Collins
Launched: 1975 Bass River, MA
Owner(s): James & Elaine Carter
Year boat took possession of current owner: 1988

The photo of ANGELUS was taken the day after Hurricane Bob '92. This picture was submitted and published in Cape Cod Life June/July 1993 as part of a photo contest. She looks much better today.
(See page 79)

154

Muscongus

LOD: 28'
Homeport: Bridgeport,CT
Builder: Albion F. Morse
Launched: 1909 Cushing, ME
Owner(s): Bruce Williams
Former name(s): Yankee Trader,
 Altair, Racer, Raider

Information provided from Friendship Sloop Society records, believed to be correct, but we were unable to get verification from the owner.

155

Queequeg

LOD: 25' Beam: 8'8" Draft: 4'3"
Homeport: Boothbay, ME
Builder: Newman (P11) / Morris, Tom
Launched: 1975 Southwest Harbor, ME
Owner(s): Richard & Beth Langton
Former name(s):The Wisdom of Solomon
Year boat took possession of
 current owner: 2000

We first discovered QUEEQUEG in a Friendship Sloop Society yearbook advertisement, announcing she was for sale in Florida. That was about the time we were getting tired of sanding and painting our wooden sloop CONTENT (#5). We had owned CONTENT for fifteen years and had been awarded the youngest crew member trophy at the annual homecoming four times. Ruthie was seven months old when she first joined our crew and Robert was eight months, but he continued to be the youngest crew member for three years on three different sloops. Not wanting to own two sloops at the same time, we put CONTENT on the market and sailed several more years until Noel March bought her. We then called the number in Florida from the old QUEEQUEG ad, but the phone was no longer in service. We finally connected when we realized that the Florida area codes had been changed. Unfortunately QUEEQUEG had been sold!

However, we found her, several owners later, sitting in the yard with a broken bowsprit. QUEEQUEG had originally been sailed to Florida and, as the story goes, was going to sail to the Bahamas. We don't think she ever made that trip, but she was set up to be sailed single-handedly. Her little coal stove was still aboard, originally installed to ward off those cool Maine evenings, and was testament to the fact that she belonged in New England. As fate seemed to dictate, QUEEQUEG was trucked back to Maine and she started the 21st century where she belonged in Boothbay Harbor. Since then our family has grown up, but we have continued to get together to sail every summer as time has allowed. We are not racers, but just enjoy the coast of Maine, the annual sloop homecoming, and the friends we have made in the Friendship Sloop Society. Now we await grandchildren so we can get back into the trophies. (See page 70)

Namaste

LOD: 31' Beam: 10'8" Draft: 5'
Homeport: Padanaram, MA
Builder: Newman (D03) / Morris, T.
Launched: 1975 Southwest Harbor, ME
Owner(s): Jerry & Penny Kriegel
Former name(s): Laperouse, Departure

Picture above taken while filming a television comercial.

Liberty

LOD: 31' Beam: 10'8" Draft: 5'
Homeport: Suttons Bay, MI
Builder: Newman (D04) / Salter, Richard
Launched: 1980 Manchester, MA
Owner(s): Inland Seas
Education Association
Year boat took possession of
current owner: 2004

Currently for sale through Jarvis Newman Marine.

(See pages 65, 73, 85)

159 *Pacific Child*

LOD: 30'6" Beam: 10' Draft: 4'6"
Builder: Bruno & Stillman (03)
Launched: 1969 Newington, NH

Whereabouts unknown.
While we presume that this sloop is still in existence, we were unable to verify the location, condition, or the owner of the sloop.

160 *Defiance*

LOD: 22'
Homeport: Chamberlain, ME
Builder: McKie W. Roth Jr.
Launched: 1973 Southport Island, ME
Owner(s): Morgan Hendry
Year boat took possession of
 current owner: 1974

In 1974, I purchased DEFIANCE, a 22' wooden Friendship Sloop, built by McKie W. Roth for Mr. Carlton Brown. Carlton Brown had the spars and rigging built by a retired Captain Kelley in Boothbay; not Mr. Roth. Carlton Brown was a family friend of the Hendry family and it was through my father I came to know about the sloop (I was only 23 at the time).

I kept the sloop at his mooring in the Gut until 1976, and then I moved it from the Gut at Southport Island to Chamberlain where my family has a summer house.

I moved the boat to Havre de Grace, Maryland in 1976 and kept it in the mouth of the Susquehanna River for about ten years. We had a great time sailing the upper Chesapeake Bay although depth of water in the flats of the upper bay was always a problem.

In 1984, I moved DEFIANCE back to Maine and sailed her until the mid-1990s when college tuitions took priority over maintenance. She was left in our garage until 2011 when I began a two-year overhaul (the Carpenter's Workshop, Bristol, and now Pemaquid Marine, New Harbor). DEFIANCE was re-launched last July and we sailed her a few times August and September, 2012; mostly in John's Bay and moored her near Fort William Henry.

161

Jenny

LOD: 22'
Homeport: Rockport,ME
Builder: Sam Guild & William Cannell
Launched: 1976 Thomaston, ME
Owner(s): Tim Clark
Former name(s): Summerwind, Damien

Information provided from Friendship Sloop Society records, believed to be correct, but we were unable to get verification from the owner.

Picture taken before Tim bought the boat and restored her.

T.B.R. Walsh

Whereabouts unknown.
While we presume that this sloop is still in existence, we were unable to verify the location, condition, or the owner of the sloop.

Reward

163

LOD: 25'
Builder: William A.Greene
Launched: 1975 Rocklin, CA

Vera Jean

164

LOD: 30'
Homeport: Choctawhatchee Bay, FL
Builder: Charles A. Morse
Launched: 1906 Friendship, ME
Owner(s): Dennis Mayhew
Former name(s): Jessie May
Year boat took possession of current owner: 1978

Have now owned VERA JEAN for 35 years. In 1978, I restored (rebuilt) her. Over the past 35 years, I have sailed her about 20,000 miles. Right now I am about 95% finished with her second rebuild with some modifications and upgrades. Hope to go cruising this winter.

(See pages 15, 32)

Reunion

165

LOD: 25'
Builder: Clifford G. Niederer
Launched: 1975 Inverness, CA
Former name(s): Skimmer

Whereabouts unknown.
While we presume that this sloop is still in existence, we were unable to verify the location, condition, or the owner of the sloop.

166

Schoodic

LOD: 25'
Homeport: Portland, ME
Builder: Concordia Co.
Launched: 1967 MA - Padanaram
Owner(s): Phineas & Joanna Sprague, Jr.

Information provided from Friendship Sloop Society records, believed to be correct, but we were unable to get verification from the owner.

167

Freedom

LOD: 28'
Homeport: Islesboro, ME
Builder: Ralph W. Stanley
Launched: 1976 Southwest Harbor, ME
Owner(s): Maldwin Drummond
Year boat took possession of
current owner: 2014

Information provided from Friendship Sloop Society records, believed to be correct, but we were unable to get verification from the owner.

(See pages 73, 75)

168

Loon

LOD: 30' Beam: 10' Draft: 5'
Homeport: Brewer, ME
Builder: Newbert & Wallace / Jacob
Launched: 1974 Thomaston, ME
Owner(s): Bruce Brown
Year boat took possession of
current owner: 2010

According to the original owners (Jacob), the name and some of the hardware were transferred from the original LOON built in the early 1900's to the new LOON built by Newbert and Wallace just before the original hull was burned. The second LOON was built on speculation during a winter lull at the boatyard and bought unfinished by the Jacobs who completed it. It was kept in the water year round in Robin Hood until the late 1980s, when it was sold and fell on hard times (and hard ground).

LOON was purchased by the current owner out of Uncle Henry's and is currently undergoing slow rehabilitation, anticipating a 2015 re-launch.

(See page 97)

Defiance

LOD: 22'
Homeport: Winthrop, MA
Builder: Eric Dow
Launched: 1976 Brooklin, ME
Owner(s): Fran Daley

Information provided from Friendship Sloop Society records, believed to be correct, but we were unable to get verification from the owner.

(See page 68)

Lady of the Wind

LOD: 31' Beam: 10'8" Draft: 5'
Homeport: Southwest Harbor, ME
Builder: Newman (D05) / Morris, T.
Launched: 1976 Southwest Harbor, ME
Owner(s): Karl Brunner
Year boat took possession of
current owner: 2004

LADY OF THE WIND has sat idle for almost nine years as I continue the endless search for time and money in the same moment so I can spend both getting her finished. She sailed for a time as a marconi rigged Friendship sloop but will now be returned to a proper gaffer. Stand by but don't hold your breath for the relaunching of LADY OF THE WIND.... In the meantime come sailing with us at Sail Acadia on one of our other two sloops here in Acadia National Park.

171 *Resolute*

LOD: 31' Beam: 10'8" Draft: 5'
Homeport: Marblehead, MA
Builder: Newman (D06) / Morris, T.
Launched: 1976 Southwest Harbor, ME
Owner(s): Alan Leibovitz
Former name(s): Golden Anchor

Information provided from Friendship Sloop Society records, believed to be correct, but we were unable to get verification from the owner.

172

Amnesty

LOD: 25' Beam: 8'6" Draft: 4'6"
Homeport: Baltimore, MD
Builder: Drake, Jim
Launched: 1982 Carlise, PA
Owner(s): Jim & Brooke Drake
Year boat took possession of current owner: 1972

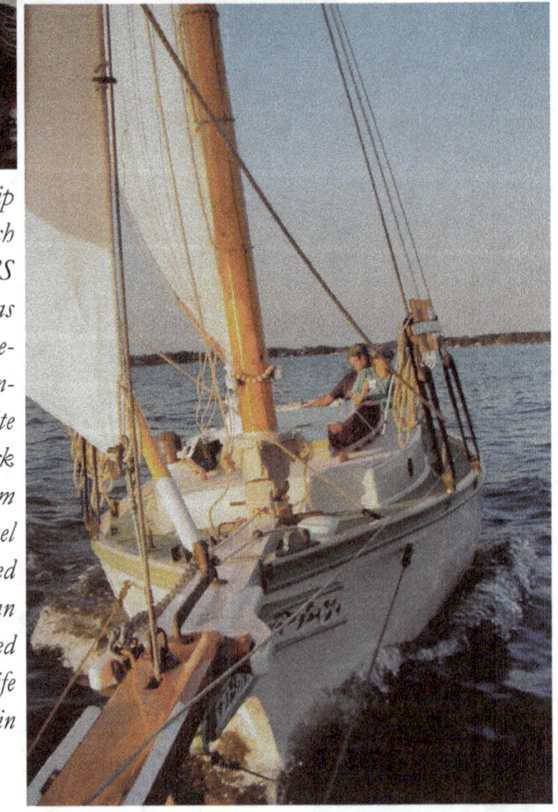

In keeping with the tradition of Friendship sloops having names that reflect traditional values such as LIBERTY, CHARITY, etc., AMNESTY'S name reflects the owner/builder's conviction that as fallible human beings, one of our greatest and most needed attributes is a capacity for forgiveness. She was built outdoors in an apple orchard in south-central Pennsylvania; the serpentine of apple blossoms on her trailboards celebrates that birthplace. She is framed with white oak and strip-planked with western red cedar. Spars are red spruce and interior woodwork is white pine and black cherry. The oak, spruce, pine, and cherry were harvested locally from trees donated by friends and family. Her deadeyes are fashioned from an offcut of the keel stock of the first PRIDE OF BALTIMORE. Her staysail club is set from a sheet-tensioned traveller that varies the draft of the sail as the sheet is set or eased - the so-called Anglemann rig. Originally rigged with topsails, she is now bald-headed, the result of a dotage-induced quest for simplicity. Auxiliary power is a Beta 14. Though she has spent most of her life on the Chesapeake, AMNESTY has made one trip to Maine for the homecoming back in 1986. We look forward to bringing her back to her home waters again one of these years.

Paul Revere

LOD: 31' Beam: 10'8" Draft: 5'
Homeport: Camden, ME
Builder: Newman (D07) / Pease
Owner(s): Dan & Kathy Pease
Year boat took possession of
 current owner: 2001

When I saw the pictures of the bare hull (Newman DICTATOR hull#7), so clean and perfect, I knew I had to have her. We had to move her sideways to avoid trees that had grown up in front of her in her 25 years of lying in wait. On the truck delivery from Brunswick to Rockport, we were running a little late and it was getting dark. The truck driver told me to follow close as he had one tail-light out. It was then that I knew what we would name her, PAUL REVERE, One if by Land... Get it? We built a temporary shed to finish her off, had to replace the plastic four times; things always seem to take longer than I think. Hmmm, now eleven years. Projects completed: Pour #6000 lead keel, twice, Whoops, Hollow Mast and boom laminated from douglas fir, all salvaged from Penobscot Bay! Full set of blocks hand-made from phenolic and stainless steel. Deck frame of black locust from downed trees in Rockport, ME. Antique store find of helm (wheel) rebuilt with new hub from old Gloucester fishing schooner; brass shaft and spoke handles from wood salvaged from HESPER and LUTHER LITTLE, ex of Wiscasset, my childhood playground! Much help from family and neighbors. There are certain milestones many home-built boats have to endure. Now we have moved, from Rockport to Camden, so that part of home building process has been completed. Move the unfinished boat. The good news is that we have a new permanent building in which to do the rest of the work. Often life gets in the way of a home building project. For example: we were unexpectedly given the use of a 28 foot sloop to use for a couple years, make that 6 years. Our young family made a lot of great memories on that boat. Then along came a little motor-sailor that was just too good to be true. Now Kathy and I plan to make an extended cruise on that boat as it seems to favor the Down-East Circle Loop and the Intercoastal Waterway. We will get back to PAUL REVERE eventually.

Edelweiss

LOD: 15'
Homeport: Friendship,ME
Builder: David Major
Launched: 1976 Friendship, ME
Owner(s): David Major

Information provided from Friendship Sloop Society records, believed to be correct, but we were unable to get verification from the owner.

Whereabouts unknown.
While we presume that this sloop is still in existence, we were unable to verify the location, condition, or the owner of the sloop.

Trumpeter

LOD: 28'
Builder: Charles A. Morse
Launched: 1878 Friendship, ME

177 *Liberty*

LOD: 19' Beam: 7' Draft: 3'6"
Homeport: Saugus, CA
Builder: Ahern (B5)
Launched: 1974
Owner(s): Tom Mehl
Year boat took possession of
current owner: 1996

I was living in Texas when I bought the boat from Tim Hoffman of Camden, Maine. I sailed it for a season on a lake, then moved to California where I undertook what became a 15-year project to completely rebuild her from the bare hull up. She was relaunched in May of 2012 and presently is berthed (year round) in Marina del Rey in sunny Southern California, where she stands out from the rest of the boats by quite a bit. She now has a topmast and a small Yanmar diesel (inboard).

178 *Nesaru*

LOD: 25' Beam: 8'8" Draft: 4'3"
Homeport: U.S. Military
Builder: Newman (P13) / C. Chase
Launched: 1977
Owner(s): Arieyeh & Barbara Austin
Former name(s): Dolphin
Year boat took possession of
current owner: 2003

NESARU was originally christened "DOLPHIN," and was owned by the Robinson family of Boston, MA. We originally referred to her as an aphrodisiac for the deprived soul as she came to us in a blessing, restoring the void created by our families' first separation by war in Iraq. When we purchased her, she had some want of repairs, and so an extensive refurbishment began from the waterline up. We renamed her "NESARU," which translates to "Wind Spirit" in a North West Native American tongue, and then transported her to Olympia, Washington, where we sailed her throughout the Puget Sound and the San Juan Islands. As the service to our country has dictated, we have continued to move her with us as we would any member of our family. She has been with us through duty stations at Fort Lewis, Washington, Fort Drum, New York, Fort Leavenworth, Kansas, and Fort Campbell, Kentucky - she has been our friend and companion. She has graced the waters of the western United States and Pacific, the Atlantic, the Great Lakes of Canada, New York and Michigan, as well as the brown waters of Perry Lake, Kansas and Lake Priest, Tennessee. She has been beaten, broken, repaired, and beaten again—but she has never failed us. Through deployments to Iraq, Afghanistan and Korea, she has always been a steady companion. To those skippers who yearn for the sweet embrace of their vessels' touch and stories yet to be made, we hope to meet up with you soon — sailing on soft winds toward a warm sunset.

Whereabouts unknown.
While we presume that this sloop is still in existence, we were unable to verify the location, condition, or the owner of the sloop.

Celene
179

LOD: 22'

180

Banshee

LOD: 25' Beam: 8'8" Draft: 4'3"
Homeport: Mattapoisett, MA
Builder: Newman (P12) / John Wojcik
Launched: 1978 Fairhaven, MA
Owner(s): John & Carole Wojcik
Year boat took possession of
 current owner: 1976

BANSHEE is named after Ben Waterworth's sloop #8, which was kept at the boatyard in Fairhaven where my dad worked. We purchased hull #12 from Jarvis Newman in November 1976 and spent over a year and a half finishing the sloop in July 1978. Our first trip to Homecoming was to Friendship in 1979, and except for three or four years, have been sailing back to homecoming as well as to events in Southwest Harbor, New London and Marblehead. For the last 20 years, BANSHEE has cruised along the Maine coast from the Cape Cod Canal with GAIVOTA #214, and more recently HEGIRA #230. We figure we have sailed BANSHEE nearly 28,000 miles along the New England coast.

(See pages 67, 68, 73)

Aurora
181

LOD: 19' Beam: 7' Draft: 3'6"
Homeport: Deer Isle, ME
Builder: Ahern (B3) / Brownie
Launched: 1975
Owner(s): Dale Young
Former name(s): Surprise, Robra

Information provided from Friendship Sloop Society records, believed to be correct, but we were unable to get verification from the owner.

Muscongus
182

LOD: 22'
Homeport: Shelter Island, NY
Builder: Apprenticeshop
Launched: 1977 Bath, ME
Owner(s): Donald Verrecchia
Former name(s): Charity

Information provided from Friendship Sloop Society records, believed to be correct, but we were unable to get verification from the owner.

183

Tara Anne

LOD: 25' Beam: 8'8" Draft: 4'3"
Builder: Newman (P14) / T. Morris
Launched: 1978 Southwest Harbor, ME
Former name(s): Silver Heels

Whereabouts unknown.
While we presume that this sloop is still in existence, we were unable to verify the location, condition, or the owner of the sloop.

184

Perseverance

LOD: 27' Beam: 9'6" Draft: 4'6"
Homeport: Montrose Harbor, Chicago, IL
Builder: Simms Yacht Yard
Launched: 1963 Scituate, MA
Owner(s): Denis & Kathie Paluch
Former name(s): Dottie G.
Year boat took possession of
  current owner: 1986

The re-build of PERSEVERANCE formerly "DOTTIE G" (An Eldridge-McInnis Design) continues to slowly progress. In 2003, at the end of the Chicago season - she sprang a leak while on her can in Montrose Harbor and went down. Turns out a plank we had the yard refasten before her spring launch seemed to be the culprit. Further inspection showed cracked ribs resulting from her previous submersion and raising when Bill Reed owned her. Initially trucked on recommendations to a boat yard in Northern Michigan - for re-building. After finding the initial work not to our liking - we called in Bruce Malone of Rockport, ME - who was highly recommended - to visit her and give us his opinion. We subsequently trucked her to Malone Boat Building Company in Rockport. The oak ribs have been replaced or sistered. The new African mahogany planking begun. The 1" teak deck has been lifted off for access and we continue to save for the final stage of restoration. We do miss the yearly varnishing of the Pigeon spruce mast and booms and hope to get her in the water in the near future. PERSEVERANCE was recently mentioned in the 314 pg. hard bound book <u>William Ernest Simms - Master Wooden Yacht Builder 1896-1986</u> by Harold G. Simms. I included pictures of "DOTTIE G." next to the 71' schooner DOROTHY G. also owned by Joseph H. Plumb—PERSEVERANCE'S first owner.

Ocean Roar

LOD: 27'
Homeport: Union, ME
Builder: J. Philip Ham
Launched: 1978
Owner(s): Leslie Taylor
Former name(s): Saro, Sine Die, Calypso
Year boat took possession of
current owner: 2002

This Friendship sloop, then called "SINE DIE", was formerly owned by U.S. Senator Christopher Dodd of Connecticut, who was one of the candidates for President in 2008. He and Senator Ted Kennedy were great friends and sailing buddies, and shared many sailing adventures on this vessel.

"SINE DIE" was also featured in two national TV commercials, one for Zocor and one for Kleenex.

Information provided from Friendship Sloop Society records, believed to be correct, but we were unable to get verification from the owner.

Ragtime Annie

LOD: 27'
Homeport: Camden, ME
Builder: Bolger / Apollonto
Launched: 1975 Camden, ME
Owner(s): Bartlett Stoodley

187

Peregrine

LOD: 26'10" Beam: 8'11" Draft: 4'6"
Homeport: Southwest Harbor, ME
Builder: Ralph W. Stanley
Launched: 1977 Southwest Harbor, ME
Owner(s): Paul & Carol Lidstrom
Year boat took possession of
current owner: 2004

Ralph W. Stanley built PEREGRINE six years after opening his boat shop. She was designed to be a replica of the AMOS SWAN, which Ralph had rebuilt with lines similar to an earlier boat, the Ventura. Two families have been owners of PEREGRINE, first Peter P. Blanchard III and his father, followed by Paul and Carol Lidstrom. PEREGRINE has won the Danforth trophy, placing in the middle of the fleet after three days of racing in Rockland. Another year she was awarded the Stanley Cup for being the best maintained wooden Friendship sloop. Adventures on PEREGRINE are never ending, ranging from thrilling to sublimely tranquil, often in the same day. One personal accomplishment was sailing without use of the engine from Rockland to Southwest Harbor, arriving safely before sunset. As simple as it sounds, it was exhilarating.

(See pages 73, 75, 92)

189

Jabberwocky

LOD: 31' Beam: 10'8" Draft: 5'
Homeport: Center Harbor, ME
Builder: Newman (D9) / Nehrbass
Launched: 1981 Port Washington, WI
Owner(s): Brad Wilkinson
Former name(s): Tradition
Year boat took possession of
current owner: 2006

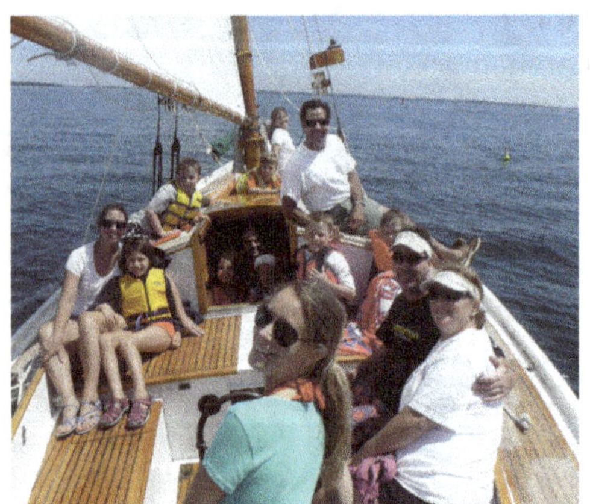

The hull was hand-laid fiberglass by Jarvis Newman in Southwest Harbor, Maine in 1981. It was then shipped to Port Washington, Wisconsin, and completed by master carpenter Roger Nehrbass over four years. She sailed the Great Lakes for twenty years, then was acquired again by Jarvis Newman. She was purchased by myself in 2006 and renamed JABBERWOCKY (from TRADITION) and loved by me and my family ever since.

Whereabouts unknown.
While we presume that this sloop is still in existence, we were unable to verify the location, condition, or the owner of the sloop.

Annabelle

LOD: 22'
Builder: Apprenciceshop
Launched: 1978 Bath, ME
Former name(s): Bauneg Beg, Muscongus, Pearle

Kervin Riggs

LOD: 22'
Homeport: Nantucket, MA
Builder: McKie W. Roth Jr.
Launched: 1977 Westport, ME
Owner(s): Bill Joyner

Information provided from Friendship Sloop Society records, believed to be correct, but we were unable to get verification from the owner.

Lady M

LOD: 32' Beam: 10' Draft: 4'7"
Homeport: South Bristol, ME
Builder: Harvey Gamage
Launched: 1978 South Bristol, ME
Owner(s): Martin Thomas & Myrna Snider
Former name(s): Lady
Year boat took possession of
current owner: 2001

I purchased "LADY," now LADY M., in 2001 from Lynwood Gamage, Harvey Gamage's son. She was Harvey's personal sloop that he had built for himself and sadly passed away before he launched her. He persuaded the Lash brothers to sell him the set of plans, which they did, but only if he swore to burn the plans after he built her AND he promptly did just that!

194

Huckleberry Belle

LOD: 25'
Homeport: Gloucester, VA
Builder: Clifford G. Niederer
Launched: 1977 Inverness, CA

Whereabouts unknown.
While we presume that this sloop is still in existence, we were unable to verify the location, condition, or the owner of the sloop.

196

Endeavor

LOD: 25'
Homeport: Southwest Harbor, ME
Builder: Ralph W. Stanley
Launched: 1979 Southwest Harbor, ME
Owner(s): Betsey Holtzmann

ENDEAVOR sank in a Rockland race in 2001. She was found, salvaged and repaired after spending 32 days on the bottom. She reverted to a bald-headed boat rig. ENDEAVOR is as good as new and a blessing to family and friends.

(See pages 73, 75, 87, 89, 90 and sidebar on page 88)

Natanya

LOD: 31' Beam: 10'8" Draft: 5'
Homeport: Greenwich, CT
Builder: Newman (D11) / Davis
Launched: 1978 Five Islands, ME
Owner(s): Joe Hliva
Former name(s): Christania

NATANYA was storm damaged when we purchased her. She was totally rebuilt to higher standards by Malcolm Pettigrow of Southwest Harbor, Maine in 1988-89, including all new Sitka spruce spars.

Bay Lady 198

The BAY LADY started carrying passengers as a new boat in Bar Harbor in 1979 under Gary Moore. Capt. Bob Fish bought her in 1983 and brought her to Boothbay Harbor. In 1985, the Witt brothers took ownership and sailed her until fall of 1994. Then Capts. Bob and Bill Campbell, of BALMY DAYS CRUISES, bought her. She is still carrying passengers from Pier 8 in Boothbay Harbor on 1-½ hour trips.

LOD: 31' Beam: 10'8" Draft: 5'
Homeport: Boothbay Harbor,ME
Builder: Newman (D12) / Bruce Lanning
Launched: 1979 Winter Harbor, ME
Owner(s): Balmy Days Cruises-
Capt. Bill Campbell
Year boat took possession of current owner: 1994

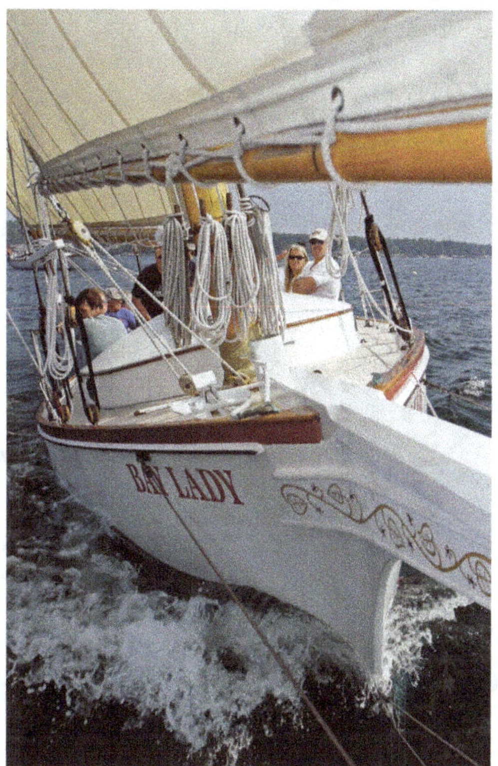

199

Wild Rose

LOD: 31' Beam: 10'8" Draft: 5'
Homeport: Newport Beach, CA
Builder: Newman (D13) / L. Thompson
Launched: 1979 Bristol, RI
Owner(s): Mike Dulien
Former name(s): Liberation, Trinity
Year boat took possession of
current owner: 2014

Information provided from Friendship Sloop Society records, believed to be correct, but we were unable to get verification from the owner.

200

Estella A.

LOD: 34'
Homeport: Mystic Seaport, CT
Builder: Robert E. McLain
Launched: 1904 Breman Long Island, ME
Owner(s): Mystic Seaport
Former name(s): New Venture
Year boat took possession of
current owner: 1957

ESTELLA A. came from Bremen Long Island, Maine. Her builder was R.E. (Rob) McLain. She was restored in 1970-72 by Newbert & Wallace in Thomaston, Maine. She was donated to Mystic Seaport by Mrs. Duncan I. Selfridge.
(See pages 18, 28)

201

Endeavor

LOD: 31' Beam: 10'8" Draft: 5'
Homeport: Nantucket, MA
Builder: Newman (D08) / James Genthner
Launched: 1979 Fairhaven, MA
Owner(s): Jim & Sue Genthner
Built by and for current owner: 1979

Jim Genthner bought the hull and deck from Jarvis Newman in 1977, and spent two years building ENDEAVOR in his parents' backyard in Fairhaven, Massachusetts. He worked as a deckhand on a research vessel from Woods Hole Oceanographic Institute to earn the money to build ENDEAVOR. He was a deckhand on the schooner BILL OF RIGHTS where he learned how to sail. After an unsuccessful attempt to charter out of the mainland, he came to Nantucket in 1982 to charter. Thirty years later, he is operating a very successful business taking out locals and visitors. Last year, Sailing Nantucket Sound- Captain Jim's Endeavor was published chronicling his journey of building ENDEAVOR and his business.

(See page 73)

202

Arrival

LOD: 31' Beam: 10'8" Draft: 5'
Homeport: Rebuilding, MA
Builder: Newman (D14) / R. Niedrach
Launched: 1981 Amherst, NH
Owner(s): John and Carole Wojcik
Year boat took possession of
 current owner: 1988

We purchased ARRIVAL in 1988 in Marion, MA where the sloop was stored after a few years of non-use. This resulted in her needing a complete rebuild as a result of over three feet of water that had accumulated in her hull. The rebuild is almost completed; a set of spars is the next and final phase of this long project.

204

Marie-Anne
LOD: 27' Beam: 7'6" Draft: 4'
Homeport: Seattle, WA
Builder: Jason Davidson / Echeverria
Launched: 1977 Stoneham, MA
Owner(s): Diana Echeverria

Information provided from Friendship Sloop Society records, believed to be correct, but we were unable to get verification from the owner.

205

Daystar
LOD: 28'6" Beam: 8'6"   Draft: 5'
Homeport: Kalamazoo, MI
Builder: Richard E. Mosher
Launched: 1989 Kalamazoo, MI
Owner(s): Richard & Sally Mosher
Year boat took possession of
current owner: 1989

DAYSTAR has sailed on Lake Michigan since she was launched on August 20, 1989. Her home port is in South Haven, Michigan, where she has sailed alongside of the Michigan Maritime Museum as a pirate ship, many times being chased and fired upon by the museum brig (FRIENDS OF GOOD WILL). DAYSTAR is now being re-caulked and seams sealed, for the next 25 years of sailing on Lake Michigan and beyond.

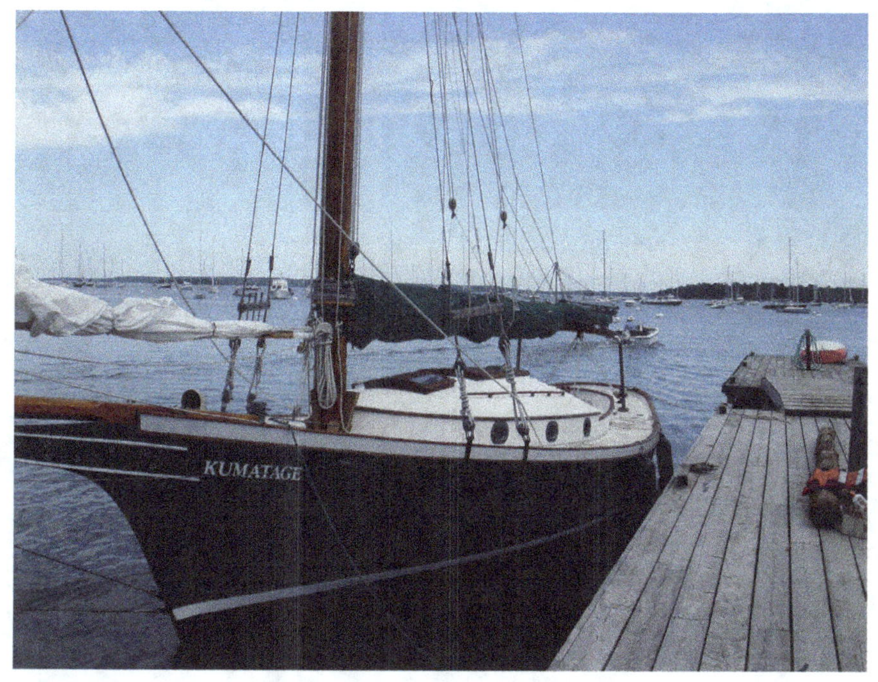

206

Kumatage

LOD: 31' Beam: 10'8" Draft: 5'
Homeport: Falmouth, ME
Builder: Newman (D15) / Chase
Launched: 1979
Owner(s): James Salmon
Former name(s): Mary Eliza, Legacy, Granuaile
Year boat took possession of current owner: 2007

KUMATAGE means the reflection of a celestial body on the sea.

208

Tupelo Honey

LOD: 31' Beam: 10'8" Draft: 5'0"
Homeport: Boston, MA
Builder: Newman (D16) / Bruce Lanning
Launched: 1981 Winter Harbor, ME
Owner(s): Donald Benoit
Former name(s): Friendship, Ladyship, Lisa K
Year boat took possession of current owner: 2009

TUPELO HONEY has become an integral figure in the social life of Boston Harbor. We offer private and public sailing adventures of various durations. She's a magical sloop. Come and join us! Our website is www.comesaila-waynow.com

209

Friend Ship

LOD: 31' Beam: 10'8" Draft: 5'
Homeport: Burlington, VT
Builder: Newman (D17) / Pettegrew
Launched: 1981 Winter Harbor, ME
Owner(s): Mike Crowley Whistling
Man Schooner Company
Year boat took possession of
current owner: 2012

The Friend Ship was built and has been used as a tour/charter boat. It was moved to Burlington, VT around 2002. We use it to offer sailing tours on Lake Champlain. It is the only sailing vessel on Lake Champlain to hold a USCG Certificate of Inspections and can carry up to 17 passengers. It is considered a prominent feature of the Burlington waterfront and listed as one of the top things to do while in Vermont.

210

Sloop John B.

LOD: 22' Beam: 7'3" Draft: 3'8"
Homeport: Canandiagua Lake, NY
Builder: Quoddy / E. Oliva
Launched: 1974
Owner(s): Russ Perrin
Former name(s): Betsy Darlin'

SLOOP JOHN B. can be found at the city pier at the north end of Canandaigua Lake. The finger lakes are 11 lakes in western New York. Canandaigua Lake is 16 miles long. I say a boat is like a horse. You don't own it, you just take care it! Why? We love it!

Left Al Perrin Right Russ Perrin and Laura Perrin rigging the boat

211

Wakeag

LOD: 22' Beam: 8' Draft: 3'6"
Homeport: Belfast, ME
Builder: Hamilton, James D.
Andover, MA
Launched: 1982
Owner(s): Dean & Robin Parker
Former name(s): Ansa,
Year boat took possession of
 current owner: 2006

Rebuilt by The Apprenticeshop in Rock-land, Maine in 2006-2007 from the keel up. We have many pictures of the rebuild and launching. Plans for new sails next year. She has a low-hour diesel 13 horsepower Kubota engine. The Apprenticeshop put over 6,000 hours into the rebuild. She is up for sale by owner due to health problems. I want a lover of these boats to own her and will price very fair. Her home port is Belfast, Maine, very near Islesboro. She is in my yard.

212

Achates

LOD: 22'
Builder: McKie W. Roth Jr.
Launched: 1980 Westport, ME

Whereabouts unknown.
While we presume that this sloop is still in existence, we were unable to verify the location, condition, or the owner of the sloop.

213 *Amie*

LOD: 25' Beam: 8'5" Draft: 4'5"
Homeport: Seattle, WA
Builder: Bob Holcomb
Launched: 1978 Ketchikan, AK
Owner(s): Harvey & C.R. Nobe
Year boat took possession of
current owner: 1995

AMIE was built between 1974 and 1978 in Ketchikan, AK and was sailed down to Puget Sound in 1980. AMIE is moored at the Center for Wooden Boats in Seattle and gives free public boat rides on Sundays.

214 *Gaivota*

LOD: 31' Beam: 10'8" Draft: 5'
Homeport: Cataumet, MA
Builder: Newman (D19) / Pettigrew
Launched: 1982 Southwest Harbor, ME
Owner(s): Colin & Kathy Whitney
Year boat took possession of
current owner: 1988

GAIVOTA came into our family a year before I retired from the US Navy in 1988, and we have been executing a "five-year-plan" for improvements ever since. We decided not to change her name to a more traditional 'Yankee' name when we were told of the origin and significance of her name in Portuguese. The original owner's family gardener, a native of Portugal, built a small sailboat for Mr. (Jack) Bush and his sister when they were children. Jack subsequently named my Friendship sloop GAIVOTA because of this childhood connection. Additionally, if you approach the name from the nautical tradition of ship names, it fits very well as a 'lucky' name. Seven letters for the seven seas, a predominance of vowels, multiple 'A's, and named after a sea creature – the enduring seagull. I've also been told that it is a gaivota that carries a lost sailor's soul to heaven, by-passing the bargeman at the River Styx, for he has no coin to pay the passage.

For the last 20+ years, we have had the privilege of cruising the New England coast in the company of John and Carole Wojcik in BANSHEE of Mattapoisett and now Laurie Raymond and Rusty Strange in HEGIRA of Woods Hole and hope to increase this Southern Massachusetts Squadron in years to come.

(See pages 68, 93)

Whereabouts unknown.
While we presume that this sloop is still in existence, we were unable to verify the location, condition, or the owner of the sloop.

Ellen Anne

LOD: 22' Beam: 7'3" Draft: 3'8"
Builder: Passamaquoddy Yachts
Launched: 1968

(See pages 79, 80)

Amity

LOD: 39' Beam: 12' Draft: 6'
Homeport: Reygades, France
Builder: W. Scott Carter
Launched: 1941 Friendship, ME
Owner(s): John F. Nichols
Year boat took possession of
 current owner: 1980

A man named Plotkin owned the boat for 30 years (maybe 1947-1977) and since he apparently owned a lumberyard and had money, he kept her in excellent shape. I think I was the 5th owner, starting in 1980, never dreaming I'd one day own it longer than Plotkin. Unfortunately, AMITY has gradually deteriorated because I haven't had the funds, the time and the skills to keep up with it. But I am gradually now making progress in retirement and just the fact that AMITY is now sitting behind my house in the middle of France is not a bad achievement. She has escaped the wrecker's ball, I'm 77 but still fairly active so I hope I'll last long enough to achieve a respectable restoration.

My vocation for the most part has been as a corporate pilot. I was working with a company in Connecticut for several years when this U.S. company sold one of its subsidiaries to a British company. I was selected to establish and manage this new flight department which was initially based at Heathrow in London and later at Farnborough. We moved to the UK in 1989, quite excited with this new life, but we were now stuck with AMITY still in the USA. We had spent so much time and money trying to restore her that we couldn't bear the idea of selling or abandoning her, so we spent the full $10,000 of our moving allowance in having her shipped to Ipswich in the UK.

Next chapter was that we had her trucked to a marina in South London on the Thames (about 1994) as we had moved to be near my wife's job. There AMITY remained until we found a special Moulin property of 30 acres in central France (the Corréze),

where she was trucked again (about 2007) to finally settle in a perfect position behind our house. If I could have known how much money I would eventually spend on maintaining and transporting her, I would probably have abandoned the project early on. Yet it is through owning AMITY that I met my wife which has been the best "thing" that ever happened to me so there is powerful sentimentality prominent in all this! My wife's employment eventually led to our gaining British nationality which enabled me to take a job as a flight simulator instructor at Le Bourget airport north of Paris. That employment and residence in France has allowed me to apply for French nationality which appears very likely to be approved eventually (takes some time to get through bureaucracy in Paris). So even if the UK makes the insane decision to pull out of the EU, we'll be untouchable!

217

Addy Claire

LOD: 33' Beam: 11' Draft: 4'5"
Homeport: Southwest Harbor, ME
Builder: Shoreline Boats
Launched: 1972 Atlantic City, NJ
Owner(s): Shane and Paula Dowsland
Former name(s): Odyssey, Ophelia's Odyssey
Year boat took possession of
 current owner: 2008

*Hoping to paint boat this winter, changed
her name to ADDY CLAIRE in 2014.*
(See page 67)

218

William M. Rand

LOD: 22'
Homeport: Cundy's Harbor, ME
Builder: John B. Rand
Launched: 1982 Lincoln, MA
Owner(s): John & Lori Rand
Year boat took possession of
current owner: 1982

*There have been many fine sails and memories
aboard the WILLIAM M. RAND. We have not had
to rebuild, but usually there is a little something to do
each spring! The boat has been in the same family for
31 years.*
(See pages 62, 68)

Yankee Belle

LOD: 23'
Homeport: Sag Harbor, NY
Builder: Paul G. Edwards
Launched: 1983 Mattituck, NY
Owner(s): Jeffrey Sander

219

220

Sorceress

LOD: 31' Beam: 10'8" Draft: 5'
Homeport: Phippsburg, ME
Builder: Newman (D20) / Pettigrew
Launched: 1984 Southwest Harbor, ME
Owner(s): Ruy & Tamara Gutierrez
Former name(s): Aikane II, Amor, Brujo

221

Seal

LOD: 22' Beam: 7'3" Draft: 3'8"
Homeport: Squirrel Island, ME
Builder: Ahern (01) / Al Zink
Launched: 1984 Andover, MA
Owner(s): John & Debby Kerr
Former name(s): Viking
Year boat took possession of
current owner: 2007

(See pages 79, 80)

222

Elspeth MacEwan

LOD: 18'
Homeport: Sebago Lake, ME
Builder: Richard L. McInnes
Launched: 1982 Belpre, OH
Owner(s): Robert C. Tupper
Former name(s): Lady Jane, Lady Jeanne

Information provided from Friendship Sloop Society records, believed to be correct, but we were unable to get verification from the owner.

223

Corregidor

LOD: 25' Beam: 8'8" Draft: 4'3"
Homeport: Salem Bay, CT
Builder: Newman (P17) / P. Chase
Launched: 1981 Blue Hill, ME
Owner(s): Brian Flynn
Former name(s): Hostess, New Venture

Information provided from Friendship Sloop Society records, believed to be correct, but we were unable to get verification from the owner.

224

True Love

LOD: 19'
Builder: Jim Wainwright
Launched: 1983 Gig Harbor, WA

Whereabouts unknown.
While we presume that this sloop is still in existence, we were unable to verify the location, condition, or the owner of the sloop.

Jim Wainwright

After I sold the boat, I lost track of the new owner. He was from the Friendship area and fell in love at first sight. I was a member of the Friendship Sloop Society for a number of years, but dropped out after the sale.
Jim Wainwright

Jim Wainwright

Whereabouts unknown.
While we presume that this sloop is still in existence, we were unable to verify the location, condition, or the owner of the sloop.

Philip J. Nichols

LOD: 28'
Homeport: Salem, MA
Builder: Philip J. Nichols
Launched: 1981 Round Pound, ME

Desireé

LOD: 31' Beam: 10'8" Draft: 5'
Homeport: Ipswich, MA
Builder: Larry Plummer
Launched: 1993 Newbury, MA
Owner(s): Jim and Janice Thoen
Year boat took possession of
 current owner: 2013

The Plumer family's love affair with Friendship Sloops started in the early 1980s when Deb and Larry Plumer had sailed up to Kennebunkport, Maine in a catboat and were fogged in for days. A beautiful Friendship named SCHOODIC asked to tie up to us. Thus began our long friendship with Bruce Lanning and the Friendship Sloop Society. Our quest to have our own Friendship was fulfilled when we purchased a cedar planked hull from the Sparrow family in 1981. We moved the hull to Larry's carpentry shop and Larry began the arduous process of building the sloop. His expertise in architectural woodwork was reflected in every piece of work completed on DESIREÉ. Over the next 12 years and 2 children later, in June,1993, DESIREÉ was launched amidst much fanfare, cannon salutes and a christening complete with the smashing of a bottle of bootleg liquor. One month later, with a crew who never sailed, we left Newburyport for a Friendship rendezvous in Bath, Maine. Our children, Carol, age 8, Kevin, age 5, and Deb quickly learned to navigate, sail, look for buoys, but, most importantly, we found out what it was like to spend true, uninterrupted quality time with family. We would drop anchor each evening and spend the night looking for constellations, playing games and being together. We were embraced by the Friendship Sloop Society as our young family would gather with other sloop families and play on the docks, play pick up whiffle ball games and 'race' our sloops. Racing was never important to us. We had much more fun throwing water balloons and enjoying the company of so many other families who enjoyed the simple pleasures in life - time with family. Our best family memories were aboard DESIREÉ. Our 3rd child, Jason, was able to join us on some trips to Jewell Island before we retired from sailing. Our children would go down below while we were underway and create endless fantasy stories with stuffed animals and look for the many treats we had stowed away for the journey! This was a treasured time for us that truly formed and strengthened our family's bonds. Upon returning from Maine one summer, we were just past the Isle of Shoals when we noticed quite a chop in the water up ahead. Knowing there were no rocks, this was a very curious sight. Soon we were sailing with hundreds of dolphins!! Can you imagine the delight of our children, sitting atop the cabin top, watching this unfold? We even had a whale surface, then go under the boat!! Amazing memories that are etched in our hearts and minds forever. On our first voyage home after spending three weeks onboard DESIREÉ, we set course for the Merrimac River, our homeport. I clearly remember saying to Larry, "Oh how I wish we could just live on this boat, home school the kids and truly enjoy life." That is how much DESIREÉ meant to our family. DESIREÉ was sold to Jim Thoen of Rowley, MA in Dec., 2013. We sincerely hope that his family enjoys the rich blessings that come with spending time with family aboard DESIREÉ.

(See page 64, 83)

227 *Celebration*

LOD: 25' Beam: 8'8" Draft: 4'3"
Homeport: Bayville, ME
Builder: Newman (P15) / G. Hodgon
Launched: 1980
East Boothbay, ME
Owner(s): Greg & Annette Merrill
Former name(s): Vesper A. Leach
Year boat took possession of
current owner: 1986

The Hodgdon yard in East Boothbay, Maine started building sailing ships in 1816 and now, more than 400 vessels later, builds high tech "mega-yachts." During a slow period in 1980, Sonny Hodgden had Newman Pemaquid hull #15 delivered to East Boothbay for finishing. Despite the speculative nature of the project, Sonny finished her to high standards including solid teak decking. John Newton, who at the time had a marine antiques business in Wiscasset, bought the finished boat and named her VESPER A. LEACH. The Merrill's bought her in 1986 and renamed her "CELEBRATION"—a name which has proven prophetic as the entire family has "celebrate(d so many) good times" over the past 27 years. Even the adventures, such as the engine burning oil off Owls Head and conversion of part of the top mast to drift wood off Port Clyde, make good stories that are now told with a smile. In addition to frequent day sails, CELEBRATION and the Merrills have attended every homecoming regatta except for the year when the owners were distracted by a barn raising. The objective during the first races was to stay as far out of the way as possible which, apparently, did not happen during the race that preceded a "barging" discussion at the next skipper's meeting. Despite usually having more crew members than any other boat in its division, CELEBRATION has had it's share of success over the years. After all, it seems that inviting everyone who wants to sail is a good way to celebrate the spirit of friendship.

228

Mermaid

LOD: 22' Beam: 7'3" Draft: 3'8"
Homeport: Boothbay Harbor, ME
Builder: Ahern (09) / Fitzgerald
Launched: 1988 Walpole, MA

Information provided from Friendship Sloop Society records, believed to be correct, but we were unable to get verification from the owner.

Capt'n George

LOD: 30'6" Beam: 10' Draft: 4'6"
Homeport: Mystic, CT
Builder: Bruno & Stillman (09)
 Launched: 1970 Newington, NH
Owner(s): Joan Durant
Former name(s): Jenniver

Information provided from Friendship Sloop Society records, believed to be correct, but we were unable to get verification from the owner.

229

230

Hegira

LOD: 25' Beam: 8'4" Draft: 4'
Homeport: Woods Hole, MA
Builder: McKie W. Roth Jr.
Launched: 1980 Westport, ME
Owner(s): Laurie Raymond
Year boat took possession of
current owner: 1997

HEGIRA, meaning "flight" or "journey" in Arabic, came to her current home port of Woods Hole, Massachusetts after sitting derelict for many years in a boatyard in Stonington, Connecticut, due to the illness of her original owner. While celebrating my father's 80th birthday in nearby Mystic, we spotted her under a heap of rotting canvas and it was love at first sight. She required some spiffing up and, since then, has frequented the waters of Vineyard Sound, Buzzards Bay and the Elizabeth Islands with many happy souls aboard. In recent years, she's grown a bit restless and has set her sails for the rugged shores of Maine in the company of like-minded sloops. She is greatly loved and pampered and returns the effort with seaworthiness, beauty and dependability.

(See pages 79, 93)

231 *Solomon Gundy*

LOD: 22'
Homeport: Branford, CT
Builder: Roth / Butcher
Launched: 1984
Owner(s): Bill Butcher

Information provided from Friendship Sloop Society records, believed to be correct, but we were unable to get verification from the owner.

232 *Compromise*

LOD: 22' Beam: 7'3" Draft: 3'8"
Homeport: Scituate, MA
Builder: Ahern (08) / White
Launched: 1979
Owner(s): Peter & Nancy Toppan
Former name(s):Carolyn
Year boat took possession of
current owner:1986

First assembled by Patrick Ahern of New England Yachts for George White, the former "CAROLYN" was substantially improved by Peter and Nancy on the recommendations of Al Zink, owner of Ahern hull #1, SEAL, and Bernie MacKenzie, founder of the Society, who quickly spotted a new Friendship sloop in town. The addition of bulkheads, deck support beams and coamings allowed COMPROMISE to become a functional daysailer. She has never been outfitted for cruising; however, she is a joy to sail along the coast outside of Scituate Harbor. The name change to COMPROMISE reflects the classic wooden boat design built of a more modern material-fiberglass. She is a true "COMPROMISE" of the old and new approaches.   Roger and Mary Duncan of EASTWARD actually gave us permission to buy her as a true Friendship when we sailed with them in August of 1986. We continue to add wooden components to the glass hull and now have the traditional tasks each year of painting and varnishing. She continues to be a great COMPROMISE.   (See pages 68, 79, 80)

233 *Princess Pat*

LOD: 22'
Homeport: Titusville, FL
Builder: Harry Armstrong
Launched: 1987 Winter Park, FL
Owner(s): Harry Armstrong

Information provided from Friendship Sloop Society records, believed to be correct, but we were unable to get verification from the owner.

Beatrice Morse

234

LOD: 22'
Homeport: Stony Creek, CT
Builder: Roth / Owens
Launched: 1985 Stony Creek, CT
Owner(s): William Owens
Former name(s): Elizabeth Jane

235

Finest Kind

LOD: 22' Beam: 7'5" Draft: 3'6"
Homeport: Whidbey Island, WA
Builder: Sam Guild / Geoff Heath
Launched: 1981 Cushing, ME
Owner(s): Mike & Karen Looram
Former name(s): Manana
Year boat took possession of
current owner: 1981

Aunty Poole

236

LOD: 25'
Builder: Harry Bryant
Launched: 1970 Westport, MA

Whereabouts unknown.
While we presume that this sloop is still in existence, we were unable to verify the location, condition, or the owner of the sloop.

237 *Christine*

LOD: 19' Beam: 7' Draft: 3'6"
Homeport: Rockland, ME
Builder: Ahern (B1) / Patten
Launched: 1975 Kittery, ME
Owner(s): Ed Glaser
Former name(s): R.V. Winkle
Year boat took possession of
current owner: 2014

(See page 79)

238 *Viking*

LOD: 22' Beam: 7'3" Draft: 3'8"
Homeport: Lynn, MA
Builder: Ahern / Ulwick
Launched: 1980 Wakefield, MA
Owner(s): Steve Ulwick

Information provided from Friendship Sloop Society records, believed to be correct, but we were unable to get verification from the owner.

(See page 79)

239 *Chebacco*

LOD: 30'6" Beam: 10' Draft: 4'6"
Homeport: Jupiter, FL
Builder: Bruno & Stillman (22) / M. Ginn
Launched: 1987 Essex, MA
Owner(s): Michael Ginn
Former name(s): Pelican

Information provided from Friendship Sloop Society records, believed to be correct, but we were unable to get verification from the owner.

(See page 68)

240 *Raven*

LOD: 26'
Builder: Rodney Reed
Launched: 1965 Boothbay, ME

Whereabouts unknown.
While we presume that this sloop is still in existence, we were unable to verify the location, condition, or the owner of the sloop.

241 *Blue Sands*

LOD: 34'
Builder: Boston Boat Boat
Launched: 1986 Gloucester, MA
Owner(s): Walt Disney Studios
Former name(s): Amaryllis

Information provided from Friendship Sloop Society records, believed to be correct, but we were unable to get verification from the owner.

Tecumseh

LOD: 36' Beam: 11'6" Draft: 6'
Homeport: Port Credit, Ontario, CN
Builder: Charles A. Morse
Launched: 1902
Owner(s): David Frid
Year boat took possession of
current owner: 1998

TECUMSEH *was a totally unplanned, spontaneous purchase in 1998 from Dan Traylor, lying in Fort Lauderdale. Three days and my life was irrevocably changed. The previous owner to Dan lived aboard* TECUMSEH *in the Miami River till the end of his life circa 1960. (some times I feel there is an oman there) She is a heavy, well-founded, seaworthy hull and we have felt secure aboard her on many a multi day offshore passage.* TECUMSEH *is the oldest registered vessel in Canada.*

(See page 94 and Preface)

Erin

LOD: 22' Beam: 7'3" Draft: 3'8"
Homeport: Orr's Island, ME
Builder: Ahern(05) Hersey Launched: 1979
Owner(s): Anne Del Borgo &
Robert Norwood
Former name(s): John Patrick
Year boat took possession of
current owner: 2001

Originally named ERIN, name changed to JOHN PATRICK, and then changed back to ERIN, which was her name at the time we purchased her.

244

Windemere

LOD: 30'6" Beam: 10' Draft: 4'6"
Homeport: Lucedale, MS
Builder: Bruno & Stillman (18)
Launched: 1971
Owner(s): Steve & Ginny Kell
Former name(s): Maui, West Indianman,
Rebecca Ames

Information provided from Friendship Sloop Society records, believed to be correct, but we were unable to get verification from the owner.

245

La Paloma

LOD: 25'
Homeport: Seattle, WA
Builder: Unknown
Launched: 1969 B.C. Canada
Owner(s): John J. Caldbick

Information provided from Friendship Sloop Society records, believed to be correct, but we were unable to get verification from the owner.

246

Dame-Mariscotta

LOD: 19' Beam: 7' Draft: 3'6"
Homeport: East Boothbay, ME
Builder: Ahern(B6) / Shelley
Launched: 1983
Owner(s): Hans P. Sinn

Information provided from Friendship Sloop Society records, believed to be correct, but we were unable to get verification from the owner.

Black Star

LOD: 35' Beam: 11'6" Draft: 5'11"
Homeport: West Boothbay, ME
Builder: Apprenticeshop
Launched: 1989 Rockland, ME
Owner(s): Ted Walsh, Judy Heininger,
and the Wilson-Charles Family
Former name(s): Rita II, Rita
Year boat took possession of
current owner: 2000

Built for Frank Snyder, the then Commodore of the New York Yacht Club, in 1989, the BLACK STAR is a copy of a 1903 Wilbur Morse Sloop RITA (evidence suggests her original name was RIETTA). Mr. Snyder had been one of the last owners of the RITA and wanted to recreate the boat he had owned in the 1940s—without the leaks and the rot.

Since we became caretakers of this boat in 2000, we rebuilt her interior to make it more functional and it has become our second home. For the first three years that we sailed the boat, we cruised from Kittery, ME to the Bay of Fundy in Canadian waters and back, and, for eleven years, BLACK STAR was known for Saxon, our ship's wolf who passed away in 2011.

(See page 81, 93)

Information provided from Friendship Sloop Society records, believed to be correct, but we were unable to get verification from the owner.

Timber

LOD: 22'
Homeport: South Lyme, CT
Builder: Rick Conant / Greg Fisher
Launched: 1979
Owner(s): Greg Hickey
Former name(s): Dolly Parton

249

Baby Blue

LOD: 25' Beam: 8'8" Draft: 4'3"
Homeport: Burlington, VT
Builder: Newman(P18) / Pettigrew
Launched: 1983
Owner(s): Scott & Sally Johnson
Former name(s): Bonnie Blue
Year boat took possession of
  current owner: 1990

BABY BLUE #249 was launched in 1983 as BONNIE BLUE and has sailed on Lake Champlain since 1990 in the company of her big sister, FRIENDSHIP hull #209, a 31' Dictator. "In 1982, the eighteenth and most recent boat of the Pemaquid class to be built by Jarvis Newman, Inc.—by then no longer owned by Newman. She was a 'super custom' model, with lots of extras such as a teak deck, Newman explains. Estimated to cost about twice that of the more conventional model of the twenty-five-footer". (Excerpt from <u>Boating Down East</u>, *May 1988, "Sitting Pretty").*

250

Belford Gray

LOD: 28'6" Beam: 9'6"   Draft: 5'4"
Homeport: Brooklin, ME
Builder: WoodenBoat School
Launched: 1992 Brooklin, ME
Owner(s): Woodenboat School
Year boat took possession of
  current owner: 1992

BELFORD GRAY was designed by Joel White and Wilbur A. Morse, and named in honor of a very special friend and former instructor at WoodenBoat School, located in Brooklin, Maine. This handsome vessel was built with the talents and dedication of many enthusiastic students working under the guidance of master builder, Gordon Swift. The boat was lofted, built, and launched over a period of 14 weeks! Launched in 1992, BELFORD GRAY has performed admirably over the years as a floating classroom for WoodenBoat School. With the feel of a real vessel under sail, BELFORD GRAY provides each student with a safe and enjoyable learning environment in which to sharpen his or her own skills afloat. With an easy motion, she deals with the wind and sea confidently - a common trait among Friendship sloops. She is fun to sail and may be the perfect boat in which to gain a better understanding of the art of seamanship.*

(See pages 80, 81)

Bucephalus

LOD: 19'
Homeport: Rubicon Bay, CA
Builder: Ralph W. Stanley
Launched: 1986 Southwest Hrbr, ME
Owner(s): Alexander J. Forbes

Information provided from Friendship Sloop Society records, believed to be correct, but we were unable to get verification from the owner.

(See pages 66, 68)

-None-

LOD: 30'
Homeport: Building, ME
Builder: Harry Quick / J.R. Sherman
Launched: TBL
Owner(s): Jeff Prosser

Information provided from Friendship Sloop Society records, believed to be correct, but we were unable to get verification from the owner.

Iolar

LOD: 26' Beam: 7' Draft: 3'4"
Homeport: Bucks County, PA
Builder: W. McCarthy & G. Richards
Launched: 1989
Owner(s): William L. McCarthy
Year boat took possession of
 current owner: 1989

My boat is a "Pemaquid" type white cedar on white oak ribs with teak sprung decks and, since I had a bout of skin cancer, I would like to sell it.

254
Northern Lady

LOD: 22' Beam: 7'3" Draft: 3'8"
Homeport: Pine Beach, NJ
Builder: Passamaquody(02)/Corea
Launched: 1972
Owner(s): Tim & Katie Crowell
Former name(s): Chaos, Whisper, Quintessence
Year boat took possession of current owner: 1997

My parents purchased CHAOS #254 in 1997-98, renamed her QUINTESSENCE, and sailed her for several years on the Toms River. They eventually bought a home in Pine Beach, NJ on the Toms River so they could sail her more frequently. A fire destroyed their house about nine years ago and they were forced to keep the sloop dry docked. The house was re-built, but the sloop never made it back in the water. Several years later, my mother threatened to sell the boat if I didn't do anything with it. So four years ago, I cut off the shrink wrap and found three feet of standing water inside the boat. The entire interior of the boat was rotted out and filled with mold. The exterior wood work had lost its varnish coating and was grayed. I was concerned she had been neglected for too long. Having worked at Eric Goetz Custom Boats in R.I. as a boat builder after college, I began pumping the water out of the boat. I restored the interior and replaced all of the running rigging so we could go sailing that summer. I had just met my wife and was glad to be able to take her sailing. I was fortunate enough to be contacted by Peter Toppan through the FSS Facebook page. Peter was able to provide me with hull and rigging plans for our boat. I have now inundated him with questions on how he has his boat set up. He was quick to reply with pictures and advice. He has been great. Every summer we take on another task. We cleaned up the exterior woodwork and varnished all of it. We had some minor damage during Hurricane Sandy, but we will look to finish repairs this spring. My wife and I welcomed a daughter in June so the boat didn't make it into the water last summer. We've decided to put her up for sale and are hoping to find a good home for her. We are undecided about putting her in the water this year with a little one. We will wait and see.

255
Genevieve

LOD: 25' Beam: 8'6" Draft: 4'6"
Homeport: San Diego, CA
Builder: Emmet Jones
Launched: 1982 Vista, CA
Owner(s): Lamonte Krause & Stacy Patterson
Year boat took possession of current owner: 2003

GENEVIEVE arrived with an old photo album documenting the cold mold process they used and the rest of her construction. We knew the builder was Emmet Jones and the photos showed an older man and two younger men working on her hull. We also got a framed set of plans that were tattered, stained and hard to read. The word "Pemaquid" was on that plan. We thought that was her original name, until we found her listed on the Friendship Sloop website and figured out it was her class. It appeared she might have been built in Costa Mesa, CA. A plaque in the boat said "commissioned in 1982." The person we bought her from was the third owner. The man who had her built sold her about a year or so after she was completed.

Two months after she came to San Diego, she was a star at the Wooden Boat Show. The third person aboard her was visiting from Arizona and couldn't believe he'd found the GENEVIEVE. He had sailed aboard the GENEVIEVE with his Uncle Vince. The family had wondered what had become of her. The boat was named after his Aunt Genevieve who was a starlet in Hollywood in the 1940s. His Uncle was an industrial architect who worked in Mideastern countries. He had been interested and charmed by the Friendship sloop design. The nephew had no specific reason why he sold the boat and informed us his uncle had passed away a few years ago.

Salty Dog

257

LOD: 28' Beam: 9'9" Draft: 6'
Homeport: Dunedin, FL
Builder: Dave Westphal
Launched: 1992 Key Largo, FL
Owner(s): Michael Shoff and Jennifer Hall
Former name(s): Toddy B.
Year boat took possession of
current owner: 2014

Whereabouts unknown.
While we presume that this sloop is still in existence, we were unable to verify the location, condition, or the owner of the sloop.

Kim

258

LOD: 22'
Builder: Harold Burnham
Launched: 1992 Essex, MA

(See pages 68,83)

Duchess

259

LOD: 28' Beam: 9'9" Draft: 6'5"
Homeport: Boston, MA
Builder: Steve Merrill / Roland Shepard
Launched: 1992
Owner(s): Christopher and
Cheryl Preston
Former name(s): Spartan
Year boat took possession of
 current owner: 2003

Owning a Friendship sloop was a dream my wife and I had after we first sailed aboard the ENDEAVOR in Nantucket back in 1991. We found DUCHESS (at that time named SPARTAN) for sale in the back of a Points East Magazine in 2003. Well, we looked at it and determined it needed a lot of work. So what did we do? We bought it. DUCHESS is a onetime take off of the original wooden boat DUCHESS, built by W. A. Morse in 1898. We have information regarding the boat's owners from approximately 1940. DUCHESS was owned by Rees Mitchell for about 40 years and it could be found on a mooring in Prettymarsh Harbor, Maine. In 1981 it came ashore from its mooring during a storm and was partially damaged and was then given to Steve Merrill in Brewer, Maine, who created a mold from the wooden hull and only one fiberglass replica of the hull was made. The boat was then sold to Mr. Frickett who sold it to Roland and Virginia Shepard. Roland and Virginia continued the rebuild by having interior work and engine installation done by B&W Marine in Brunswick, Maine. In 1992, Roland and Virginia launched the boat under the name SPARTAN. We purchased the boat in 2003 and continued the rebuild process by adding running lights, a water system, waste system and finishing off the interior. We documented the boat under its original name DUCHESS and launched it again in 2006. We have been using it as a charter boat in Boston Harbor since 2009 under Duchess of Boston Sailing Charters, LLC. We enjoyed being part of the rebuild that saved this Friendship sloop. The enjoyment it brings our customers makes the time and effort spent to bring her back to life worthwhile.

260 Nimble

LOD: 25'
Homeport: Halifax, NS
Builder: Nelson Cutler / Kim Smith
Launched: 1994
Owner(s): Christopher Zimmer

Information provided from Friendship Sloop Society records, believed to be correct, but we were unable to get verification from the owner.

261

Bluenose

LOD: 19'
Homeport: Annapolis, MD
Builder: David Holmes
Launched: 1974
Owner(s): Charly Holmes

Information provided from Friendship Sloop Society records, believed to be correct, but we were unable to get verification from the owner.

262

I Got Wings

LOD: 22' Beam: 7'3" Draft: 3'8"
Homeport: Stonington, CT
Builder: Ahern(04) / Almedia
Launched: 1980
Owner(s): Tamara Stoddard, Daniel Gordon, and Eric Austin
Former name(s): Gypsy
Year boat took possession of current owner: 2008

We took over this gorgeous sloop from Binnacle Wright in 2008. We sailed it for three seasons around Fishers Island Sound and the New London/Mystic area. We hope to bring it to New York City in the coming years. I GOT WINGS is currently in Mystic undergoing a major renovation. We hope to have it back up and sailing down in New York Harbor soon!

Ralph W. Stanley

LOD: 21'
Homeport: Olbia, Sardinia, IT
Builder: Ralph W. Stanley
Launched: 1998 Southwest Harbor, ME
Owner(s): Anne Franchetti

263

Information provided from Friendship Sloop Society records, believed to be correct, but we were unable to get verification from the owner.

(See page 83)

264

Margaret F.

LOD: 24' Beam: 8' Draft: 4'7"
Homeport: Falmouth, ME
Builder: Dave & Loretta Westphal
Launched: 1998 Falmouth, ME
Owner(s): Block Island Maritime Funding
Year boat took possession of
current owner: 2001

During our time with MARGARET F., we used her largely as a daysailer in and around Gloucester with occasional overnights in local venues. We occasionally took part in various races in Gloucester and down in Marblehead, without the success achieved by the builder, David Westphal, at the annual races in Rockland in the years after she was launched. I believe he was "first overall" one year. As of December 2013, MARGARET F. is in excellent condition with the smell of fresh cedar still strong in her cabin.

265

Maria Emilia

LOD: 25'
Homeport: Ovalle, Chile
Builder: Rafael Prohens
Launched: 1998 Ovalle, Chile
Owner(s): Rafael Prohens
Year boat took possession
of current owner: 1998

266

Malisa Ann

LOD: 22' Beam: 7'3" Draft: 3'8"'
Homeport: Winterport, ME
Builder: Ahern/Hilburn
Launched: 1992
Owner(s): Steve Blessington
Former name(s): Zazupitts

Information provided from Friendship Sloop Society records, believed to be correct, but we were unable to get verification from the owner.

267

Tristan

LOD: 25' Beam: 8'8" Draft: 4'6"
Homeport: Southwest Harbor, ME
Builder: Joe Bernier
Launched: 1980 Quebec
Owner(s): Rick & Debbie Smith

Information provided from Friendship Sloop Society records, believed to be correct, but we were unable to get verification from the owner.

Prydwyn of Lamorna
LOD: 25'
Homeport: Fremantle, AU
Builder: Unknown
Launched: 1977 Fremantle
Owner(s): Brian Cross

Information provided from Friendship Sloop Society records, believed to be correct, but we were unable to get verification from the owner.

Information provided from Friendship Sloop Society records, believed to be correct, but we were unable to get verification from the owner.

(See pages 75, 83)

Acadia
LOD: 28'
Homeport: Dartmouth, UK
Builder: Ralph W. Stanley
Launched: 1998 Southwest Harbor
Owner(s): Adrian Edmondson

Information provided from Friendship Sloop Society records, believed to be correct, but we were unable to get verification from the owner.

Josephine
LOD: 25'
Homeport: Marion, MA
Builder: Nelson Cutler
Launched: 1985
Owner(s): Ron Wisner

Jasmine
LOD: 18' Beam: 6'4"
Homeport: Alberta, CN
Builder: Pete Donahoe
Launched: 1985 British Columbia
Owner(s): Patrick S. McMahon
Former name(s): Hummingbird

Information provided from Friendship Sloop Society records, believed to be correct, but we were unable to get verification from the owner.

272 *Tamara*

LOD: 35'
Homeport: Coecles Harbor, NY
Builder: Richard Stanley, and Ralph W. Stanley
Launched: 2004 Southwest Harbor, ME
Owner(s): Sean & Tamara McCarthy

Information provided from Friendship Sloop Society records, believed to be correct, but we were unable to get verification from the owner. *(See page 94 and Preface)*

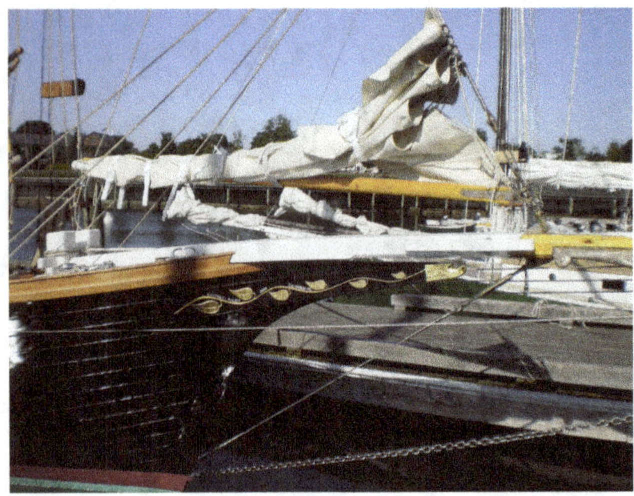

273 *Summerjoy*

LOD: 19'
Homeport: Greenport, NY
Builder: Ralph W. Stanley
Launched: 1989
Owner(s): Lyor Cohen

Information provided from Friendship Sloop Society records, believed to be correct, but we were unable to get verification from the owner.

Remedy

Accurately built to plans by Howard Chapelle from the Museum of History and Technology, part of the National Museum of American History, Smithsonian Institute.

The boat is featured on page 94 of the book <u>Down Below: Aboard the World's Classic Yachts</u> by Mathew Walker.

LOD: 25′ Beam: 8′6″ Draft: 4′6″
Homeport: Port Townsend, WA
Builder: James Lyons
Launched: 1977
Owner(s): Todd Uecker
Year boat took possession of
current owner: 2013

Viking

Information provided from Friendship Sloop Society records, believed to be correct, but we were unable to get verification from the owner.

LOD: 8′
Homeport: Cape Porpoise, ME
Builder: Wilbur Morse
Launched: 1908
Owner(s): Cordell & Janine Hutchins

Lucy Bell

LOD: 38′6″ Beam: 11′6″ Draft: 5′
Homeport: Mt. Desert, ME
Builder: Peter H. Sellers
Launched:1983 New Britain, PA
Owner(s): Peter and Lucy Sellers
Year boat took possession of
 current owner: 1971
(That's when the building began)

LUCY BELL was built in a barn in Doylestown, Pennsylvania. She has crossed, not oceans, but the George Washington Bridge. She has no motor. Peter and I have been sailing her together for thirty years.

277

Saralee

LOD: 21'
Homeport: Shalimar, FL
Builder: Craig Gleason
'Owner(s): Craig & Saralee Gleason
Launched: 2005

Information provided from Friendship Sloop Society records, believed to be correct, but we were unable to get verification from the owner.

278

Cygnus

LOD: 32'
Homeport: Seattle, WA
Builder: John Elfrey
Launched: 1976 Edgewater, MD
Owner(s): Joe Maslan

Information provided from Friendship Sloop Society records, believed to be correct, but we were unable to get verification from the owner.

279

Hand of Friendship

LOD: 22' Beam: 6' Draft: 3'6"
Homeport: Mordialloc, Australia
Builder: Tom Whitfield
Launched: 1990 Mordialloc
Owner(s): Mike & Phillip Morris
Year boat took possession of current owner: 2005

One of only two official Friendships in Australia. Winner of the Geelong Wooden Boat Show 2010 "Concourse d'Elegance." My wife Liz claims that "HoF" is the most photographed boat in Mordialloc, as every time we row out of the creek and set sail, we have a number of people stop on the pier and photograph us. Been mentioned and photographed in the <u>Australian Yachting Magazine</u> *2007 and* <u>Club Marine</u> *magazine 2010 and 2012. The sloop has impacted the location of where my father and I have bought our houses.*

(See page 83)

Retta

LOD: 24'4" Beam: 8'6 "Draft: 4'
Homeport: Key Largo, FL
Builder: David Westphal
Launched: 2008 Key Largo
Owner(s): David Westphal

Information provided from Friendship Sloop Society records, believed to be correct, but we were unable to get verification from the owner.

280

This sloop is listed as for sale through a marine broker.

Susie B.

LOD: 22' Beam: 7'6" Draft: 3'0"
Homeport: East Hampton, NY
Builder: Robert Barker
Launched: 2008 Easton, PA
Owner(s): Robert Barker

Information provided from Friendship Sloop Society records, believed to be correct, but we were unable to get verification from the owner.

281

282

Ghoti

LOD: 22' Beam: 7'3" Draft: 3'8"
Homeport: Boston, MA
Builder: Passamaquoddy / Murray
Launched: 1970 Yarmouth, MA
Owner(s): Anne-Marie Chouinard
Former name(s): Gertrude E
Year boat took possession of current owner: 2007

(See page 79)

283

Arapala

LOD: 26′ Beam: 8′ Draft: 5′
Homeport: Sorrento Victoria Australia
Builder: Unknown
Launched: 1955
Owner(s): Colin and Ginnie Bibby
Year boat took possession of
current owner: 2009

ARAPALA means full moon in Australian aboriginal language ARAPALA coincidences: We purchased her on a full moon! First sailed her to our home port on a full moon! Two years on, a storm broke her mast on a full moon! ARAPALA was built in Williamstown, Victoria, by a professional boat builder in 1955. (The builder's name is still unknown to us as there were many boat builders in Williamstown at that time.) She has had four owners, one person inadvertantly purchased her twice, the second time he purchased her sight unseen through a broker, to his surprise he had ARAPALA once again . She has spent 90% of her life in Port Philip Bay, Victoria, Australia and 10% in Sydney harbour where she partially sank due to unintentional neglect (the owner had an injury which required two years of rehabitation at which time she patiently waited in Sydney Harbour). When he was well enough she was transported back to Sorrento,Victoria. After some rehabilitation herself at The Wooden Boat Shop we purchased her. While we have had ARAPALA we have done regular maintenance in addition to stripping her hull back to bare timber then resealing and painting her. ARAPALA is most happy bouncing along in full sail flanked by a dozen or so dolphins with her current owners Colin and Ginnie.

Sloops known to be destroyed. Gone but not forgotten:

003   *Finette*
LOD: 40' Builder: Wilbur A. Morse Launched: 1915 Friendship, ME Former name(s): Right Bower

004   *Golden Eagle*
LOD: 26' Builder: Albion F. Morse   Launched: 1910 Cushing, ME Former name(s): Queequeg

008   *Banshee*
LOD: 30' Builder: Morse Launched: Unknown Friendship, ME

011   *Shulamite*
LOD: 24' Builder: W. Prescott Gannet Launched: 1938 Former name(s): Old Friendly, L'Aigle D'Or, Poor Penny

017   *Jolly Bucaneer*
LOD: 45' Builder: Eugene McLain Launched: 1906 Bremen Long Is., ME   Former name(s): Sky Pilot, Myrtle E

020   *Murre*
LOD: 30' Builder: Morse Launched: 1910 Former name(s): Moses Swann, Wanderer, Joeanna

026   *Virginia M.*
LOD: 28' Builder: Wilbur A. Morse Launched: 1917 Friendship, ME Former name(s): Swan

027   *Sarah E.*
LOD: 25' Builder: R. McKean/W.S. Carter Launched: 1939 Friendship, ME Former name(s): Red Coat, Yankee Trader, Island Trader, Peggoty

028   *Bounty*
LOD: 22' Builder: W. Prescott Gannet Launched: 1932 Former name(s): Tern

029   *Susan*
LOD: 41' Builder: Charles A. Morse Launched: 1902 Friendship, ME Former name(s): Ocean Belle

036   *Margin*
LOD: 25' Builder: Unknown Launched: Unknown

048   *Channel Fever*
LOD: 33' Builder: F.A. Provener Launched: 1939 Bronx, NY

053   *Eagle*
LOD: 32' Builder: Wilbur A. Morse Launched: 1915 Friendship, ME Former name(s): Damn Yankee

055   *Right Bower*
LOD: 47' Builder: Wilbur A. Morse Launched: 1915 Friendship, ME Former name(s): Finette III

060   *Old Salt*
LOD: 32' Builder: Robert McLain & Son Launched: 1902   Bremen Long Is., ME Former name(s): Friendship, Mammie E McLain, Ranger

068   *Robin L.*
LOD: 25' Builder: James H. Hall   Launched: 1967 Rowley, MA Former name(s): Lucy Anne

072   *Temptress*
LOD: 33' Builder: Philip J. Nichols Launched: 1934 Round Pound, ME Former name(s): Result, Pensive

076   *Packet*
LOD: 26' Builder: Charles A. Morse Launched: 1925 Friendship, ME

078   *Emmie B.*
LOD: 37' Builder: Reginald Wilcox, Launched: 1958

079   *Nimbus*
LOD: 30' Builder: A.T. Chenault III Launched: 1954 New Orleans, LA

108   *Loon*
LOD: 35' Builder: Charles A. Morse Launched: 1907 Friendship, ME

111   *Amos Swann*
LOD: 26' Builder: Wilbur A. Morse Launched: 1910 Friendship, ME

116   *Tinqua*
LOD: 30' Builder: Bruno & Stillman Launched: 1971 Newington, NH

Sloops known to be destroyed. Gone but not forgotten:

135 *Hatsey*
LOD: 25' Builder: Newman (P07) / Morris Launched: 1973 Southwest Harbor, ME Former name(s): Reef Point, Green Pepper

136 *Squirrel*
LOD: 28' Builder: Charles A. Morse Launched: 1920 Friendship, ME

148 *Sloop Out Of Water*
LOD: 38'Builder: Carter Launched: 1903Bremen, ME Former name(s): Eleda, Cubanola, Eileen, Matahasi II

158 *Eva R.*
LOD: 33' Builder: Edward Robinson Launched: 1906 Vinalhaven, ME

162 *Irene*
LOD: 38' Builder: Charles A. Morse Launched: 1917 Friendship, ME Former name(s): Fudee III, Hel-Don, New Moon, Sea Bird, Southern Cross

173 *Medusa*
LOD: 25'Builder: Ron Nowell Launched: 1982 Marshall, CA

188 *Maude*
LOD: 32' Builder: Harvey Gamage Launched: 1939 South Bristol, ME

190 *Aikane*
LOD: 31' Builder: Newman (D10) / C. Chase Launched: 1978 Brooksville, ME

195 *Princess*
LOD: 25' Builder: Wilbur A. Morse Launched: 1908 Friendship, ME

203 *Aurora*
LOD: Unknown Builder: Unknown Launched: 1898 Former name(s): Lucy S.

207 *Safe Home*
LOD: 31' Builder: H. Melquist Launched: 1980 Former name(s): Daisy Nell, Lannette M.

256 *October 4th*
LOD: 22' Builder: Edgar Knowles Launched: 1985 Former name(s): Friendship

Acknowledgements:

In taking on this project, the book committee also knew that we would be taking on the task sorting through more than half a century of Friendship Sloop Society records and archival material. Much of that material was hopelessly entangled with the local history of small Maine towns and their own records and archival material. Sorting out the correct attributions and original sources for that material would not have been possible without the generous help of many people who were willing to volunteer their time and resources to make it possible.

We would particularly like to point out the help and contributions of the following people and organizations: Bill and Caroline Zuber, who helped us weed through many early documents and photographs pertaining to the early history of the Friendship Sloop Society (many of which reside in their basement). Margaret W. Gagnon of Friendship, who offered the use of photographs in her collection. Tinker Crouch and the Deer Island and Stonington Historical Society for help tracking down several historic photographs and allowing us permission to use them in this publication. Ben Fuller and Kevin Johnson and the Penobscot Marine Museum who further sorted out the sources of the historic photographs in this book and who also allowed us to publish photographs from their extensive collection. Nathan Lipfert and the Maine Maritime Museum for helping us sort out some of our own records and lines drawings. The family of Roger and Mary Duncan who graciously donated a collection of 150 photographs to the Friendship Sloop Society, many of which appear in this book for the first time. We would also like to thank Jeff Dobbs of Jeff Dobbs Productions, Bar Harbor, Sydney Roberts Rockefeller and the Great Harbor Museum, Hannah Stevens and the Northeast Harbor Library, Louisa Watrous of Mystic Seaport, and Carl Cramer, Kim Patten, and Rich Hilsinger at *WoodenBoat*.

Finally, we would like to acknowledge the many members of the Friendship Sloop Society who contributed photographs and historical information for individual sloops and written material that appears in this book.

The members of the Friendship Sloop Society book committee:
Bill and Kathy Whitney
Peter and Nancy Toppan
Rich and Beth Langton
John and Carole Wojcik
Jim Salmon
Anne-Marie Chouinard
Greg Roth
Judy Heininger
Ralph W. Stanley
Ted Walsh

Membership information about the Friendship Sloop Society:

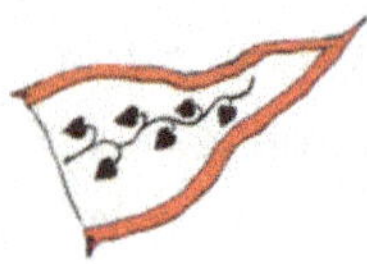

The Friendship Sloop Society is made up of sloop owners and family members, trades people, and other interested parties who share a love of these historic and seaworthy vessels. We presently have 283 registered sloops, and count as good friends many members who don't own a Sloop of their own (even some who prefer just to look at boats and keep their feet on dry land).

The Society was founded in the early 1960s. Through the years our activities have grown in number. We hold several rendezvous/regattas along the New England coast each year in Connecticut, Massachusetts, and Maine (see the "Schedule of Events" page on our website www.fss.org). We hold our annual meeting in the Portland, Maine area a couple of weeks before Thanksgiving. This is always a great time—we take care of the business end of things pertaining to the Society, trade stories, renew acquaintances, and start new friendships.

As an active member you are most welcome to participate in every one of our events and functions. July, 2013 was the nineteenth year we held our annual Homecoming Rendezvous (our major event) at the Rockland, Maine waterfront.

Membership dues are $35 a year for sloop owners and $25 a year for cooperative membership. Members receive the newsletter of the Society, FRIENDSHIPS, a decal, and may fly the burgee of the Friendship Sloop Society.

You'll find a copy of our membership application on the Web site. You can download and complete it, and mail it to me at the address below. If you have questions about the Society and its functions I will be happy to answer them for you.

I look forward to hearing from you!
Carole Wojcik, Membership Secretary
347 Lincoln Street
Norwell, MA 02061

Interested in sailing on a Friendship Sloop?

Below is a listing of boats that take out passengers with contact information.

Maine:

Bar Harbor/Acadia National Park
Helen Brooks –Karl Brunner, owner
Tel.#: (207) 266-5210
e-mail: info@downeastfriendshipsloop.com
Website: www.downeastfriendshipsloop.com

Southwest Harbor/Acadia National Park
Alice E – Karl Brunner, owner
Tel.#: (207) 266-5210
e-mail: info@downeastfriendshipsloop.com
Website: www.downeastfriendshipsloop.com

Acadia National Park / Bar Harbor
Surprise - Steve Kablinsky, owner
Tel#: - (888)-405-SAIL
 e-mail: downeastsail@acadia.net
 Website: www.downeastsail.com

Brooklin/Naskeag Point
Belford Gray –WoodenBoat School
Tel.# (207) 359-4651 Ask for courses on the Belford Gray
e-mail: school@woodenboat.com
Website: www.thewoodenboatschool.com

Belfast
Amity - Patrick Meg Reilly, owner
Tel# - (207)-323-1443
e-mail: info@belfastbaycompany.com
Website: www.belfastbaycompany.com

Rockland Harbor
Heritage - Capt. Neal Parker
Tel.# (207) 230-7083
e-mail: nep@gwi.net
Website: http://www.mainecoastsail.com

Rockland Harbor
Anna R. – Aaron Paolino
Tel.# (207) 702-3644
e-mail: rocklandsailing@gmail.com
Website: http://rocklandsailing.com/
Rockland Harbor

Persistence –Sail, Power, and Steam Museum
 Capt. Jim Sharp
Tel.#- (207) 596-0200
e-mail: ssmuseum@midcoast.com
Website: www.sailpowerandsteammuseum.org

Boothbay Harbor
Sarah Mead - Nate Jones, owner
Tel #: - (207)-380-5460
e-mail: captains@sailmuscongus.com
Website: www.sailmuscongus.com

Boothbay Harbor
Bay Lady – Balmy Day Cruises Capt. Bill Campbell
Tel.# -(207) 633-2284
e-mail: see website for form.
Website:www.balmydayscruises.com

Massachusetts:

Marblehead
Resolute- Captain Alan Leibovitz
Tel#-(978)-590-4318
e-mail: vy80@comcast.net
Website: www.atlantic-charters.com

Boston
Tupelo Honey – Capt. Don Benoit
Tel.#-(617) 828-9005
e-mail: Charters@ComeSailAwayNow.com
Website: www.comesailawaynow.com

Duchess - Captain Chris Preston
Tel.# (781)-591-9783
e-mail: Captain.chris@DuchessOfBoston.com
Website: www.duchessofbostonsailingcharters.com

Nantucket
Endeavor - Captain James Genthner
Tel# - (508)-228-5585
e-mail: endeavor@nantucket.net
Website: www.endeavorsailing.com

Vermont:

Burlington
Friend Ship - Captain Mike Crowley
Tel# - 802-598-6504
e-mail: captain@whistlingman.com
Website: www.whistlingman.com

www.ingramcontent.com/pod-product-compliance
Lightning Source LLC
Chambersburg PA
CBHW080444030726
47592CB00011B/2968